CRIME
CONTROL
Politics & Policy

2nd Edition

Peter J. Benekos
Mercyhurst College

Alida V. Merlo
Indiana University of
Pennsylvania

 LexisNexis®

 anderson publishing
A member of the LexisNexis Group

MW01053686

Crime Control, Politics, and Policy, Second Edition

LexisNexis and the Knowledge Burst logo are trademarks of Reed Elsevier Properties, Inc.
Anderson Publishing is a registered trademark of Anderson Publishing, a member of the LexisNexis Group

Library of Congress Cataloging-in-Publication Data

Benekos, Peter J.
  Crime control, politics, and policy / Peter J. Benekos, Alida V. Merlo -- 2nd ed.
     p. cm.
  Includes bibliographical references and index.
     ISBN 1-59345-347-7 (softbound)
     1. Criminal justice, Administration of--United States. 2. Law enforcement--United States.
  3. Mass media and crime--United States. 4. Corrections--United States. 5. Juvenile justice, Administration of--United States I. Merlo, Alida V. II. Title.

HV9950.B46 2006
364.973--dc22   2005036773

Cover design by Tin Box Studio, Inc./Cincinnati, Ohio   EDITOR Ellen S. Boyne
Cover photography by Olivia Grondin   ACQUISITIONS EDITOR Michael C. Braswell

Dedication

To Pat

To Kevin and Alexandra

Acknowledgments

Special appreciation to my loving wife, Pat, for her continued understanding and patience. Her encouragement supports my work and makes my efforts more successful. Thanks also to my mother, Lil, for her love and joy.

—PJB

A number of people have provided us with assistance and support throughout this project. We are delighted to have had the opportunity to work with our friends at LexisNexis/Anderson Publishing Co. We thank Mickey Braswell at LexisNexis/Anderson who first nurtured our ideas, helped us to refine them, and provided us with valuable feedback. Thanks to Frank Cullen for his review of the first manuscript. His comments were incisive and very helpful in guiding the project. Kelly Grondin provided us with the opportunity to initiate and finish this book, and we are grateful for her long-standing support. We are also very excited to again work with Ellen Boyne, who does an excellent job of making our manuscript a polished product. It was a great honor and privilege to work together, and we appreciate all that she did to facilitate this project. Thank you, Ellen.

A special thank you to my mother, Clara Merlo, for her wisdom and love, and for all that she has done throughout my life. She is truly the "wind beneath my sails." A final and especially heartfelt thank you to my husband, Kevin Ashley, whose candor, intelligence, humor, love, and support are the mainstays of my life, and to our daughter, Alexandra Ashley, who makes every day a holiday.

—AVM

Preface

One of the prevailing policy issues facing the nation is what to do about crime. For the last four decades, this has become a major social, political, and economic problem that has also generated the growth of the academic and research discipline of criminal justice. As students of this problem, you are certainly aware of the increasing amounts of information and research findings that are disseminated to legislators, administrators, and the public—and are studied by scholars of criminal justice.

As professors of this academic discipline, we are often asked by students why the "system" is not more effective and why crime cannot be better controlled. While students regularly study what the criminal justice system "should" be doing and how it "should" be doing it, questions about why these efforts are not working are often left to concluding observations or critical thinking exercises. Some exceptions are Samuel Walker's treatise, *Sense and Nonsense About Crime and Drugs: A Policy Guide*, Sixth Edition, and Jeffrey Reiman's *The Rich Get Richer and the Poor Get Prison*, Sixth Edition. In this tradition, we attempt to focus the crime and justice debate by asking you, the reader, to consider criminal justice policies that deal with crime prevention and crime control.

Our intent is to review concepts, information, and points of view that help to explain the context and constraints of the criminal justice system. From an interdisciplinary perspective, we want to engage the reader in a critique of criminal justice as a means of moving the discussion to a more informed and insightful level and to create enthusiasm and understanding about what can be done by the criminal justice system.

To accomplish this goal, we encourage you to adopt what Mills called the "sociological imagination" (1959). This requires you to read, take notes, reflect, discuss, and critique the following chapters in order to examine the implications of the information. In other words, we want to engage you in a dialogue to consider what can be done to improve the system of criminal justice. Our effort is not intended to review all the literature or present a compendium of information, but rather to select the themes and evidence that we believe reflect important, useful, and timely information. We encourage you to question the ideas and to let us know what you think about criminal justice.

This critique of criminal justice is organized into seven chapters. We begin by summarizing what we have found to be salient themes and concepts that are helpful in understanding recent developments in public policy and crime control. Three themes that are central to the discussion are the impact of ideology, the role of the media, and the politicization of crime and criminal justice. Because these perspectives will reappear throughout the book, it is worth the time to examine them carefully and to have a sense of how they can be applied to the crime and justice topics.

Chapter 2 presents a review of law enforcement initiatives and reforms, and deconstructs the "thin blue line" metaphor of policing. We critique the "war model" of crime control and assess the impact of the various wars on crime and drugs. Issues such as the excessive use of force, community policing, and the professionalization of policing are discussed. We consider some successful strategies but also see a pattern of "quick fix" schemes.

A familiar theme in criminal justice is that "sentencing drives the system." In examining the impact of sentencing reform on the system, Chapter 3 summarizes some of the sentencing philosophies, goals, and models, and considers the politicization of the courts. Sentence enhancement statutes have been enacted in a number of states, and they have affected the size of the prison population. At the same time, there is evidence of a greater reluctance to sentence offenders to death. These changes signify a possible shift in our thinking about how best to deal with offenders.

These topics are continued in Chapter 4, in which the consequences of recent sentencing reforms and the shifting philosophies of what to do with offenders are discussed. We think this chapter is especially helpful in understanding how the various concepts, ideologies, policies, and politics converge to distort the justice system and to present dilemmas for corrections systems. This discussion includes a review of the intermediate punishment phenomenon.

The issues pertaining to juvenile justice further illustrate what's wrong with the system. Chapter 5 reviews the legislative changes in juvenile justice and examines the trends and implications of how the images and definitions of adolescent offenders are being reconstructed in contemporary society. Despite the punitive and zero-tolerance policies of the 1990s, there are indications of a softening in our attitude toward juvenile offenders and a greater emphasis on informing policy with research, particularly in the areas of early intervention and prevention.

In Chapter 6, we examine four issues: overcrowding in prisons; recent Supreme Court decisions on sentencing and their potential effect on prison populations; prisoner re-entry; and collaborative efforts among criminal justice professionals and the community. Although our history indicates a strong commitment to incarceration and punitive policies, there is evidence of a softening in our approach and an emphasis on treatment-oriented strategies.

The final chapter offers our questions and reflections about alternative models of "justice." We review some public policy ideas and challenge the reader to think about what's right with the system and to evaluate beliefs about which ideas, programs, policies, and models "should" drive the criminal justice system.

After reading the book, and (hopefully) after discussing your ideas with friends, peers, mentors, and colleagues, we encourage you to let us know what you think. Because we continue to learn from our students and the questions and insights they share with us, we feel that the information and perspectives summarized in these chapters should serve the purpose of reflective and knowledgeable dialogue about what's wrong—and what's right—with criminal justice. Let us know what impact these ideas have had on your thinking. We look forward to hearing from you.

PJB: pbenekos@mercyhurst.edu
AVM: amerlo@iup.edu

Table of Contents

1

Dynamics of Criminal Justice

Since 1997, the sustained downturn in reported crime has been a major story in the United States. Even major cities like New York have experienced a continued decline in the number of violent crimes reported to police. In 2004, the number of murders in New York (570) was the lowest since 1963 (Lueck, 2005). Experts have offered various explanations ranging from better policing to tougher sentencing to stabilization of the crack drug market to an improving economy (Butterfield, 1997a, 1997b).

In the summer of 2005, however, this encouraging, optimistic news about declining crime was juxtaposed with news and television replays of the 1996 bombing at the Atlanta Olympics (which killed one woman and injured more than 100 people) and the 1998 bombing of an abortion clinic in Birmingham, Alabama (where a police officer was killed and a nurse was seriously injured) (Rahimi, 2005). These bombings were revisited because the "terrorist bomber," Eric Robert Rudolph (who was apprehended in May 2003, after a lengthy manhunt), was sentenced in July 2005 to two consecutive life terms for the Birmingham bombing and he is "scheduled to receive two life sentences without parole" for the Olympic bombing (Rahimi, 2005:par. 5). The news about Eric Rudolph included statements from Emily Lyons, the nurse who was permanently injured in the clinic bombing, and Felecia Sanderson, the widow of police officer Robert Sanderson, who was killed in the bombing (Rahimi, 2005).

During the summer of 2005, news reports were also focused in Idaho on the search for Shasta (age 8) and Dylan (age 9) Groene, who were missing since May 16, 2005, after their mother, brother, and the mother's boyfriend were found bludgeoned to death in their home (Geranios, 2005). After six weeks of disappearance, Shasta was recognized in a restaurant, and police apprehended Joseph Edward Duncan III and charged him with first-degree murder and first-degree kidnapping. Dylan's body was later found in a camp site used by Duncan. This crime also captured attention because Duncan was a convicted sex offender who had been diagnosed as a "dangerous sexual psychopath" and had served a prison sentence for raping a 14-year-old boy at gunpoint in 1980 (CNN, 2005a). Duncan was 16 years old at the time. After being paroled in 1994, he violated parole conditions, was returned to prison in 1998, then "released again in 2000 after serving his full sentence" ("Today Show," 2005). At the time he kidnapped the Groene children and murdered three people, he had "skipped out" on bail from Minnesota, where he had been charged with "second-degree criminal sexual conduct" for allegedly molesting two boys ("Today Show," 2005).

Another major "story" that captured the news throughout 2004 was the murder of Laci Denise Peterson and her fetus (baby boy, Connor). This was followed by almost daily news about the investigation, arrest, trial, conviction, and sentencing of her husband, Scott Peterson ("The Laci Peterson Case," 2005). The crime story was presented as a drama with soap opera elements, including a young, beautiful, pregnant wife, allegedly murdered by a philandering husband; another woman, Amber Frey, who had been lied to by Scott Peterson; the death of a fetus, raising issues of fetal rights; interviews with anguished parents; news briefings by opposing attorneys; a media frenzy focusing on Modesto, California; the suspense of jury deliberations; and the final sentencing verdict (death by lethal injection) ("The Laci Peterson Case," 2005).

These stories are not a representative sampling of crime in the United States for 2005, but they do suggest a few salient generalizations and themes about crime and criminal justice:

1. Obviously, crime is news, and a significant segment of the public gains its information and understanding of crime and criminal justice from news stories presented by the media.

2. News about crime and criminal justice is frequently general, reflecting broad trends and issues. For example, aggregate data are used to report that the national crime rate is down, the number of offenders incarcerated in state and federal prisons is up, the number of law enforcement officers killed in the line of duty is down, and the number of cities with teen curfews is up.

3. On the other hand, the news can be specific and detailed, including childhood photos and crime scene pictures. Details about the crime, the life of the victim, and the status of the investigation all reinforce a familiarization with the crime incident. For example, Emily Lyons, the nurse who was injured by the bombing of the Woman All Woman abortion clinic, lost an eye and had more than 20 operations as a result of the explosions. After Rudolph's sentencing, she posted an "8-page statement . . . on the Web" calling Rudolph a "monster" and declaring that "she had not received justice" (Rahimi, 2005:par. 10). Duncan's criminal record was quickly broadcast, documenting that he was 12 years old when he committed his first sexual assault.

4. News stories often include commentary from public officials or "state managers" (Welch, Fenwick & Roberts, 1998) and experts. Former New York City Mayor Rudolph Giuliani credited tough policies and police crackdowns on minor crimes as the reason for the decrease in crime in New York City (Goldberg, 1998). DiIulio suggests that mandatory and longer prison sentences have removed more offenders from the streets (1992). These statements reflect perspectives and conclusions that are not always shared. As a result, opposing views may be solicited to "balance" the reporting. For example, an improved economy may dissuade youth from entering the drug business, thus subtracting from the pool of offenders and potential victims.

5. Elected public officials are politicians who may capitalize on the news to further their political agendas and to gain support of voters. In 1996, in response to media reports of youth crime and increasing public fear of youth violence, Senator Mike Fisher (Rep. PA) proposed tougher penalties for youths using weapons when committing a felony. He also introduced legislation to lower the age to 15 for the transfer of violent youths to criminal court. Senator Fisher was elected attorney general of Pennsylvania on the promise to "get tough" on crime and offered the new state law, ACT 33, which he sponsored as evidence of his commitment to go after criminals (Durantine, 1996).

In April 2005, Florida lawmakers responded to the kidnapping and murder of 9-year-old Jessica Lunsford by proposing legislation that would require longer sentences and life-time electronic monitoring for designated sex offenders (CNN, 2005b). In May 2005, three months after Jessica Lunsford was found dead, Florida Governor Jeb Bush signed the Jessica Lunsford Act, which "establishes a mandatory sentence of 25 years to life behind bars for people convicted of certain sex crimes against children 11 and younger" (*New York Times*, 2005a:18).

Also in April 2005, H.R. 1505, the Jessica Lunsford Act, was introduced in the U.S. House of Representatives, with provisions to tighten registration requirements for sex offenders (Thomas, H.R. 1505). Similarly, in July 2005, the U.S. Senate introduced the Jessica Lunsford and Sarah Lunde Act, which would provide funding to assess the effectiveness of the electronic monitoring of sexual predators (Thomas, S. 1407). With this focus on sex offenders, the Department of Justice announced in July 2005 that a national sex offender database, with more than 500,000 registered sex offenders, was available for online searches (*New York Times*, 2005b).

In examining these general observations, three dynamic dimensions of criminal justice that influence crime control policy in the United States can be identified. These are helpful in explaining the dilemmas and destiny of the criminal justice system. First, the news media are instrumental in "constructing" crime stories and using celebrated cases to portray crime as a prominent social issue. One of the realities of the news industry (e.g., limited space and time to reach and attract as many consumers as possible) requires the emphasis on "extreme, dramatic cases" to generate interest in the stories (Chermak, 1994:580). Based on his content analysis of crime stories and news production, Chermak described how both the public and politicians develop distorted images and perspectives on crime (p. 580):

> Although these (dramatic) incidents represent crime in its most extreme form, the public is more likely to think they are representative because of the emphasis by the media. . . . Yet the media overemphasis of celebrated cases and moral panics may be influential because people are more likely to recall these events when thinking about crime. . . .

Consequently, as will be discussed below, the public is sensitized— or oversensitized—to the crime issue and, based on distorted representations, is preoccupied with crime and fearful of being victimized. With this zeitgeist of crime as a major social issue, a second dynamic— ideology—reflects the need to explain and make sense of this social problem and to do something about it.

Attributions of crime, however, reflect different—and often opposing—assumptions and concepts of human behavior. Later discussion will suggest how ideas about crime and criminals are reflected in ideologies and public policies on crime control. It is important to note that ideology influences individual and public perspectives on crime and that the media have an important role in shaping the prevailing ideology.

However, society's dominant crime ideology also influences how the media construct crime news. In other words, "though crime news exists as a product manufactured by the media, it is shaped significantly by state managers who contribute to its distinct ideological qualities (Welch, Fenwick & Roberts, 1998:220).

This points to the final dynamic of criminal justice: politics and the politicization of crime and criminal justice. Fairchild and Webb explain that this "suggests that crime and fear of crime are being used by politicians as issues in which rhetorical and symbolic policy initiatives can enhance their popularity and electability" (1985:8). As students of United States politics understand, politicians have differing ideological perspectives regarding crime causation and control. Among the dynamics of media, ideology, and politics, it is not surprising that politicians attempt to promote their views and agendas, which tend to influence how crime news is distorted by the media. More directly stated, "crime news therefore tends to be ideological insofar as it represents a worldview of state managers (e.g., political leaders) who distort the reality of crime" (Welch, Fenwick & Roberts, 1998:220). The dynamics of these dimensions of criminal justice will be discussed further.

MEDIA

The role of the media in informing public opinion and influencing citizen reaction to crime issues is central to understanding the framing of crime policy. With round-the-clock, up-to-the-minute news, the television viewer not only learns about local crimes but also sees victims, offenders, and crime news from around the nation and the world. Just as the news coverage of the Vietnam War influenced public sentiments about the war, the news helps to keep crime issues high on the list of public concerns and serves to heighten fears and apprehensions about victimization and public safety.

Increased technology and changes in local and national media environments have significantly altered the portrayal of crime in America. The growth of cable stations, the live broadcast of court proceedings (e.g., that of Louise Woodward, the au pair accused of killing eight-month-old Matthew Eappen), and the changing societal mores governing what is appropriate media coverage (consider Paula Jones's sexual harassment lawsuit against President Bill Clinton, as well as Clinton's inappropriate relationship with Monica Lewinsky), coupled with changes in programming that rely heavily on news stations, magazines, talk shows, and re-enactments of real-life crime dramas, have all affected the public's perception of the crime problem (Sacco, 1995:145). As a result, the public has developed a "fixation on crime."

Potter and Kappeler describe the growth of the new genre of programming called "reality TV," which is a "genetic cross between entertainment and the news" (e.g., "America's Most Wanted," "Unsolved Mysteries") (1998:3).

In addition, because crime stories are presented as entertainment, viewers develop a distorted understanding of criminal investigation and "unrealistic expectations" about forensic evidence (Stockwell, 2005). For example, Stockwell described a phenomenon called the "CSI effect" (2005:29):

> Prosecutors say jurors are telling them they expect forensic evidence in criminal cases, just like on their favourite television shows, including "CSI: Crime Scene Investigation." In real life, forensic evidence is not collected at every crime scene, either because criminals clean up after themselves or because of a shortage of resources. Yet, increasingly, jurors are reluctant to convict someone without it, a phenomenon the criminal justice community is calling the "CSI effect."

Clearly, the media, the government, politicians, and other special interest groups have benefited from the news coverage of crime. Our perceptions of crime and its victims are largely shaped by the presentations that are made through these various media. The television news stations, newspapers, and news magazines selectively determine which aspects of official police incident reports, crimes, victims, and court proceedings merit attention. Television news programs do not have unlimited amounts of time to detail every aspect of the official versions of crime provided by the police department. Therefore, decisions are made to feature the most sensational, emotional, significant, and universally appealing aspects of the crime stories for the public's viewing (Sacco, 1995:146-147).

The adage, "if it bleeds, it leads," is well-known in the television news industry. Data suggest that violent crime news is disproportionately broadcast on major networks (Potter & Kappeler, 1998). Chermak concludes that "seriousness" of the crime is "an important variable, influencing decisions about selection and production" of crime news (1994:568). Based on his content analysis of crime news, Chermak found that celebrated cases and "crimes with the greatest audience appeal are emphasized similarly across media" (p. 571). With limited opportunity to sell news in a competitive industry, the media bias is toward crime news that sells.

The presentation of these crimes and their seeming randomness in society heightens the public's sensitivity to the crime problem, reinforces emotional reactions, and encourages the "quick fix" mentality regarding solutions. For example, parents of murdered children seeking to bring some closure to their tragedies often work with politicians to pass "laws in memory of their murdered children" and are "forming a swelling procession from children's graves to legislatures" (Russakoff, 1998:27). Examples include:

- Megan's Law (New Jersey), which requires states to notify communities when a sex offender moves in.

- Jenna's Law (New York), which proposed to end parole for all violent felons.

- Stephanie's Law (Kansas), which allows for commitment of repeat sex offenders to mental hospitals if they are deemed too dangerous to release after a prison term.

- Joan's Law (New Jersey), which imposes a life-without-parole sentence for murder of a child under 14 during a sexual assault.

- Amber's Law (Texas), which is imposed on repeat, federal child sex offenders.

- Jessica Lunsford Act (Florida), which requires lifetime electronic monitoring for sex offenders.

This "personalized" legislation demonstrates how visible and significant crime has become in the United States and also illustrates the dynamic between politicians, the electorate, the media, and the dominant get-tough ideology (Russakoff, 1998:27):

> Disparate social forces have propelled passage of these laws. They include the rise of the victims' rights movement, the spread of "if-it-bleeds-it-leads" television news, the currency of humanizing anecdotes as politicians clamor for the attention of an alienated electorate and the salience of crime as a political issue, even as crime rates drop.

This type of emotional, quick-fix response plays well for the public and advocates of deterrence theory (discussed below), but it tends to misdirect crime policy and distort explanations of crime causation. For example, sex offender registration laws may sound good, but "the system relies on the offenders themselves to register" and enforcement is inconsistent (Okwu, 2005:par. 7). Although early explanations of particular crime patterns or incidents may point to several causes (gangs, unemployment, racism, unequal access to quality public education and health care), later news accounts tend to identify a single factor as the cause of the problem (e.g, guns, drugs, or gangs). This monocausal approach is attractive because it is simple and straightforward; it concentrates responsibility on a single actor or actors and disassociates the rest of society from the problem. Moreover, the "single cause" can be briefly stated, whether it is in the print or television

Florida Governor Jeb Bush signs into law the Jessica Lunsford Act during ceremonies on May 2, 2005, in Tallahassee. The bill enhances penalties for sexual crimes against children. The presence of the family members of Sarah Lunde and Jessica Lunsford (who were victims of sexual predators) at the enactment of such "personalized" legislation highlights the dynamic between politicians, the electorate, and the media. *(AP Photo/Phil Coale)*

media (Stallings, 1990:90). Reiman (1998) also provides evidence that it keeps the focus on "street crimes" rather than on organizational and corporate crimes that present more risk to employees and the general public.

Additionally, the media have the capability to create for the viewing public the perception of an epidemic or a crime wave regarding certain social problems like drugs, child sexual victimization, or serial murder. The media, according to Kappeler, Blumberg, and Potter, are part of the myth-making process whereby a crime is not only reported but is portrayed as pervasive (1996:15). During those periods of time when there are no "crime waves" to report, Barak contends that the mass media deal with the void by "providing a steady diet of the growing and omnipotent danger of impersonal crime" (1995:133).

However, the media are not solely responsible for society's perceptions regarding the extent of violent crime and the potential risk of victimization. In their quest to make sense of the actual criminal act, the media rely on the government and the experts to interpret the events for them and to provide some rationale for a particular crime. In short, we rely on others (stakeholders, elected officials, government bureaucrats) to frame the news for us and to relate it to our world (Stallings, 1990:91).

In their study of the dynamics between print media and crime news sources, Welch, Fenwick, and Roberts (1998) observed a reciprocity between the state managers who control access to crime information—that is, the gatekeepers (political leaders and law enforcement officials) and journalists who need the information to do their work. In the process of selecting information to share, state managers present their views and ideologies on crime causation and crime control, which reinforce their organizational and professional interests. Not surprisingly, the researchers found that state managers, as compared to "intellectuals" (i.e., professors and researchers), were more likely to emphasize crime control perspectives than crime causation statements. While this may also reflect a "selection bias" or self-fulfilling prophecy in that journalists seek out state manager sources to reinforce crime control policy, it underscores the role of media in supporting the dominant crime ideologies.

The media's role in helping us to interpret and analyze crime is not inconsequential. The media are largely responsible for determining which social problems merit greater attention and then finding the stories and experts to contextualize them for us. For example, the media may initiate newspaper or television news series on youth violence after a dramatic, highly publicized incident such as the school shootings in Jonesboro, Arkansas (see Chapter 5) or Littleton, Colorado.[1] The media not only inform the public about a specific problem or (as in this case) crime but also identify community experts and services to deal with it, thus attempting to further influence or inform public understanding. Unfortunately, with crime news, the information—or misrepresentation of information—reinforces the public's sense of the dangers of crime as "immediate, omnipresent, and almost inescapable"; this results in support for "more police, more arrests, longer sentences, more prisons, and more executions" (Potter & Kappeler, 1998:3).

In discussing this crime news phenomenon and its impact, Diana Gordon (1990) describes the "vicarious victimization" effect that tends to make citizens hypersensitive to perceptions of vulnerability. Even as nonvictims, citizens who watch and identify with stories and images of crime and victimization react as if they too have been victimized. This is consistent with "cultivation theory," which maintains that "heavy television watchers have their views of the real world shaped by what they see on the screen" (Schor, 2004:64). Fears and insecurities are exacerbated, anger and outrage are expressed, and frustration results with the failures of the criminal justice system to control crime. In the context of a dominant ideology that supports punishment and incapacitation, the public can be easily encouraged to support the "draconian" responses noted by Potter and Kappeler.

Because of an overload of information, and the conflicting and competing points of view about crime and criminals, individuals often rely on frames of reference to make sense of the issues. "Frames are mental structures that shape the way we see the world" (Lakoff, 2004:xv). That is, people select language that helps them thread the information and fit it "into the contexts of broader story lines" that they understand (Bai, 2005:40). The framing of crime issues reflects this generalized perspective or world view.

In this context, Theodore Sasson's study of how citizens react to crime news suggests five crime frames or categories of interpretation that aid individuals in making sense of the information about crime: (1) the faulty system, (2) blocked opportunities, (3) social breakdown, (4) media violence, and (5) racist society (1995). He found that a popular mental set for interpreting crime news is the "faulty system frame" (p. 13):

> This frame regards crime as a consequence of impunity: People do crimes because they know they can get away with them. The police are handcuffed by liberal judges. The prisons, bursting at their seams, have revolving doors for serious offenders.

In other words, if the criminal justice system were improved, if more police were on the streets, if more offenders were sentenced to longer sentences, if more prisons were built, and if offenders served their sentences, then dangerous criminals would be removed from society, potential criminals would be deterred, crime would be reduced, and citizens would feel safer. This crime frame or perspective implies certain assumptions about crime causation and principles of crime control. Based on the information and findings from Chermak (1994), Potter and Kappeler (1998), and Welch, Fenwick, and Roberts (1998), these ideas about crime and policy are influenced by the media, which construct crime news to reflect the dominant ideology (Welch, Fenwick & Roberts, 1998). Sometimes this is referred to as "spin," which is the "manipulative use of a frame" (Lakoff, 2004:100).

IDEOLOGY

Most studies of criminology and criminal justice include some review of the basic ideas or schools of thought regarding crime and punishment. (For example, see Allen & Simonsen, 1995; Cullen & Gilbert, 1982; Hagan, 2002.) Discussion generally focuses on major elements of the classical and positivist models, which are summarized below.

The ideas of Cesare Beccaria (1738-1794) are consistent with classical ideology and reflect principles for improving the practices of punishment and establishing a more humane and utilitarian penal system (1981). A primary emphasis is that punishment, if properly administered, can be an effective deterrent of crime. Beccaria also stressed certainty rather than severity of punishment and was opposed to excessive, unfair, and torturous punishment.

An opposing perspective was oriented toward studying the causes of crime and identifying antecedents of criminal behavior. Cesare Lombroso (1835-1909) was a leader in using science to study characteristics of criminals. He advanced the principle that biological factors (as measured by physiognomy) could be located to identify criminals as a subclass of humankind (Lombroso, 1912/1968). This scientific perspective has developed into a more general search (i.e., of social, psychological, economic factors) to explain motives for criminal behavior. It is known as positivism.

Classical Perspective:

1. Behavior is based on free will, which is explained using the rational choice model. This emphasizes a voluntaristic understanding of criminal behavior.

2. Based on this rational perspective, a "hedonistic calculus" is offered as a heuristic to explain a pleasure-pain formula for decisionmaking. That is, individuals seek to maximize pleasure and enjoyment and to avoid or minimize pain and punishment.

3. To control or deter criminal behavior, punishment must exceed pleasure. Therefore, if crime is committed, it is attributed to weak enforcement or not enough punishment. The deterrence model, as well as related concepts of punishment and crime control through system improvements, are characteristic of this school of thought.

Positivist Perspective:

1. Behavior is the consequence of circumstances and situations that surround and influence the individual. This view proposes a deterministic explanation of criminal behavior.

2. In this developmental model, efforts focus on identifying elements of the environment that adversely affect behavior and contribute to antisocial acts.

3. In order to control or prevent criminal behavior, corrective intervention is necessary to undo the effects of negative experiences and to promote and reinforce acceptable, prosocial behavior. This incorporates a medical model analogy that seeks to find the relevant and effective treatment or rehabilitative strategy.

These statements oversimplify the respective ideologies and exaggerate differences in their assumptions and operating models.

While advocates of each model emphasize crime control, their ideological differences serve to frame different conceptualizations of the problem and how best to respond to crime. For example, the "faulty system" perspective noted above is more consistent with the classical model and also with more conservative ideas about crime and punishment. This ideology calls for reducing "loopholes and technicalities that impede the apprehension and imprisonment of offenders" and increasing the "swiftness, certainty, and severity of punishment" that is consistent with Beccaria and classical thought (Sasson, 1995:14).

Table 1.1
Classical versus Positivist Principles of Criminal Behavior

Classical		Positivism
voluntaristic	vs.	deterministic
rational choice	vs.	developmental
deterrence model	vs.	medical model
punishment	vs.	rehabilitation

In contrast to the conservative "faulty system" view, another frame identified by Sasson is "blocked opportunities." This frame "depicts crime as a consequence of inequality and discrimination, especially as they manifest themselves in unemployment, poverty, and inadequate educational opportunities" (1995:14). These ideas are more consistent with the positivist model and align more closely with a liberal ideology that calls for both social reform and individualized interventions or rehabilitative programs.

In defining the government's role in responding to crime, these left-right, liberal-conservative ideologies are incorporated into policy perspectives and rationales. Politicians who operate with partisan affiliation demonstrate these ideological assumptions in their legislative proposals, in the rationales they use to argue the validity of policy recommendations, and in their explanations for crime.

POLITICS

Standing before his colleagues in the Senate, Byron Dorgan (Democrat, North Dakota) began his address by acknowledging that (1997):

> [T]here are a good many issues that come to the floor of the
> Senate that cause debate between Republicans and Democrats.
> Some are partisan, some cause great rancor, but there is one
> issue that ought not ever be a partisan debate. That is the issue
> of crime and how we in our country address it.

Dorgan is correct that political debate is generally absent in recognizing that crime is a national problem; the question of what to do about it, however, has been a more contentious and divisive matter that reflects the dynamic nature of crime policy in the United States. Politicizing the crime issue has distorted rational policies and resulted in the co-optation of criminal justice initiatives.

Reviewing how crime has emerged into the national consciousness illustrates three important themes of politicization: (1) crime can be utilized as an effective surrogate for social anxieties, (2) concepts of crime and criminals reflect ideological assumptions that polarize (and therefore distort) policy considerations, and (3) politicians get elected by using the crime issue in political campaigns.

Crime as a Surrogate Social Problem

In the early 1960s, the nation was becoming alarmed (and divided) by the Vietnam War, civil rights issues, urban unrest and riots, student protests, assassinations, and a growing sense that the post–World War II prosperity was giving way to social upheaval and disorder (Cronin, Cronin & Milakovich, 1981). As discussed earlier, the role of the media—especially television—in bringing images of these developments to homes around the country served to capture national attention and to raise public anxieties. The news media presented images of crime and lawlessness and the public looked to the federal government for solutions.

When Lyndon Johnson and Barry Goldwater campaigned for the presidency in 1964, they debated on how best to confront and correct these social concerns (Rosch, 1985). Crime was an emotional issue that became personalized as the public focused on concerns about personal safety (Cronin, Cronin & Milakovich, 1981:5). Goldwater, a Republican, advocated "law and order" to quell the unrest and to restore order in society. His vision of the government's role was to use authority to define the limits of behavior and to win back the peace. Johnson, a Democrat, looked to underlying aspects of the problems and proposed a "war on poverty" to help the disenfranchised by providing temporary relief and by removing obstacles to opportunities for social and economic participation.

Two lessons were learned from this election. Crime was an issue that condensed the public's anxieties and fears (Gordon, 1990), and the candidates were able to define this issue in simplified terms. As campaign strategists recognized that "crime could symbolize more than people being robbed or mugged," they used the issue to heighten public concern about social and civil conditions, and then to define their candidate's vision or government's role in restoring American society (Rosch, 1985:25).

In assessing this theme of crime and campaigns, Marion reviewed how crime can become three types of issues: personal, positional, and symbolic (1995:94-95). A personal issue is one that has no opposition. As in the case of crime, it is "opposed" by all candidates. This is consistent with Dorgan's statement that crime is not a partisan issue. A positional issue, however, reveals that candidates have different ideas or positions regarding the correct response to the problem. Capital punishment is certainly an example of a positional issue: candidates are either for or against the death penalty. Finally, crime is also a symbolic issue because candidates avoid serious discussion of both the complex nature of crime and the commitment of time and resources necessary to confront this social problem adequately. Consequently, candidates use "bumper sticker" slogans to announce solutions to crime.

Crime is also considered a symbolic issue because it is often synonymous with the issue of race (Rosch, 1985:25). The call for "law and order" in the 1960s was a not-so-discreet appeal to control urban riots and to impose law on civil rights demonstrators. Suggesting that these issues commingled in the public's perspective, Baker concluded that "race and crime were often scrambled in the public mind, their common denominator, fear—fear of being mugged on a street corner and fear of being mugged economically by the newcomer in the labor market" (1983:42). The fear of crime became synonymous with the fear of minorities and threats to the prevailing social and economic order of the times.

Ideology and Crime

In proposing an agenda to control crime, candidates reveal their political ideologies and define the "positional" debate by identifying the assumptions and perspectives that are used to rationalize crime control policy. For example, beginning with the Johnson-Goldwater campaign in 1964, Barry Goldwater characterized the crime problem as "the result of a weakened morality and a decline in discipline" (Marion, 1995:95). His "conservative" response was to improve the criminal justice system with more police, fewer restrictions on police authority, and tougher laws (Marion, 1995). Although Republicans generally oppose federalism, Goldwater advocated a stronger federal role in the case of crime policy, and his campaign served to raise the issue of crime from the state and local level to the federal level (Marion, 1995:96).

President Lyndon Johnson, on the other hand, conceptualized crime as a consequence of social and economic conditions. He focused his crime campaign on defining the "root causes" of crime and using the government to develop programs to correct them. Like Goldwater, he proposed an expanded federal role but he envisioned a "great society" as opposed to a "law-and-order society."

The crime control policies of Republicans and Democrats generally parallel the continuum of conservative/classical versus liberal/positivist models presented earlier. Republican-conservative assumptions, for

example, are more consistent with the classical school of cı
which recognizes individual free choice, rational decisionn
the deterrence model, and emphasizes punishment, inca̤ṵ̈ṵ̈ṵ̈,
and the expansion of the criminal justice system. The Democratic-lib-
eral perspective incorporates positivist assumptions, including deter-
minism and developmentalism, the medical model, and an emphasis on
rehabilitation and therapeutic intervention (Hagan, 1998). Liberals also
advocate social reforms and more prevention and treatment programs
as opposed to prisons.

In a review of presidential campaigns since 1964, Marion (1995)
has identified how the crime issue was used by various candidates:
Richard Nixon wanted to "get tough" in 1968; Gerald Ford was concerned about victims' rights as opposed to offenders' rights in 1976;
Ronald Reagan wanted tougher penalties and more anti-crime legislation in 1980 and 1984; and George Bush and Michael Dukakis
debated the issue of furloughs in 1988 as the Willie Horton incident
served to exaggerate and magnify crime as a salient public concern (see
page 16 for further discussion of Willie Horton). In the 1992 presidential election, Bill Clinton remembered the Horton lesson and took
the crime agenda away from George Bush by supporting capital punishment and promising to put 100,000 more law enforcement officers
on the street. In fact, Clinton again co-opted the crime issue from the
Republican candidate Robert Dole in 1996 by advocating a "conservative" agenda on crime.

In each of these elections, crime was an important issue, and the candidates proposed policies that could be dichotomized as either liberal or
conservative. The public was presented with choices and, in five of the
nine elections (1964-1996), a Republican candidate was elected. An interesting observation regarding the 1992 and 1996 elections is that candidate
Bill Clinton presented a crime control agenda that consisted of "liberal
policies with a conservative thrust," which gained him the label of
"conservative liberal" regarding crime control (Marion, 1995:43).

The relevance of this election study is not only to reinforce the significance of crime control policy as a national issue but also to demonstrate that explanations for crime and rationalizations for anti-crime
policies are understood in the context of ideology. Evidence of a convergence of liberal and conservative views about crime control in
1996 suggests that such ideologically grounded debate on crime may
be waning. This is not necessarily the end of liberalism, but being tough
on crime and espousing classical concepts of crime control now appear
to be realities of the politics of elections.

Getting Elected

From Lyndon Johnson to Bill Clinton (1964-1996), crime and criminal justice became salient features of campaign rhetoric and debate. The politics of the 1988 election between George Bush and Michael Dukakis, however, epitomize the politicization of crime and the cooptation of criminal justice.

In the 1988 presidential election, the name Willie Horton became synonymous with "dirty politics" and a lesson in how politics, ideology, and the media have a significant impact on the public, on crime policy, and on the criminal justice system. The story of William Horton is now well-known. The fact that some of "the memories are factually inaccurate does not diminish their power" (Jamieson, 1992:16).

Horton was a convicted murderer serving a life sentence in Massachusetts. He "escaped" while on furlough and went to Maryland, where he raped Angela Miller and stabbed her fiancé Clifford Barnes (Anderson, 1995). In seeking evidence to discredit the Democratic candidate, Michael Dukakis, the governor of Massachusetts, Republican strategists discovered the Horton news story, presented it to a focus group, and found that the information and images turned the voters against Dukakis. While the Bush election aides (Lee Atwater, a strategist, and Roger Ailes, a media advisor) "were telling the literal truth" in the campaign ad, it was the "symbol" of Willie Horton that captured the voters and helped turn the public toward Bush (Jamieson, 1992:23).

The symbolic messages addressed the public's anxieties about crime and criminal justice policies. They included the following: (1) the portrayal of Dukakis as a "liberal" politician who supported furlough programs, even for murderers, and thus a candidate who was soft on crime; (2) the public's fear of crime, especially violent crime such as rape; and (3) the race issue, which reinforced the image of black criminals (e.g., Horton) preying on white victims (i.e., Angela Miller and Clifford Barnes).

Incomplete and false statements about furlough programs and the Horton case fueled the drama and reinforced the significance of the crime issue in shaping voters' preferences. Even when facts regarding the overall successes of the Massachusetts and federal furlough programs were presented, or when information about Horton's previous successful eight furloughs were reported, the public's image and judgment of the liberal, anti–death penalty candidate (Dukakis)—and what federal crime policies he might propose—were resistant to change. As Jamieson observed, "messages that induce fear dampen our disposition to scrutinize them for gaps in logic" (1992:41).

While the Horton case was atypical and exaggerated, it was effectively utilized to condense the public's worst fears about crime and criminals in order to identify Dukakis with those negative images and emotions and to persuade voters to elect Bush as a get-tough champion of law and order. In diminishing the significance of other campaign issues, "'crime' became a shorthand signal to a crucial group of white voters, for broader issues of social disorder, evoking powerful ideas about authority, status, morality, self-control and race" (Edsall & Edsall, 1991:77).

Jamieson's compelling analysis of how the Horton incident was used by both the media and the Bush strategists illustrates how

Conservative activist Floyd Brown announces a television advertising campaign designed to damage the campaign of Democratic presidential candidate Bill Clinton. Brown was the admaker who turned Willie Horton into a political lia- bility for Michael Dukakis in 1988. (*AP Photo/Barry Thumma*)

the complex issue of crime can be distorted and co-opted. In this case, a candidate who was trailing in the opinion polls was able to surge ahead on a popular anti-crime message and win the election. A decade later, candidates remember the four important lessons of Willie Horton.

(1) *Don't be soft on crime.* For example, support capital punish- ment. During his first term as governor of Arkansas, Bill Clinton opposed capital punishment. After losing in one election, he became an advocate of capital punishment and was re-elected. In 1994, Tom Ridge, a Republican candidate for governor of Pennsylvania, cam- paigned to enact more anti-crime legislation and to use the death penalty. In his first year as governor, he kept his campaign promise and executed two offenders, the first executions in the state since 1967.

(2) *Portray your opponent as soft on crime.* A Republican televi- sion campaign advertisement in 1988 pictured prisoners going through a revolving turnstile door in front of a prison and ended with the state- ment, "Weekend prison passes. Dukakis on crime." In Pennsylvania in 1994, candidate Ridge labeled his opponent Mark Singel as soft on crime because of Singel's support of commutation for an offender who was released and subsequently killed an elderly women.

(3) *Simplify the crime issue.* First, use dichotomies. Dukakis opposed the death penalty; Bush supported the death penalty. Dukakis was "for" offenders; Bush was "for" victims. "Whenever issues are framed in such a divisive way, it is clear what the outcome will be" (The Sentencing Project, 1989:3). Second, use people and incidents rather than facts and statistics. The public identified the furlough issue with Willie Horton, the criminal; Clifford Barnes, the stabbed fiancé; and

Angela Miller, the rape victim. Notwithstanding the tragedy and violence of these crimes, Horton's furlough was one of 76,455 furloughs granted while Dukakis was governor and only one of 275 that resulted in escape (Jamieson, 1992:20). This information on the furlough program's success rate of 99.6 percent could not compare with the emotion and visceral reaction to one furlough and the real people involved.

(4) *Reinforce messages with emotional content.* The campaign advertisements using the Horton incident associated the words "liberal," "rape," "furlough," "escape," "violent," and "brutal" with Dukakis.

As a result of the Horton experience and the politics of the 1988 Presidential election, furlough programs, which were used by several states and the federal government, with average success rates of 95 percent (*Criminal Justice Newsletter*, 1992:4), fell under criticism. Eligibility and availability were restricted. In Massachusetts, the state with the most drastic reductions, prison furloughs decreased 76 percent, from 5,857 in 1987 to 1,423 in 1990. The federal prison system went from 17,860 furloughs in 1987 to 5,245 in 1990, a 71 percent reduction (*Criminal Justice Newsletter*, 1992:4).

In reviewing these themes, it is evident that what to do about crime and criminals is a significant public concern. Therefore, candidates' platforms must be consistent with public sentiment, perspectives, and expectations. However, if being tough on crime is a prerequisite for candidates, then the defining question for them is how tough are you. This tends to distort rational discussion about crime policy by escalating punitive impulses and rhetoric, and by generating more severe anti-crime legislation, longer sentences, and more emphasis on incarceration and prisons. As a result, crime policy becomes skewed toward the conservative ideological end of the policy continuum and legislated sanctions become vehicles for the posturing of get-tough politicians.

WAR MODEL

In the context of this get-tough posturing, an anti-crime concept that is consistent with the simplification of the crime problem and that also captures punitive attitudes toward criminals is the war model of crime control. The war metaphor was evident during Prohibition and eventually became the model for the war on drugs in the early 1970s, reaching a zenith in the late 1980s (Walker, 1998:250). The images and media reporting of crime and drugs (especially cocaine) fueled alarm about a growing drug epidemic that was contributing to the nation's crime problem.

Capitalizing on the get-tough momentum and targeting drugs and drug offenders, the Bush administration, through the Office of National

Drug Control Policy and its "czar," declared war on this scourge upon the nation (Brownstein, 1996). The policy of this war on drugs was to "disrupt, dismantle and ultimately destroy the illegal market for drugs" (Brownstein, 1996:45). A critical assessment of this model of crime control, however, suggests that not only is it inappropriate, but the latent effects are harmful to society.

A declaration of war suggests an imminently threatening national crisis or open conflict requiring the use of extraordinary power and authority, and the mobilization of massive resources to curb the threat and vanquish the enemy. In war, an enemy is identified as well as demonized, and the line between the front-line soldier of national defense—between "them and us"—is clearly drawn. War is recognized to be a brutal affair that will expectedly result in a victory and the return to normalcy. The expectations also include a short conflict during which "wartime" powers must be exercised to ensure victory. Strategies may require escalation of efforts, additional forces, and intensified fighting. War also challenges the limits of legitimate authority and tests concerns about human rights.

These elements of war also characterize the intensive police crackdowns on street-level drug dealers; the collaboration of federal, state, and local law enforcement (including the use of the military); and more punitive sentencing policies toward drug offenders (Walker, 1998:250). In addition, images and stereotypes of the drug offender portray the enemy of the drug epidemic and the target of the war effort as young, inner-city, minority males who join gangs to terrorize communities and innocent citizens while conducting illegal drug deals and committing related crimes.

Unintended Effects

The latent consequences of the war model approach to crime control, however, include: (1) intensified racial tensions resulting from targeting minorities; (2) concerns about the erosion of civil rights as aggressive law enforcement strategies are encouraged; (3) increased costs of criminal justice, especially for prisons; and (4) continued fear of crime and criminals because efforts to reduce the correlates of crime are generally minimal.

In a discussion of civil rights, Treaster noted the racial overtones of the drug war, which targets "poor black sections where most of the police action takes place" (1990:E5). In addition, fearful citizens and potential victims of drug crime violence dismiss concerns about constitutional principles, citing more immediate concerns about public safety. As a result, law enforcement policies and actions that infringe on Fourth (search and seizure), Fifth (self-incrimination), and Sixth (legal representation) Amendment rights are viewed as a necessary price in the war on drugs (Treaster, 1990). Sensational incidents such as those involving Rodney King in Los Angeles and Abner Louima in New York (see Chapter 2, page 37) reveal glimpses of racial tension, excessive use of force, and the mentality of a "thin blue line" between "them and us"—all of which seem to be encouraged by the war model (Herbert, 1997). In New York City, "complaints about police misconduct are up more than 56 percent" but citizens tend to "look the other way because they believe this strategy (aggressive policing) helps reduce crime" (Harden, 1997:10). In spite of some public approval for the outcomes, law enforcement abuses tend to erode authority and to contribute to a siege mentality.

Furthermore, the legislative policies that established a 100-to-1 ratio between sentences for trafficking crack cocaine and powder cocaine also underscore the resulting racial disparity in fighting the drug war (Wren, 1997). In this case, the federal

> mandatory minimum sentence applies to thresholds of 5 grams of crack and 500 grams of powder. But critics have attacked the disparity, saying that it puts far more blacks than whites behind bars for five years or longer, because whites are statistically more likely to snort or inject cocaine, while blacks are likelier to smoke cocaine in its cheaper crack form (pp. A1, A14).

The targeting of crack cocaine and the existence of disparate drug sentences have significantly contributed to the increasing number of incarcerated offenders and to prison overcrowding. With more than 2.1 million offenders in state and federal prisons, drug offenses have been a driving force behind the crowding (Harrison & Beck, 2005). By 1995, approximately 60 percent of federal prisoners were incarcerated for drug offenses (Mumola & Beck, 1997). Between 1985 and 1995, the number of state prisoners sentenced for drug offenses increased 478 percent, from 38,900 to 224,900 (Mumola & Beck, 1997:10). Explaining the growing number of female prisoners, which increased from 44,065 in 1990 to 103,310 in 2004 (Harrison & Beck, 2005), is the fact that about one in three women is serving time for drug-related offenses compared to one in eight in 1986. In federal prisons, about 80 percent of female prisoners are incarcerated for drug-related offenses (Owen, n.d.). In 1999, about 90 percent of offenders convicted of a drug offense in federal courts "received a sentence that included imprisonment" (Scalia, 2001:8). Regarding the implication of racial disparity,

> during the 10-year period, the number of black inmates serving time for drug offenses rose by an estimated 117,400, while the number of white inmates in for drug offenses rose

by 64,900. Overall, the increasing number of drug offenders accounted for 42 percent of the total growth among black inmates and 26 percent of the growth among white inmates (p. 10).

The image of the male minority as the "enemy" of the war on drugs is further reinforced by the disproportionate incarceration rates for whites and blacks. The data in Table 1.2 indicate that in 1995 black males were seven times more likely to be in prison than were white males. In addition, "on December 31, 1995, an estimated 3.2 percent of all black males were in prisons, compared with less than half of 1 percent of all white males" (Mumola & Beck, 1997:9). By the end of 2003, "9.3 percent of black males (age 25-29) were in prison compared to 2.6 percent of Hispanic males and 1.1 percent of white males (Harrison & Beck, 2004:1).

Efforts to reduce the disparity between federal sentences for crack cocaine and powder cocaine were initiated by former Attorney General Janet Reno and former drug-policy director Barry McCaffrey. While McCaffrey "had wanted to propose eliminating the sentencing disparity entirely," he joined the Attorney General in proposing a 10 to one gap (e.g., 25 grams of crack and 250 grams of powder cocaine) (Wren, 1997:A14). Although this recognizes the apparent injustice in the sentences, the political ramifications raise doubt about acceptance of the proposal. An earlier recommendation from the United States Sentencing Commission to eliminate the disparity was rejected. As was discussed earlier, politicians do not want to appear "soft" on crime, and they are "particularly sensitive to accusations of being soft on drugs" (Wren, 1997:A14).

Table 1.2
Estimated Number of Sentenced Male Prisoners per 100,000 Male Residents

Year	White	Black	Hispanic
1985	246	1,559	542
1990	339	2,376	817
1995	461	3,250	1,174
2000	449	3,457	1,200
2003	465	3,405	1,231

Source: Christopher J. Mumola and Allen J. Beck (1997). *Prisoners in 1996*. Washington, DC: Bureau of Justice Statistics. Allen J. Beck and Paige M. Harrison (2001). *Prisoners in 2000*. Washington, DC: Bureau of Justice Statistics; Paige M. Harrison and Allen J. Beck (2004). *Prisoners in 2003*. Washington, DC: Bureau of Justice Statistics.

In its 2002 Report to Congress, the United States Sentencing Commission again recommended revisions to statutory sentences that would reduce the crack–powder disparity: "Congress has not acted on those recommendations" (2002:v). To support the recommendations, the following findings were reported to Congress (2002:Chapter 8):

1. The current penalties exaggerate the relative harmfulness of crack cocaine.

2. Current penalties sweep too broadly and apply most often to lower-level offenders.

3. Current quantity-based penalties overstate the seriousness of most crack cocaine offenses and fail to provide adequate proportionality.

4. Current penalties' severity mostly impacts minorities.

With the escalation of crime control and criminal justice efforts, especially for drug control, the total expenditures for anti-crime policies continue to increase. For example, between 1981 and 1996, the United States spent $290 billion on the war on drugs (Frankel, 1997:6). This included budget increases of 40 percent for the Federal Bureau of Investigation and 33 percent for the Drug Enforcement Agency, and a military budget for patrolling United States borders that has grown from $1 million in 1980 to $958 million in 1997 (Frankel, 1997:7).

Of the $180.5 billion economic costs of drug abuse in 2002 (compared to $107.5 billion in 1992), about $36.4 billion was attributed to costs associated with criminal justice, including $14.2 billion for the operation of prisons (Office of National Drug Control Policy, 2004:xi). According to the Office of National Drug Control Policy (ONDCP), "another $9.8 billion was spent on state and local police protection" (2004:xi). In the 2006 Fiscal Year budget request for federal drug control, 61 percent of $12.4 billion is designated for law enforcement and interdiction, 26 percent for treatment, and 13 percent for prevention (Office of National Drug Control Policy, 2005:7). Essentially, based on data reviewed by Harrison (2004:par 2):

> Each year, the U.S. government spends more than $30 billion on the drug war and arrests more than 1.5 million people on drug-related charges. More than 318,000 people are now behind bars in the U.S. for drug violations. This is more than the total number of people incarcerated for all crimes in the United Kingdom, France, Germany, Italy and Spain combined.

The increased concentration of resources in fighting the war on drugs and the emphasis on enforcement and crime control have contributed to the federalization of the criminal justice system and to positioning toward a national police system (McGee, 1997). The joint efforts (especially of the FBI, DEA, and CIA) in sharing information, technology, and agents is continuing to support the juggernaut of criminal justice that Gordon described as a manifestation of conservative enforcement, control, and pro-punishment policies (1990). The results of these efforts include 13.7 million arrests in 2002, of which 1.54 million arrests were for drug charges (11.2%) and "another 590 thousand (4.3%) were for offenses deemed attributable to drug abuse" (Office of National Drug Control Policy, 2004:III-22).

In this context, the juggernaut reflects how misplaced belief in the war model as crime policy contributes to the escalation of control, expansion of the criminal justice system, and encroachment on—and potential threats to—civil rights. The view that more police (100,000) and more prisons to confine the "prisoners of the war on drugs" are needed to fight crime overlooks some of the lessons of the Vietnam War. Commitment to failed policy not only contributes to increases in human and resource costs but also to further dehumanization of the "enemy" and to desperate acts of inhumanity. For example, 45,941 United States soldiers were killed in combat (an additional 10,420 died in noncombat-related deaths) in Vietnam before the war ended in 1973 but this was not until after Lt. William Calley, Jr. was convicted for his role (personally killing 109 Vietnamese) in the My Lai massacre, in which 347 people, including "old men, women, boys, girls, and babies" were killed (Sheehan, 1988:689).

The potential for this type of tragedy was seen in Texas, where a United States Marine Corporal involved in military anti-drug operations fatally shot a teenager on the Texas-Mexico border. In response, the Pentagon suspended its border operations (Verhovek, 1997). In addition, the brutal assault of Abner Louima by police officers not only suggests a racially motivated attack against a Haitian immigrant but also raises questions about the consequences of "zero tolerance" crime fighting and concerns about the patterns of police brutality (Beals & Bai, 1997).

In reviewing the lessons of Prohibition and police crackdowns on drugs, Walker is also skeptical about the effectiveness of war-model policies (1998:251, 253). Aside from their limited intended effects, the unintended consequences included: (1) law enforcement abuses and corruption, (2) "social damage . . . in loss of respect for the law" (Walker, 1998:254), and (3) angry and hardened attitudes toward offenders. All of these warrant a reassessment of current crime control policy.

CYCLES OF SOCIAL CONTROL AND CRIME POLICY

Various ideas about crime, criminal behavior, and philosophies of punishment have already been reviewed. In the context of this earlier discussion, consider that social thinkers have also speculated on the nature of society, including the concept of a "social contract" and the need for a "collective use of force" to preserve social and moral order (Collins & Makowsky, 1993). From revenge to restoration, seeking the "right" justification for punishment has been important to society (Clear, 1994).

For example, while revenge is still expressed as an individual, emotional impulse to retaliate against criminals, this motive has been co-opted and redirected by the more important need to maintain social order. As a result, the United States has moved away from informal, personal responses to crime and has developed a more cumbersome, formal, and rational system to maintain social order. Historically, one of the first "socially" imposed punishments—and a move away from the practice of personal revenge vendettas—was exile. This was significant as a form of punishment because (1) it established banishment from the social group as a legitimate means to preserve the social order, and (2) it was the "beginning of criminal law as we know it" (Allen & Simonsen, 1995:7). Rather than trying to reform the individual and keep him or her in good standing with society, this "exclusionary" practice reflects what has become a cyclic pattern of exclusionary and inclusionary policies of social control (Cohen, 1985).

In the twenty-first century, the exclusionary-inclusionary concept includes policies of incarceration and decarceration. For example, the 1960s included initiatives to deinstitutionalize and reintegrate offenders (as well as the mentally ill). In contrast, the 1980s and 1990s witnessed a significant increase in incarceration rates and the use of prisons for punishment and incapacitation. This exclusionary policy of control was also facilitated by three concurrent developments: (1) the discrediting of rehabilitation as a goal of criminal justice—a media message that "nothing works," (2) the view of criminals as free-willed individuals making rational decisions to commit crime—a shift in the ideology of crime, and (3) the emphasis on public safety and victims' rights rather than concerns with offenders' rights—politics and politicization of crime.

As in the nineteenth century, which included a period of "great incarcerations" (Cohen, 1985:33), the late twentieth century cycled back to a new era of even greater incarcerations and exclusions. For example, in 1999, prison population growth reached new records—2 million prisoners with 5.2 percent annual growth (The Sentencing Project, 1999)—"in spite of 6 straight years of declining crime" (Butterfield, 1998: A14). Based on his report and interviews of corrections officials, Butterfield observed that "the imprisonment boom has developed a built-in growth dynamic independent of the crime rate" (p. A14). We suggest that this dynamic is the confluence of media, ideology, and politics.

This type of cyclic policy pattern has also been recognized by Archambeault and Archambeault (1982) in what they call a "perturbated spiral compression" model of policy change. The authors describe five stages of policy evolution in which new ideas emerge, reach a point of maximum impact, begin to decline, and then become integrated into collective knowledge. In the final state, reconceptualized and redefined ideas re-emerge and the cycle continues (pp. 158-160). This process is irregular (perturbated) and continuous (spiral), and the evolution of policy changes is occurring more quickly (compressed).

These concepts—cycles of crime control policy—are relevant to understanding criminal justice and social control because they show that competing ideologies and theories provide the momentum for policy change. As Cohen observed, "the problems, inconsistencies, contradictions and unintended consequences" of crime control policies provide opponents with a rationale to begin dismantling and replacing discredited and bankrupt policy (1985:35). The "nothing works" rationale propelled the decline of rehabilitation and the emergence of just deserts and the justice model (Archambeault & Archambeault, 1982; Cullen & Gilbert, 1982). In a similar pattern, by the mid-1990s, concerns about (1) increasing costs, (2) irrationality of sentencing policies, (3) disproportionate minority imprisonment, and (4) continuously increasing prison populations provoked more intense criticism of exclusionary, incarcerative policies and skepticism with the get-tough justice model (Merlo & Benekos, 1992).

The control-by-confinement approach, while still well-entrenched at the beginning of the twenty-first century, was beginning to unravel enough to allow alternative theories and ideologies to re-emerge as suggested in Archambeault and Archambeault's model. As the pendulum of incarceration and exclusion was beginning to slow, the rationale for new, more inclusionary models was being developed in the form of a "balanced approach" for juveniles (Bazemore & Umbreit, 1994) and "restorative justice" for adults (Van Ness & Strong, 2002).

Seeking Balance

Even though fear and frustration with juvenile crime persist, and news headlines continue to portray egregious examples of youth violence, a rational response to youth crime is offered with the "balanced approach" to the juvenile justice system. The model incorporates elements of treatment and punishment for the offender as well as concern for victims and public safety. As explained by Bazemore and Umbreit (1994:1):

> [R]estorative justice, the guiding philosophical framework for
> this vision, promotes maximum involvement of the victim, the
> offender and the community in the justice process and presents
> a clear alternative to sanctions and interventions based on ret-
> ributive or traditional treatment assumptions.

In the context of the cycles of social control discussed above, a salient
element of the balanced approach model is the effort to "transcend
unproductive conflicts between crime control and treatment" (Bazemore & Umbreit, 1994:2). In addition, the balanced approach mitigates
the urge to banish the offender (exclusion) and presents a vision of
restoring the offender to a responsible role in the community (inclusion) by responding to the harm suffered by victims and to victim needs
while still holding the offender accountable to the community.

Similarly, the restorative justice model attempts to "transform" the
focus of criminal justice away from punishment, deterrence, and incapacitation toward "justice that promotes healing." It involves and
includes the community in the process (Van Ness & Strong, 2002:37).
Van Ness and Strong explain that one criticism of government control
of criminal justice is that it often does harm not only to the offender
but also to the victim. In effect, this formal, rational control becomes
what Miller terms "iatrogenic punishment," by which intervention
intended to do good actually worsens the condition (Miller, 1996:119).
The criminal justice intervention (e.g., incarceration) "further alien-
ates [the offender] from the community, strains family relationships,
and may lead to long-term employment disadvantages or prevent them
from making amends to their victims" (Van Ness & Strong, 2002:40).

The restorative justice approach integrates previous policies of
rehabilitation and reintegration and emphasizes an inclusionary model
of social control. As victims' movements have worked to interject
their concerns into the crime control and criminal justice processes, the
restorative initiatives seek to involve the entire community in working
for justice, order, and peace. Van Ness and Strong conclude that
restorative justice encourages offenders "to take responsibility for
their actions and for the harm they have caused, by providing redress
for victims, and by promoting reintegration of both within the community" (2002:49). This clearly embraces inclusionary ideology and
is consistent with the juvenile justice efforts to achieve a balanced
response to the harm done by youthful offenders.

In contrast to the get-tough, incarcerative momentum of the 1980s
and 1990s, these models—balanced justice and restorative justice—suggest that, at least philosophically and conceptually, a rationale is being
promoted to slow the punitive, vengeful character of criminal justice.

Race and Exclusion

The exclusionary and punitive themes that have characterized public attitudes and policies toward criminals have been even more evident in the treatment of African-American offenders. Throughout United States history, race has been a pernicious and pervasive issue underlying criminal justice reforms. Lazarus has noted that in the context of Supreme Court reviews of constitutional law, one of the most consistent and deeper rifts that has plagued the nation is race (1997:23). From minority voting rights and school desegregation to conflicts over affirmative action laws and policies, the Court has wrestled with this "American dilemma" (Myrdal, 1962). Dionne describes this as the "American paradox" because the nation "began with a Constitution that permitted slavery and a Declaration of Independence whose core ideas subverted slavery" (1997:27).

Today, the issue of race reflects more pragmatic concerns for the criminal justice system. For example, while blacks comprise 13 percent of the population, they represent approximately 44 percent of prisoners in state and federal institutions while whites account for 35 percent and Hispanics for 19 percent (Harrison & Beck, 2004). In fact, "at the end of 1996, there were more black men in prison than whites, 526,200 to 510,900" (Butterfield, 1998:A14). In 2003, the number of black men sentenced to prison increased to 586,300 compared to 454,300 white males (251,900 Hispanic males were sentenced) (Harrison & Beck, 2004). In addition, the United States incarceration rate was 445 per 100,000 Americans in 1997; for black males, it was 3,096 per 100,000 compared to 370 per 100,000 for white males (Butterfield, 1998:A14). By 2003, the U.S. incarceration rate climbed to 486 per 100,000: the incarceration rate for white males was 465 per 100,000; for black males it was 3,405 per 100,000 (Harrison & Beck, 2004).

According to data compiled by The Sentencing Project (1997b), while white males have a 4 percent lifetime chance of serving time in prison, black males have a 28 percent chance of doing so. From 1988 to 1994, in state prisons the black incarceration rate increased from 6.88 times to 7.66 times the incarceration rate of whites. Moreover, while one in 15 young white males (20-29 age group) was under some type of correctional control (prison, jail, probation, parole), approximately one in three young black males was under similar control. This represents an increase from the one in four black males (age 20-29) under correctional control that was reported in 1990 (The Sentencing Project, 1997b). Clearly, these data demonstrate racial disparity and reflect one of the consequences of the war on drugs and determinate sentencing policies that targeted street-level drug crimes. The consequences will be further discussed in Chapter 3.

This disparity is also a consequence of differences in poverty levels and income inequality for whites and blacks (Wilson, 1996). In examining the impact of a global economy on inner-city, disadvantaged blacks, Wilson argued that the decline of legitimate employment opportunities can destabilize social institutions, create preconditions for crime, and put poor blacks at higher risk for deviance.

In response to this evidence of racial disparity, Miller (1996) has been critical of the criminal justice system and policies that disproportionately target and punish young black men, especially for less serious offenses. His concerns include the aggravated deterioration of race relations and the harm done to African-American families by the politics of crime control and the war on drugs. His scholarly treatise provides evidence to support the contention that the growth of the crime control industry has not only targeted black males but also contributed to conditions that will increase the likelihood that this pattern will be perpetuated.

It is against this backdrop of media, ideology, and politics that we present the remaining chapters. Lest you conclude that there are no signs of optimism in the criminal justice system, let us assure you that this is not the case. On the contrary, there are many manifestations of successful and innovative programs and policies in existence. For example, community policing, intensive supervision probation, early childhood intervention programs, and collaborative juvenile delinquency prevention programs demonstrate that the society and the system are capable of preventing and curbing crime. As we begin the twenty-first century, the debate continues regarding which strategies to employ.

NOTE

[1] In March 1998, Andrew Golden, age 13, and Mitchell Johnson, age 11, waited outside Westside Middle School in Jonesboro, Arkansas, and shot and killed four students and one teacher as they evacuated the school after an alarm had been triggered. In April 1999, in Littleton, Colorado, Eric Harris, age 18, and Dylan Klebold, age 17, entered Columbine High School and methodically opened fire on students and teachers, killing 12 students and one teacher before shooting themselves. Several explosive devices and weapons were found at the scene.

DISCUSSION QUESTIONS

1. In reporting crime, why do the media focus on "extreme, dramatic" cases? What are the consequences of this style of reporting? Discuss recent sensational cases of crime and examine the elements and themes of the crime reporting.

2. Examine the relationship between the prevailing political "ideology" and the media in constructing crime stories.

3. Explain the dynamics that have produced "personalized" legislation.

4. Discuss the consequences of the relationship between gatekeepers and journalists.

5. Discuss the concept of "vicarious victimization." What are the implications for crime policy? Consider the effects of emotion versus rationality in understanding crime.

6. Compare the assumptions and perspectives of the classical and positivist schools of thought. What crime control strategies are suggested by each school? Which school is more consistent with your views and assumptions?

7. Examine the concept of crime as a surrogate social problem. Discuss the implications that this phenomenon has for the development of public policies and crime control strategies. What does the practice of "racial profiling" suggest about this concept?

8. Critique the observation that the "ideologically grounded debate on crime may be waning." What does this suggest about the politicization of crime?

9. Discuss the lessons that the 1988 presidential campaign and the Willie Horton incident have had on politics, politicians, and crime policies.

10. Examine the limits and unintended consequences of the "war model" as a crime policy. What is the appeal of this approach? What alternative crime policy "models" can you suggest?

11. Using the concept of cycles of social control, discuss the future of crime control policies in the United States. What do you expect will be the future of crime control?

REFERENCES

Allen, Harry E., and Clifford E. Simonsen (1995). *Corrections in America: An Introduction*, 7th ed. Englewood Cliffs, NJ: Prentice Hall.

Anderson, David C. (1995). *Crime and the Politics of Hysteria*. New York: Random House.

Archambeault, William G., and Betty J. Archambeault (1982). *Correctional Supervisory Management: Principles of Organization, Policy, and Law*. Englewood Cliffs, NJ: Prentice Hall.

Bai, Matt (2005). "The Framing Wars." *The New York Times Magazine* (July 17):38-45, 68-71.

Baker, L. (1983). *Miranda*. New York: Atheneum.

Barak, Gregg (1995). "Between the Waves: Mass-Mediated Themes of Crime and Justice." *Social Justice* 21(3):133-147.

Bazemore, Gordon, and Mark S. Umbreit (1994). *Balanced and Restorative Justice*. Washington, DC: Office of Juvenile Justice and Delinquency Prevention.

Beals, Gregory, and Matt Bai (1997). "The Thin Blue Line." *Newsweek* (September 1):52-53.

Beccaria, Cesare (1981, 1764). *On Crimes and Punishment*. Trans. by Henry Paulucci. Indianapolis: Bobbs-Merrill.

Beck, Allen J., and Paige M. Harrison (2001). *Prisoners in 2000*. Washington, DC: U.S. Department of Justice, Office of Justice Programs.

Brownstein, Henry H. (1996). *The Rise and Fall of a Violent Crime Wave: Crack Cocaine and the Social Construction of a Crime Problem*. Albany: Harrow and Heston.

Butterfield, Fox (1997a). "Property Crimes Steadily Decline, Led by Burglary." *New York Times* (October 12):A1, A26.

Butterfield, Fox (1997b). "Drop in Homicide Rate Linked to Crack's Decline." *New York Times* (October 27):A10.

Butterfield, Fox (1998). "Prison Population Growing Although Crime Rate Drops." *New York Times* (August 9):A14.

Chermak, Steven M. (1994). "Body Count News: How Crime is Presented in the News Media." *Justice Quarterly* 11(4):561-582.

Clear, Todd R. (1994). *Harm in American Penology: Offenders, Victims, and Their Communities*. Albany: State University of New York Press.

CNN (2005a). "Evidence Examined in Idaho Kidnapping." July 3. *http://www.cnn.com/2005/US/07/03/idaho.children/index.html*

CNN (2005b). "Congress Gets Lunsford Legislation." April 21. *http://www.cnn.com/2005/POLITICS/04/21/lunsford.act/index.html*

Cohen, Stanley (1985). *Visions of Social Control*. Cambridge, UK: Polity Press.

Collins, Randall, and Michael Makowsky (1993). *The Discovery of Society*, 5th ed. New York: McGraw-Hill.

Cronin, Thomas E., Tania Z. Cronin, and Michael E. Milakovich (1981). *U.S. v. Crime in the Streets*. Bloomington, IN: University of Indiana Press.

Cullen, Francis T., and Karen E. Gilbert (1982). *Reaffirming Rehabilitation*. Cincinnati: Anderson.

Criminal Justice Newsletter (1992). "Prisons Grant More Furloughs, But Eligibility Is Tighter." (January 2):4.

DiIulio, John J., Sr. (1992). "The Value of Prisons." *The Wall Street Journal* (May 13):A16.

Dionne, E.J., Jr. (1997). "Tolerating Our Differences." *The Washington Post National Weekly Edition* (August 18):27.

Dorgan, Byron L. (1997). "Crime in America." *Congressional Record—Senate* (March 14):S2317-S2319.

Durantine, Peter (1996). "Tougher Sentencing Rules for Juveniles Go Into Effect." *Erie Morning News* (March 19):A5.

Edsall, Thomas Byrne, and Mary D. Edsall (1991). "Race." *The Atlantic Monthly* (May) 267:5, 53-86.

Fairchild, Erika S., and Vincent J. Webb (eds.) (1985). *The Politics of Crime and Criminal Justice*. Thousand Oaks, CA: Sage.

Frankel, Glenn (1997). "The Longest War." *The Washington Post National Weekly Edition* (July 7):6-8.

Geranios, Nicholas K. (2005). "Idaho Kidnap Suspect Charged with Murder." ABC News. July 12. *http://abcnews.go.com/US/wireStory?id=933002*

Goldberg, Jeffrey (1998). "Sore Winner." *The New York Times Magazine* (August 16):30-33.

Gordon, Diana (1990). *The Justice Juggernaut: Fighting Street Crime, Controlling Citizens*. New Brunswick, NJ: Rutgers University Press.

Greenfield, Lawrence A., and Tracy L. Snell (2000). *Women Offenders* (Revised). Washington, DC: U.S. Department of Justice, Office of Justice Programs.

Hagan, Frank E. (2002). *Introduction to Criminology: Theories, Methods and Criminal Behavior*, 5th ed. Belmont, CA: Wadsworth/Thomson Learning.

Harden, Blaine (1997). "In Fighting Crime, Thinking Small Can Pay Off Big." *The Washington Post National Weekly Edition* (July 28):10.

Harrison, Ann (2004). "Counting the Costs of the Drug War." AlterNet. *http://www.alternet.org/drugreporter/18641/*

Harrison, Paige M., and Allen J. Beck (2004). "Prisoners in 2003." *Bureau of Statistics Bulletin*. Washington, DC: U.S. Department of Justice, Office of Justice Programs.

Harrison, Paige M., and Allen J. Beck (2005). "Prison and Jail Inmates at Midyear 2004." *Bureau of Statistics Bulletin*. Washington, DC: U.S. Department of Justice, Office of Justice Programs.

Herbert, Bob (1997). "Connect the Dots." *New York Times* (August 24):E13.

Jamieson, Kathleen Hall (1992). *Dirty Politics: Deception, Distraction, and Democracy.* New York: Oxford University Press.

Kappeler, Victor E., Mark Blumberg, and Gary W. Potter (1996). *The Mythology of Crime and Criminal Justice,* 2nd ed. Prospect Heights, IL: Waveland.

"The Laci Peterson Case" (2005). CourtTV.com. *http://www.courttv.com/trials/peterson/*

Lakoff, George (2004). *Don't Think of an Elephant! Know Your Values and Frame the Debate.* White River Junction, VT: Chelsea Green.

Lazarus, Edward (1997). "The Geography of Justice." *U.S. News & World Report* (July 7):20-27, 32.

Lombroso, Cesare (1912/1968). *Crime: Its Causes and Remedies.* Montclair, NJ: Patterson Smith.

Lueck, Thomas J. (2005). "Serious Crime Declines Again in New York at Rate Outpacing the Nation's." *New York Times* (June 7). *http://www.nytimes.com*

Marion, Nancy E. (1995). *A Primer in the Politics of Criminal Justice.* New York: Harrow and Heston.

McGee, Jim (1997). "Is the FBI Too Charged Up?" *The Washington Post National Weekly Edition* (August 11):6-9.

Merlo, Alida V., and Peter J. Benekos (1992). "Adapting Conservative Correctional Policies to the Economic Realities of the 1990s." *Criminal Justice Policy Review* 6(1):1-16.

Miller, Jerome G. (1996). *Search and Destroy: African-American Males in the Criminal Justice System.* Cambridge, UK: Cambridge University Press.

Mills, C. Wright (1959). *The Sociological Imagination.* New York: Oxford University Press.

Mumola, Christopher J., and Allen J. Beck (1997). "Prisoners in 1996." *Bureau of Justice Statistics Bulletin.* Washington, DC: U.S. Department of Justice, Office of Justice Programs.

Myrdal, Gunnar (1962). *An American Dilemma,* 2nd ed. New York: Harper and Row.

New York Times (1998). "Silence Envelops Cosby Murder Case." June 30. *http://www.nytimes.com*

New York Times (2005a). "Tough Law on Child Molesters." (May 3):18.

New York Times (2005b). "Sex Offender Registry Available on Web." July 22. *http://www.nytimes.com*

Office of National Drug Control Policy (2004). *The Economic Costs of Drug Abuse in the United States, 1992-2002.* Washington, DC: Executive Office of the President.

Office of National Drug Control Policy (2005). *National Drug Control Strategy, FY 2006 Budget Summary*. Washington, DC: Executive Office of the President.

Okwu, Michael (2005). "How Effective in Megan's Law?" MSNBC (July 5). *http://www.msnbc.msn.com/8476294/*

Owen, Barbara (n.d.). *Women in Prison*. Drug Policy Alliance. *http://www.drug policy.org*

Potter, Gary W., and Victor E. Kappeler (1998). *Constructing Crime: Perspectives on Making News and Social Problems*. Prospect Heights, IL: Waveland.

Rahimi, Shadi (2005). "A Remorseless Rudolph Gets Life Sentence for Bombing at Clinic." *New York Times* (July 18). *http://www.nytimes.org*

Reiman, Jeffrey (1998). *The Rich Get Richer and The Poor Get Prison: Ideology, Class, and Criminal Justice*, 5th ed. Boston: Allyn & Bacon.

Rosch, Joel (1985). "Crime as an Issue in American Politics." In Erika S. Fairchild and Vincent J. Webb (eds.), *The Politics of Crime and Criminal Justice*. Thousand Oaks, CA: Sage.

Russakoff, Dale (1998). "The Power of Grief." *The Washington Post National Weekly Edition* (June 22):27.

Sacco, Vincent F. (1995). "Media Constructions of Crime." *The Annals of the American Academy of Political and Social Science* (539):141-154.

Sasson, Theodore (1995). *Crime: How Citizens Construct a Social Problem*. New York: Aldine de Gruyter.

Scalia, John (2001). *Federal Drug Offenders, 1999 with Trends 1984-99*. Washington, DC: U.S. Department of Justice, Office of Justice Programs.

Schor, Juliet B. (2004). *Born to Buy*. New York: Scribner.

The Sentencing Project (1989). *The Lessons of Willie Horton: Thinking About Crime and Punishment for the 1990s*. Washington, DC: The Sentencing Project.

The Sentencing Project (1997a). *America Behind Bars: A Comparison of International Rates of Incarceration*. Washington, DC: The Sentencing Project.

The Sentencing Project (1997b). *Facts About Prisons and Prisoners*. Washington, DC: The Sentencing Project.

The Sentencing Project (1999). *Facts About Prisons and Prisoners*. Washington, DC: The Sentencing Project.

Sheehan, Neil (1988). *A Bright Shining Lie: John Paul Vann and America in Vietnam*. New York: Random House.

Stallings, Robert A. (1990). "Media Discourse and the Social Construction of Risk." *Social Problems* 37(1):80-95.

Stockwell, Jamie (2005). "The 'CSI Effect.'" *The Washington Post National Weekly Edition* (May 30-June 5):29.

Thomas: Legislative Information on the Internet. *http://thomas.loc.gov*

"Today Show" (2005). "Police Detail 8-Year-Old's Kidnap Ordeal." July 15. *http://www.msnbc.msn.com/id/8582503/*

Treaster, Joseph B. (1990). "Is the Fight on Drugs Eroding Civil Rights?" *New York Times* (May 6):E5.

United States Sentencing Commission (2002). *Report to the Congress: Cocaine and Federal Sentencing Policy* (May). *http://www.ussc.gov*

Van Ness, Daniel, and Karen Heetderks Strong (2002). *Restoring Justice*, 2nd ed. Cincinnati: Anderson.

Verhovek, Sam Howe (1997). "Pentagon Halts Drug Patrols After Border Killing." *New York Times* (July 31):A1, 9.

Walker, Samuel (1998). *Sense and Nonsense About Crime and Drugs: A Policy Guide*, 4th ed. Belmont, CA: West/Wadsworth.

Welch, Michael, Melissa Fenwick, and Meredith Roberts (1998). "State Managers, Intellectuals, and the Media: A Content Analysis of Ideology in Experts' Quotes in Feature Newspaper Articles on Crime." *Justice Quarterly* 15(2):219-241.

Wilson, William Julius (1996). *When Work Disappears*. New York: Knopf.

Wren, Christopher S. (1997). "Reno and Top Drug Official Urge Smaller Gap in Cocaine Sentences." *New York Times* (July 22):A1, 14.

2

Police: Maintaining a Delicate Balance

When the problem is crime, one of the first responses is to think about the police. After the attack on New York's World Trade Center on September 11, 2001, the use of "first responders" to characterize the front-line defenders of public safety (and freedom) captured media attention. Heroic images of police, firefighters, and emergency medical technicians, arriving at the scene to provide aid and establish order, elevated the stature of uniformed personnel. The images reinforced the police mission to protect and defend and portrayed police in a very positive role.

These images of police are also part of the popularized story of "cops and robbers" and crime fighting. This classic image, however, misinforms public expectations, distorts understanding of the police, and disappoints police recruits. In his study of police and responses to street crime, Scheingold (1991) presented evidence to challenge this myth of good cops catching bad criminals and attempted to explain how law enforcement and crime control are more complex social phenomena involving politics, politicians, and police. He concluded that punitive values (i.e., ideology) and political interest (i.e., politics) "transcend the practicalities of crime control and the empirical findings of criminological research" (1991:15). Policy and policymaking, therefore, are about controlling and influencing "competing social visions" of crime (i.e., media) and perpetuating myths of crime and punishment (p. 14). This chapter reviews some of the dynamics and dichotomies of the police and policing in an effort to focus on the practicalities of crime control.

IMAGES

The media have had profound consequences on criminal justice by focusing public and political attention on police behavior and by shaping and reinforcing images of the police. Weitzer concluded that "celebrated incidents of police misconduct may color citizens' attitudes toward the police" (2002:397). For example, in July 2005, the Los Angeles Police Department (LAPD) was involved in a hostage situation in which a suspect, Jose R. Pena, used his 17-month-old daughter, Suzie Pena, as a shield while shooting at police. Both Pena and his daughter were killed after a three-hour shootout with police (Broder, 2005).

According to LAPD Chief William Bratton, this was "only the second hostage to be killed in a case involving the department's special weapons and tactics team in its 38-year history" (Broder, 2005:par. 8). While police said Pena (who was allegedly depressed, taking medication, and drunk) "left them no choice . . . there was little sympathy for the police at the child's mother's house" (Broder, 2005:par. 18). The televised news of the crime scene included statements of fact from police officials, which were contrasted with emotional reactions from neighbors, family, the child's mother, and statements of grief from the mayor of Los Angeles, Antonio Villaraigosa.

Citizen protests about the child's death and the minimal efforts taken by police to protect her safety were countered with official information about the "extraordinary volatile situation" and the failed opportunities given to Pena to surrender (Wittmeyer & Winton, 2005:par. 9). Tensions in this Watts area of Los Angeles were high as protestors carried signs calling police "baby killers." This same neighborhood was the subject of similar notoriety in the past. In 1965, it experienced the infamous Watts riots that started when a white police officer stopped a black driver, and in 1992, the area received national attention when the Rodney King incident became a flashpoint for police-citizen tensions.

The 81-second videotape that captured LAPD officers "arresting" Rodney King is not easily dismissed. The behavior raised questions about police brutality, racism, and the effectiveness of police training and supervision. The role of the media in perpetuating this "news" story by inviting expert commentary and rebroadcasting the videotape illustrates how a local critical incident can become a national issue capable of polarizing the public. For some, the image was the police at its worst, using excessive force to brutally attack and beat a minority motorist. For others, it was the police subduing a fleeing suspect who was later determined to be a convicted felon on parole. After a jury acquitted four police officers in April 1992, the riots in Los Angeles offered more news stories and televised reports that provided the opportunity to replay the videotape of the Rodney King beating. During the riots, 38 people were killed and more than 1,200 were injured (Staten, 1992).

While this incident "triggered" new policing reforms (Fyfe, Greene, Walsh, Wilson & McLaren, 1997), it also was reminiscent of the images of police during the social unrest and civil rights protests of the 1960s. It reinforced the negative image of police and prompted new questions about the nature of police behavior. In August 1997, in New York City, another incident of alleged police brutality (or criminality) captured the headlines, became national news, and again reinforced the negative police stereotype.

Abner Louima, a Haitian immigrant, alleged that after he was arrested for disorderly conduct, he was taken to the 70th Precinct in Brooklyn, where four police officers beat him and sexually assaulted him with the wooden handle of a toilet plunger (Kocieniewski, 1997a). Louima was hospitalized for serious internal injuries; four officers and one sergeant were indicted; and questions were raised about supervisors' responses. In addition, after being given limited immunity from prosecutors, only two officers of the almost 100 who were interviewed provided any "valuable information" about the alleged stationhouse brutality (Barry, 1997). Louima later filed suit against the New York Police Department and the Patrolmen's Benevolent Association because "they had jointly encouraged a 'blue wall' of silence that fostered police misconduct" (Fried, 1998:1).

In response, former Police Commissioner Howard Safir maintained that this incident was not reflective of the police department (Goldberg, 1998:33):

> But most police officers understand their role and how they're held accountable. The Louima case was a separate crime. It wasn't related to police activity. Police brutality by definition is, I go to arrest you, and you resist. I can use reasonable force. But after you're down, I hit you on the head five times. That's brutality. But taking someone 30 minutes after an event, taking them into a room and brutalizing them the way it allegedly happened, that's criminal.

Contrast this image of police with the one from almost a year later, in July 1998, in the United States Capitol building, where two police officers, Jacob Chestnut and John Gibson, were killed in the line of duty while trying to protect tourists and staffers from an alleged mentally ill gunman (Thomas & Annin, 1998). While the nation mourned with the officers' families, the officers' heroism for selflessly protecting others underscored the serious and dangerous nature of police work and reinforced the "thin blue line" metaphor of policing (i.e., the image that law enforcement officers stand as the last defense between law-abiding citizens and dangerous criminals). [A Bureau of Justice Statistic report released in July 1998 identified that law enforcement officers had the highest rate of occupational victimization: 306 per 1,000 workers, compared to 218 for corrections officers, 184 for taxi drivers, and 117 for security guards (Warchol, 1998). In 2003, 52 law enforcement officers were feloniously killed (Federal Bureau of Investigation, 2004)]. The Capitol incident presented an opportunity for the media to report on the courageous, positive image of police and the bravery and dedication of all law enforcement officers (*The Washington Post National Weekly Edition*, 1998:25):

> Last week, the city and nation singled out for praise two brave U.S. Capitol Police officers whose lives were taken as they served at their appointed posts. It was a senseless and unforgettable crime. But because Jacob Chestnut and John Gibson—and men and women serving in critical posts like theirs—everyone who visits or works at the Capitol's cherished monuments and buildings is safer.

This incident (1) reinforced the public's fear of random, senseless violence, (2) aggravated the experience of vicarious victimization, and (3) drew attention to other "lonely desperadoes" and "mentally ill" violent offenders of notoriety: John Hinckley, who shot and wounded President Ronald Reagan; Theodore Kaczynski, the "Unabomber"; and Timothy McVeigh, perpetrator of the Oklahoma City bombing (Thomas & Annin, 1998:22).

DICHOTOMY AND DISTORTION

This type of media coverage makes the public more aware of police behavior (Griffin & Ruiz, 1998) but also serves to perpetuate and exaggerate two images or dichotomies of the police: one of pubic servants holding a thin blue line of protection as in first responders after 9/11 (the good cop), and the other, of sociopathic personalities hiding behind a blue wall of silence as in the assault of Abner Louima (the bad cop). In this sense, police can be likened to a two-headed or "Janus" figure. As adapted from Bortner's discussion of the bifurcated juvenile justice system, the Janus figure refers to a Roman god who has a head with two opposing faces (1988:364). In addition to this bifurcated image, the media (especially television and movies) emphasize the good-cop "face" by promoting the crime-control, law-and-order image of police that accentuates crime-fighting expectations. "Presentations of police are often overdramatized and romanticized by fictional television crime dramas while the news media portray the police as heroic, professional crime fighters" (Dowler, 2003:111). Dowler's assessment is that "media portrayals of police officers and (research) findings reveal two conflicting views. Some researchers argue that the police are presented favourably in the media, while other research suggests that the police are negatively portrayed in the media" (2003:111). As reviewed in Chapter 1, since the 1960s, the issue of street crime has become a public problem in search of solution. While it may be an intractable problem, the police crime-fighting role has been exaggerated to the extent that the public has unrealistic expectations of what police can do about the crime problem.

> This is so because, in our search for a simple solution to the problem of crime, we have tried to unload this social problem on the police and the rest of the criminal justice system. This has been a mistake (Fyfe, Greene, Walsh, Wilson & McLaren, 1997:39).

In documenting the realities of police work, researchers have found that "law enforcement" represents a small element of patrol officer duties characterized by reactive efforts to restore order. (See Fyfe, Greene, Walsh, Wilson & McLaren, 1997, Chapter 2, for a discussion of the police role in society.) As Dowler concludes, "the public's perception of victims, criminals, deviants, and law enforcement officials is largely determined by their portrayal in the mass media" (2003:109). Essentially, the media contribute to a misunderstanding of police work by reiterating the crime-fighting image and by portraying a "supercop" as a symbol of the police. As a result, when politicians respond to the crime problem by putting more police on the streets, as was the case with the 1994 Crime Bill, the public has false expectations of the outcomes. Police become politicized as the rhetoric of crime control obscures the parameters and limits of law enforcement. In addition, fighting crime has a tendency to take on characteristics of "punitive policy" (Scheingold, 1991:80) and to contribute to the imbalance between crime control and due process by emphasizing crime control objectives (Packer, 1968). This model underscores the protection of society from offenders who have violated the rules of order and have threatened the safety of citizens. The criminal is portrayed as an evil character who must be apprehended and removed from society.

In his study of how citizens "frame" or construct and make sense of crime issues, Sasson found that more emphasis on civil rights rather than on public safety was viewed as having handcuffed the police; this was perceived by respondents as having contributed to a "faulty" criminal justice system unable to respond to criminals adequately (1995:45). In other words, as the citizen respondents in the study used their understanding of crime, arguably based on "bits of media discourse" (p. 9), some indicated that police needed to be able to do more crime fighting. This reflects the public's understanding of—and support for—the law-and-order strategy of dealing with crime. While citizens have other sources for crime information (personal experience, friends, vicarious victimizations), the media reinforce the crime-fighting scenario and contribute to how citizens define their expectations for the police. This is suggested by English's observations of law enforcement officers in a study of organized crime and Vietnamese gangs (1995:289):

> When speaking frankly, most federal agents and cops admit that their mandate as lawmen is all too often determined by what the media and, by extension, the public designate as a priority.

Politics also contributes to this construction of public expectations.

POLITICS AND REFORM

From the early evolution of municipal policing in the United States, politics has been a salient force in police behavior. As Fyfe and colleagues describe, "police departments were used as a source of political patronage that provided jobs for the people the (political) machines needed for their vote" (1997:10). Consequently, police officers derived their authority from the local "political power structure" and often used physical force to coerce and control citizens of lesser position and culture. Decentralized departments facilitated the exercise of discretion and personal style to maintain order in the neighborhoods. Over time, this dynamic of politics and police led to corruption, inefficiency, and discrimination. It is from these antecedents that police reforms have developed.

In an effort to depoliticize police departments and professionalize policing, reforms that began in the twentieth century attempted to use the "bureaucratic-efficiency" model to centralize control and to develop a rational-legal approach to police administration (Fyfe, Greene, Walsh, Wilson & McLaren, 1997:14-15). The objective of these reforms was to identify principles and procedures that would dictate police work and make departments more independent from political manipulation. This effort to disengage from political control "called for the kind of professionalism in which power was lodged predominantly in the chiefs of departments and in which training, discipline, and impartiality in enforcing the law were stressed" (Fairchild & Webb, 1985:10).

This was the direction of reform until the social and civil unrest of the 1960s raised new questions about police policies and precipitated a new wave of reforms, including court interventions that put "restrictions on investigation and interrogation practices" (Scheingold, 1991:76). In addition to the changing social, legal, and political conditions, Fyfe and colleagues also noted the importance of other factors that provided impetus for a new era of reforms (1997:24): (1) empirical research on the effectiveness of police strategies, (2) the due process revolution that countered the crime control emphasis, (3) the public's increasing alarm over crime and disorder, and (4) the politicization of crime as a national issue. This shift from the legalistic to the professional was characterized "by emphasis on closer ties between police and public and less social and occupational isolation, and greater accountability of the police" (Fairchild & Webb, 1985:11). Concern with accountability and police-community relations encouraged new strategies such as team policing, foot patrols, community relations programs, and problem-oriented policing. From the traditional era to the legalistic and more recent community policing developments, these twentieth-century reforms have attempted to improve efficiency, accountability, and professionalism as a means to achieve more effective crime control and crime prevention (Fyfe, Greene, Walsh, Wilson & McLaren, 1997).

One of the characteristics of the community policing movement (to be discussed below) that is most evident in the problem-oriented policing (POP) approach proposed by Goldstein (1990) is commitment to working with the community and other agencies to reduce the problems that contribute to crime. In part, this was an effort to shift from a crime fighter (i.e., catching the criminal) to a problem solver (i.e., crime prevention). As a general model incorporating various elements, community policing signals a change "from a closed, incident-driven and reactive bureaucracy to a more open, dynamic, quality-oriented partnership with the community" (Taylor, Fritsch & Caeti, 1998:1). Even with this recent reform, however, there are still opportunities for politics to insinuate into police work. For example, one of the questions about this and other police strategies is how to measure their effectiveness. Traditionally, if police were supposed to fight crime, then the number of arrests and the clearance rate would be a good annual measure of effectiveness—or at least a reflection of police activity. In contrast, with preventive and community policing, a reduction in the number of arrests and reported crime would indicate desired outcomes. In either case, Fyfe and colleagues caution that "overreliance on result-based performance measures tends to reinforce unreasonable and inappropriate behavior" (1997:47). An example of this is the manipulation of crime data to facilitate a "reduction" in crime.

As crime in the 1990s and early 2000s continued to decline, this good news put "new pressure on police departments to show ever-decreasing crime statistics" (Butterfield, 1998:1). This resulted in charges that in some major cities (Philadelphia, Boca Raton, New York, and Atlanta), police administrators were "falsely reporting crime statistics" by downgrading property crimes in order to demonstrate continued reduction of felony crimes. For example, in Boca

Raton, burglaries were recorded as vandalism or missing property; as a result, the reported felony crime rate declined 11 percent in 1997 (Butterfield, 1998).

In the case of New York City, former Mayor Rudolph Giuliani claimed in 1997 that "his crime-fighting strategies" had saved lives and reduced crime "to the lowest level since the mid-1960s" (Kocieniewski, 1997c:1). Giuliani advocated that police officers be more aggressive and crack down on minor street offenses to improve the quality of life. His involvement and investment in police matters may be atypically visible in the 1990s, but his presence illustrates how political pressure still influences police policy and demonstrates the politicization of crime. From President Clinton, who signed legislation authorizing 100,000 additional police officers for community policing, to Mayor Giuliani, who merged Housing and Transit Police with the New York Police Department to centralize New York policing, the politicization of the police is an important dimension of criminal justice in the United States.

IDEOLOGY

As noted, ideas and expectations about what police should do and how they should do it have characterized the reforms of the twentieth century. It is not surprising, then, that these expectations about the proper role for police have been reflective of certain ideologies and are "always a part of the political agenda" (Fairchild & Webb, 1985:8). For example, during the more liberal era of the 1960s, concern about due process and suspects' rights was evident in the safeguards established by the courts. The concerns about police-community relations were directed at accountability of the police to the community. That is, the police were "expected to subject themselves to community standards of behavior and to minimize coercive practices" (Scheingold, 1991:77). This was the so-called "handcuffing" of the police.

As crime became more of a national issue in the 1970s and 1980s (i.e., more politicized) and political leaders continued using the "war on crime" metaphor, some shifting from due process to crime control was inevitable, as were efforts to reinvest in and promote the crime-fighter image of the police (Scheingold, 1991:76). At the same time that community policing was evolving and attempting to define itself, parallel efforts to fight the war on drugs raised questions about civil liberties (i.e, due process) and "no-knock" searches. The get-tough ideology and accompanying rhetoric of the 1980s and 1990s reinforced a dualistic fallacy (i.e., society comprised of two distinct groups: good people and evil people) that portrayed criminals as bad individuals making rational decisions to pursue illegal activities—individuals who needed to be apprehended at whatever cost and removed from society for as long as possible. (This is reflected in the "three strikes and you're out" movement discussed in the next chapter.)

In other words, the due process model was considered an obstacle to fighting crime. Even President Clinton supported the "routine" use of no-knock entry for drug searches (*New York Times*, 1997). In this context—the police as warriors, criminals as enemies—the potential for abuse of authority is present. In New York City, where an "aggressive assault against drugs" was defended by the mayor and the police, concerns were raised about the number of police drug raids and the use of "terroristic" tactics, sometimes against innocent citizens who were wrongly identified by "confidential informants" (Cooper, 1998). In these anti-drug efforts, one tactic is to trade reduced charges against criminals for information that can be used to obtain search warrants. The accuracy of the information and the feasibility of the procedure have been questioned, and some citizens believe:

> [I]t may be time to rethink a policy in which the word of a single criminal, who is often paid for his information, can be enough to send armed police officers to break down doors and invade the homes of innocent people (Cooper, 1998:2).

Although these search mistakes are rare, they are costly in terms of lawsuits, good will, and public image. According to former NYPD Police Commissioner Howard Safir, "of the more than 3,000 search warrants executed last year (1997), the police raided only 6 wrong apartments" (Goldberg, 1998:33). Similarly, the "war" against illegal immigrants has also resulted in controversy. The Border Patrol has been charged with cruel and degrading treatment of illegal immigrants, including "beatings, sexual assault, racially derogatory comments and denial of medical care and food" (Verhovek, 1998:A12). In correctional institutions, the punitive, get-tough, exclusionary ideology and negative image of criminals as evil people has also evidenced cases of unnecessary force and abuse of inmates. In one maximum-security state prison, 40 officers were involved in 36 separate incidents of beating inmates and using excessive force to transfer inmates to segregated housing units (*Newsfront*, 1998). Some of these incidents were videotaped by institution cameras that officers knew were recording.

It is relevant to note these extreme cases because they illustrate the behavioral consequences predicated on a get-tough, punitive ideology that rationalizes the war-model metaphor. These cases of excessive use of force may be due to more than just the war-model metaphor or the characterization of criminals (including illegal immigrants) as evil people who deserve the "beatings" they receive. The authors maintain, however, that this is one important dimension that contributes to organizational and peer culture facilitating these behaviors (e.g., see McAlary, 1988). While there is always concern with police officer deviance, the concepts of criminal justice and the values that support a retributive philosophy do influence law enforcement policy and officer attitudes and behaviors. The fear of being victimized by street crime and the anxiety over social disorder are easily manipulated by politicians and translated into repressive policies and practices. Police are part of this dynamic as they respond to community expectations. A U.S. General Accounting Office (GAO) report on drug-related police corruption in the 1990s, for example, identified "job cynicism" and "dissatisfaction" with how they were perceived by the public as motivating factors in police corruption (1998:9). The report suggested that frustration with the "war on drugs" has given some police—and police departments—an attitude "that vigilante justice was the way to punish those who might otherwise go unpunished" (U.S. General Accounting Office, 1998:9). In attempting to explain how emphasis on drug enforcement has impacted on the nature of police corruption, the report recognized that "drug-related police corruption differs in a variety of ways from other types of police corruption" (p. 3). Some characteristics included (p. 8):

- Stealing money and/or drugs from drug dealers.
- Selling stolen drugs.
- Protecting drug operations.
- Submitting false crime reports.

In New York City, the "profit" motive also involved "small groups of officers who protected and assisted each other in criminal activities" (p. 3). In a sense, unrealistic expectations and goal frustration contribute to cynicism and help police to "rationalize" their behavior.

Although data on police corruption is incomplete, using FBI data on corruption cases from 1993 to 1997, the GAO (1998:35) identified a 51 percent increase in the number of drug-related cases opened for criminal investigation (61 to 92). Of all the corruption cases opened in 1997, the drug-related cases represented 48 percent of the total (92 of 190). This compares to 33 percent of all cases in 1993 (61 of 186). Of the law enforcement officers convicted in 1997, 53 percent were for drug-related offenses (79 of 150). In 1993, it was only 46 percent (59 of 129).

These data reveal that the number and proportion of drug-related corruption cases and criminal offenses by police have increased, thus reflecting another casualty of the war-model approach to the social problem of drug use and abuse. The context suggests that putting police on the front line of the war has been a factor in more corruption by increasing both the opportunity for illegal behavior and fostering the culture to tolerate it (U.S. General Accounting Office, 1998:4):

> One commonly identified factor associated with drug-related corruption was a police culture that was characterized by a code of silence, unquestioned loyalty to others, and cynicism about the criminal justice system.

The GAO recommended that in addition to raising the age and educational requirements for police recruits and requiring command accountability to control corruption, community policing could be an effective strategy to reduce corruption as well as to deal with the causes of crime and reduce the fear of victimization. Therefore, in contrast to reaction and retribution (wars and warriors), the ideology of community policing and its models offer a promising approach for policing.

COMMUNITY POLICING

As noted above, the most recent reform in policing has been the promotion of the community policing "philosophy." Fyfe and colleagues explain that this model supports "proactive crime prevention, problem solving, and community engagement . . . in efforts to obtain community cooperation and support in controlling crime and disorder" (1997:20). Others have also noted that because this is a general approach that includes various activities and programs, there is a lack of consensus on exactly what community policing is (Breci & Erickson, 1998; Taylor, Fritsch & Caeti, 1998). Nonetheless, about one-half of police agencies with populations of more than 50,000 have implemented this model. Moreover, the Violent Crime Control and Law Enforcement Act of 1994 provided funding for 100,000 officers to encourage communities to adopt community policing (Breci & Erickson, 1998:16). Since the bill was passed, more than $9 billion has been allocated to 10,537 law enforcement agencies (of more than 19,000 eligible agencies). According to Roth and Ryan (2000:2), preliminary estimates indicated that "between 84,700 and 89,400 (officers) will have been deployed by 2003." Koper, Moore, and Roth projected "that COPS (Office of Community Oriented Policing Services) will add 98,000 officers to the nation's communities on a temporary basis between 1994 and 2005, within a likely range of 93,400 to 102,700 officers" (2002:3-2).

Breci and Erickson question whether these agencies are "truly implementing community-oriented policing (COP), or are they merely trying to obtain the available federal funding?" (1998:16). In other words, has this "new" ideology of policing been politicized and favorably endorsed by the media to promote the impression of collaborative, decentralized reform? Taylor, Fritsch, and Caeti (1998) argued that this may be the case and cautioned that without systemic and structural changes in police organizations and administration, it may be premature to conclude that community policing is anything more than a concept. In their discussion of core challenges to community policing, they believe that it has already become too politicized:

> If a department was not involved in community policing then it was labeled backward, stationary, non-progressive, or worse, Neanderthal . . . police chiefs and academicians have too much at stake in criticizing community policing . . . and those individuals managing police departments understand, all too well, the political ramifications of heading a movement against what is deemed somehow more progressive and better than the status quo (p. 4).

They also criticize the "facade of success" that is being promulgated and the unrealistic expectations of police that are being presented to the public. While they endorse the principles and procedures of this concept, they remain skeptical that without meeting some tough challenges (e.g., the lack of empirical evidence that community policing has a positive impact on community perceptions of police; the need for systemic changes in all of city government; the actual rather than academic implementation of community policing), community policing will remain a rhetoric of buzzwords. Perhaps the recommendation of creating "a new class of higher-paid, more highly decorated community patrol officers," as suggested in New York City (Kocieniewski, 1998:1), is consistent with the challenges (i.e., structural changes) raised by Taylor, Fritsch, and Caeti. Without such changes, at best, community policing becomes what Griffin and Ruiz caution will only be a "positive step towards improving community relations," while its long-term effects remain in doubt (1998:38).

In fact, the issues and concerns regarding the strategies that are necessary in order to "maintain" the popularized initiatives collectively called community policing have been addressed by others (Breci & Erickson, 1998; Fyfe, Greene, Walsh, Wilson & McLaren, 1997; Glensor & Peak, 1998; Sherman, 1997). In a study of law enforcement in Virginia Lake (Reno, Nevada), Glensor and Peak assess Goldstein's model (1990) of police problem solving—scanning, analysis, response, and assessment—and conclude that in order for community policing to make a lasting impact, a long-term commitment based on the following efforts is necessary to sustain the successes of initial intervention (1998:7):

continuing to assess and respond to emerging problems; maintaining regular liaison with community leaders, business groups and municipal agencies; and viewing the success of any initial problem-solving intervention not as the end but as the beginning.

In his critique of community policing and problem solving, Manning argued that while media, politicians, some scholars, and some law enforcement administrators have claimed the success of these policy initiatives, the evidence suggests otherwise (2005:150):

> Community policing was always a blurred, undefined label in search of a social location. It was a solution searching for a problem. The implication of the fashionable political rhetoric was that it was not, but would soon be, current practice.

Manning's review of the evidence indicates that the rhetoric of the reforms is "unsupported" and the realities of police culture, department organization, and social ideology discourage full commitment to problem-oriented, community-based policing policy. Based on interviews and a survey of the San Diego Police Department, Cordner and Biebel also concluded that problem-oriented policy was not fully implemented, and they recognized a "distinction between every day problem solving and problem-oriented policy" (2005:177). Essentially, even though "problem solving and community engagement has been embraced by many police departments with apparent success in improving police-community relations and reducing community problems," the implementation and practicality of this model is questioned (Cordner & Biebel, 2005:177).

Collectively, the authors noted above have serious concerns and questions about: (1) the politicization of community policing, (2) the rhetorical endorsement of a concept or ideology without commitment to adequate implementation strategies, and (3) the exaggerated expectations about the effectiveness of problem-oriented and community policing in curbing crime. They are not critical of the model but of the dynamics that seem to co-opt substantive transformation of the police. While there is wide support for the elements of this model—for example, community collaboration and partnership (see Chapter 6)—and their ability to focus on quality-of-life concerns, social services, and problem solving, there is also a recognized need "for a fundamental rethinking of the police role and a redesign of police services to respond to changing social conditions" (Fyfe, Greene, Walsh, Wilson & McLaren, 1997:24).

Even with these concerns and criticisms of community policing, gains have been made in police community relations, and some departments have demonstrated success in using the strategies of preventive policing (Harris, 2005). Recognizing that "there are almost as many definitions of community policing and its fundamental principles as there are police departments," Harris observed that "every successful community policing effort has looked at the connection to local residents as an essential pillar of its philosophy" (2005:23-24). After September 11, 2001, however, as the Department of Justice began using state and local law enforcement agencies as "an adjunct force in the federal effort to fight the war on terror," some of the gains in community relations were eroded (Harris, 2005:3). According to Harris, the use of local police in "immigration control" and "police questioning of 'nonsuspects'" (what Harris refers to as "Ashcroft policing" in reference to John Ashcroft who was the Attorney General after 9/11) was counterproductive to community policing (p. 4). Immigration enforcement alienated police from the communities and the citizens that could be instrumental in counterterrorism efforts (e.g., Arabs and Muslims) (p. 10). Interviews with nonsuspects, especially in Dearborn, Michigan, "home to the largest Arab and Muslim community in the United States," resulted in "massive squandering of goodwill and relationships with the community" (Harris, 2005:11).

As politicians keep the focus on crime reduction as a salient political issue and take credit for the effectiveness of get-tough, law-and-order criminal justice policies, the pressure on police administrators to demonstrate success (i.e., more decline in crime) will increase. While the two perspectives on policing—crime-fighting and problem-solving—are not incompatible, as crime rates begin to rise (as they eventually will), the politics of crime will turn toward warriors, not problem solvers. Therefore, to overcome the challenges and concerns identified above, it has been suggested that community policing needs to emphasize "restoration" as one of the core elements of policing as well as include strategies for problem solving and partnerships (U.S. General Accounting Office, 1998:5). (See Table 2.1.)

What Works?

As Scheingold concluded in his study of politics and the police, "it is difficult to distinguish the appearance of change from the substance of change" (1991:114). Taylor, Fritsch, and Caeti (1998), in a critique of the community policing reform movement that was discussed earlier, caution that this "style over substance" phenomenon may be occurring, thus explaining why community policing programs are not necessarily or consistently achieving their stated objectives. On a broader scale, Walker's (1998) review of various police strategies, which included adding more police and eliminating "technicalities" of procedure, suggests that "unleashing" the police is not likely to reduce crime. Similar conclusions were presented by Sherman (1997), who cau-

Table 2.1
Community Policing

Goal: Solve problems—improved relations with citizens is a welcome by-product.

Line Function: Regular contact between officers and citizens.

A department-wide philosophy and department-wide acceptance.

Internal and external influence and respect for officers.

Well defined role—does both proactive and reactive policing—a full-service officer.

Direct service—same officer takes complaints and gives crime prevention tips.

Citizens identify problems and cooperate in setting up the police agenda.

Police accountability is ensured by the citizens receiving the service in addition to administrative mechanisms.

Officer is the leader and catalyst for change in the neighborhood to reduce fear, disorder, decay and crime.

Chief of police is an advocate and sets the tone for the delivery of both law enforcement and social services in the jurisdictions.

Officers educate public about issues (like response time or preventive patrol) and the need to prioritize services.

Increased trust between the police officer and citizens because of long-term, regular contact results in an enhanced flow of information to the police.

Officer is continually accessible in person, by telephone, or in a decentralized office.

Regular visibility in the neighborhood.

Officer is viewed as having a "stake in the community."

Officer is a role model because of regular contact with citizens (especially youth role model).

Influence is from "the bottom up"—citizens receiving service help set priorities and influence police policy.

Meaningful organizational change and departmental restructuring—ranging from officer selection to training, evaluation, and promotion.

When intervention is necessary, informal social control is the first choice.

Officer encourages citizens to solve many of their own problems and volunteer to assist neighbors.

Officer encourages other service providers like animal control, fire fighters, and mail carriers to become involved in community problem solving.

Officer mobilizes all community resources, including citizens, private and public agencies, and private businesses.

Success is determined by the reduction in citizen fear, neighborhood disorder, and crime.

All officers are sworn personnel.

Source: Robert C. Trojanowicz and Bonnie Bucqueroux (1994). *Community Policing: How to Get Started*, pp. 133-134. Cincinnati: Anderson.

tioned against the simplistic notion that more cops mean less crime. He concluded that "how" police are used is more important in preventing crime than "how many" police are used (pp. 8-33). For example, he notes that four "focused" police strategies appear to be relatively effective (pp. 8-33):

1. Increased directed patrols in street-corner hot spots of crime.

2. Proactive arrests of serious repeat offenders.

3. Proactive drunk driving arrests.

4. Arrests of employed suspects for domestic assault.

In addition, some "promising" strategies include (pp. 8-34):

1. Police traffic enforcement patrol against illegally carried handguns.

2. Community policing with community participation in priority setting.

3. Community policing focused on improving police legitimacy.

4. Zero tolerance of disorder, if legitimacy issues can be addressed.

5. Problem-oriented policy generally.

In a review of numerous studies on the effectiveness of various police strategies, it is interesting that "legitimacy" was identified by Sherman as an important and salient element of the strategies that can make a positive difference; he explains (pp. 8-11):

> One of the most striking recent findings is the extent to which the police themselves create a risk factor for crime simply by using bad manners. Modest but consistent scientific evidence supports the hypothesis that the less respectful police are toward suspects and citizens generally, the less people will comply with the law. . . . Making both the style and substance of police practices more "legitimate" in the eyes of the public, particularly with high-risk juveniles, may be one of the most effective long-term police strategies for crime prevention.

Sherman's observation is consistent with one of the characteristics of community policing: involving the police in "partnerships" with citizens to focus on reducing the problems and conditions that can lead to crime. This type of social interaction has the potential of changing the image of police and enhancing the legitimacy of police work in the community. Replacing the 911 system with a one-on-one system has the potential to "reform" policing from crime fighting to problem solving and may correct the distorted image of police that media and politicians have promoted. Implementing the structural and substantive changes necessary to achieve this ideology of policing is the challenge for police administrators in the twenty-first century.

In spite of the challenges presented by the models of community policing and their implementation, this approach represents an important initiative for police and policing. Some evaluations of community policing programs have identified related effects, such as improved police–community relations and more positive citizen attitudes toward the police. For example, an evaluation of Chicago's Alternative Policing Strategy (CAPS) indicated "that police and residents have successfully negotiated various effective partnerships and that CAPS has reduced levels of crime and serious neighborhood problems" (National Institute of Justice, 1995a:1). One of the significant characteristics of CAPS and other community policing models is the "partnerships" and collaborative efforts between police and citizens. This is further discussed in Chapter 6.

Citizen involvement is important to the success of resolving neighborhood problems and this underscores different expectations of police. In fact, in the Chicago program, "the development and implementation of solutions were most successful when citizens were organized, developed strong leadership, and initiated problem identification" (National Institute of Justice, 1995a:2). In addition, a survey of law enforcement agencies found that while "no single approach emerged as a model," community partnership and problem solving were recognized as "core components" of community policing (National Institute of Justice, 1995b:2). In a commentary on what to do about crime, Wilson cautiously endorsed this community-policing approach because it focused on proactive, directed efforts to address real problems associated with crime (1994). In endorsing the ideas of Goldstein (1990), Wilson proposed that "problem-oriented" policing was a more appropriate name for the strategies identified as community-based policing.

While the endorsements of this policing strategy are encouraging, concerns about implementation (as noted above by Taylor, Fritsch, and Caeti [1998]) present lessons for both police and citizens. For example, implementation requires a long-term view of the process and the need to develop the support from citizens, elected officials, and community agencies (National Institute of Justice, 1995b:2). In an ongoing study of policing, Mastrofski, Parks, and Reiss (1998) found that even though community policing improves cooperative efforts between police and citizens, an evaluation of police in Indianapolis revealed that they were still oriented toward reactive policing (i.e., responding to calls for service). Police concerns about "reducing citizens' fear of crime, reducing public disorder, [and] encouraging public involvement in neighborhood improvements" were rated among the lowest goals (p. 2). It is not surprising that police are more oriented toward law enforcement than problem solving. The nature of training, field experiences, and occupational socialization tend to reinforce the crime-fighter image.

In his summary of the role that police can play in crime prevention, Skogan discussed how police can help: (1) maintain social control and (2) support "development of community organizations" (1997:93). While endorsing community policing strategies and recognizing the importance of training police, Skogan cautioned that an overlooked obstacle to successful implementation is "difficulty getting neighborhood residents involved" (p. 93). Citizens often fail to understand what police are doing and may remain skeptical and suspicious. Based on his ongoing assessment of community policing, Skogan offered three recommendations to facilitate more effective community policing (p. 94):

1. The support of the public must be won, not assumed.

2. Train citizens, not just police.

3. Get organizations involved.

Skogan's observations address the need for a true commitment to making this strategy successful rather than simply reacting to political pressure and popular rhetoric. As discussed above, this is commitment to a process not a program. This perspective is also underscored by Innes, who emphasized that "the importance of obtaining community input in defining problems has not been sufficiently appreciated" (2005:191). Without incorporating community into the process, problem-oriented policy will only lead to policing problems.

Third-Party Policing

Another policing strategy that recognizes the importance of both process and place on crime-reduction efforts is "third-party policing" (Buerger & Mazerolle, 1998). Consistent with Sherman's emphasis on targeting "hot spots" and "hot dots" of crime (1997), third-party policing attempts to "decrease opportunities for crime and disorder" by targeting "an intermediate class of nonoffending persons who are thought to have some power over the offenders' primary environment" (Buerger & Mazerolle, 1998:301). Police encourage (or coerce) "capable guardians" to improve control over places where deviant behaviors are probable, thus discouraging (or displacing) individual criminality.

According to Buerger and Mazerolle, third-party policing uses sanctions or threats of sanctions (often civil penalties) "against persons responsible for conditions that encourage lawlessness on the part of marginal persons" (p. 302). This includes landlords, commercial businesses, and bar owners. The authors reviewed two programs, the Beat Health program of Oakland, California, and the Minneapolis Repeat Call Address Policing (RECAP). They found evidence that place-based policing, which entailed working with property owners and landlords to "regain control" over at-risk areas, was effective in reducing drug nuisance problems (Beat) and calls for police service (RECAP). Buerger and Mazerolle concluded that: "The police actions merely provide a formal framework for the informal social control that better-endowed neighborhoods take for granted" (p. 321).

This strategy demonstrates problem-oriented policy and contributes to crime prevention and reduction by discouraging conditions and activities that facilitate criminal behaviors. Third-party policing is consistent with crime prevention goals and strategies such as "opportunity reduction" and "informal social control" programs that have been discussed by Fyfe and his colleagues (1997). They, thus, reinforce the proactive capacities of policing.

Homeland Security

After September 11, 2001, law enforcement agencies took on added responsibilities of preparing for terrorism. In addition to the creation of the Department of Homeland Security (DHS) in November 2002, and realignments in the Federal Bureau of Investigation (FBI), Central Intelligence Agency (CIA), and National Security Agency (NSA), state and local agencies also shifted personnel and resources into developing counterterrorism capabilities (Davis et al., 2004). At the local policing level this included (Davis et al., 2004:xvii):

- Expanding emergency response planning and mutual aid agreements.

- Planning for chemical, biological, and radiological (CBR) attacks.

- Reallocating and/or increasing spending to focus on terrorist preparedness.

The New York City Police Department (NYPD) not only increased the number of officers working "the terrorism beat" from about two dozen to about 1,000, it also assigned detectives to countries around the world to collect intelligence (e.g., Israel, Pakistan, Afghanistan, Russia, Britain) (Finnegan, 2005). Since the attacks of 2001, the Department has also been reorganized and includes a Deputy Commissioner for Intelligence and a Deputy Commissioner for Counter Terrorism who meet every morning with the NYC Police Commissioner, Ray Kelly (Finnegan, 2005:58). The NYPD also established "Operation Nexus," which is "a program that tracks terror-sensitive business" by making regular visits to talk with business personnel who may have useful information (e.g., hotels, religious clothing suppliers, financial institutions) (Finnegan, 2005:64). After the July 2005 subway bombings in London, four detectives (from Intelligence and Counter Terrorism) were sent to London (p. 65). In addition, other cities (e.g., Seattle, Boston, Los Angeles, Washington) have sent officers to other countries such as Israel to learn about counterterrorism and to receive training in "suicide bomber intelligence gathering and apprehension" (Kershaw, 2005:par. 5).

In Finnegan's report, it is evident that terrorism is a major "worry" for the NYPD and, notwithstanding federal efforts (e.g., FBI, CIA, DHS), the streets and subways of New York City are protected primarily by the NYPD. After the London bombings, "the New York City police began randomly searching bags and backpacks at subway stations and other travel hubs" (Kershaw, 2005:par. 3). As one sergeant observed, "9/11 is never over" (p. 64). These issues are not just the concern of major cities. In his assessment of "challenges" facing law enforcement, Carter concluded that law enforcement executives must "recognize that every law enforcement agency—regardless of size or location—has a stake in this global law enforcement intelligence initiative and, as such, must develop some form of an intelligence capacity in order to be an effective consumer of intelligence products" (2004:xi).

One initiative that received renewed attention and prominent coverage after the July 2005 subway bombings in London was the use of surveillance cameras to monitor public areas (e.g., streets, parks, airports). Several cities expanded surveillance networks by adding more cameras in more locations (Moore, 2005). With more than 2,200 cameras installed by July 2005, Chicago has one of the largest "homeland security grids" and has plans not only to increase the miles of fiber-optic grid throughout the city but also to add listening devices (Electronic Privacy Information Center, 2005). Video surveillance has been embraced as a "response to the threat of terrorism" and as a way to reduce crime and make cities safer (Kinzer, 2004:par. 14).

With funding from the Department of Homeland Security, cities and their law enforcement agencies are eager to install the technology and to use electronic surveillance to combat crime and prevent terrorism. Even though studies indicate that the systems have "little effect on crime," fear of terrorism is used to justify the millions of dollars being spent for surveillance projects (Electronic Privacy Information Center, 2005:par. 2). Even as cities rush to expand the number of cameras in use, some cities (e.g., Detroit, Miami, Oakland) are abandoning their systems because they have "little effect on crime prevention" (Electronic Privacy Information Center, 2005:par. 7). It is also important to remember that while the video images in London confirmed the identities of the bombers, they were not able to prevent the bombings (Weiss, 2005).

In addition to questions about utility and effectiveness, concerns about privacy, civil liberties, and misuse/abuse of camera surveillance have also been raised (Kinzer, 2004; Moore, 2005; Weiss, 2005). Some Muslims have been critical and "fear that American police will engage in religious or ethnic profiling" (Kershaw, 2005:par. 7). Instead of DWB (driving while black), the reference is to MEWC—"Middle Eastern with a camera" (Kershaw, 2005:par. 8). However, when images of terrorist activities (e.g., bodies and carnage from bombings) are repeatedly presented in television news, citizens dismiss concerns about "Big Brother" and place safety and security above privacy and freedoms (Kinzer, 2004). "For politicians, there is the temptation to hype it (terrorism), to practice the politics of fear" (Finnegan, 2005:71). In the case of city mayors, they promote video technology as a tool to help police do their job of monitoring the streets and protecting the public. In Washington, DC, after the announcement that more cameras would be installed in the city, mayor Anthony Williams downplayed threats to civil liberties and pointed to the lessons from the July 2005 London bombings (Weiss, 2005:B1).

For post-9/11 law enforcement, and in the era of the Department of Homeland Security, Polk and MacKenna recognize dilemmas that will continue to face policing in the twenty-first century (2005). A major issue is the increase in service expectations while fiscal resources diminish or are reallocated to other public needs. In discussing the supply–demand equation of policing, Polk and MacKenna see a weakening local tax base at the same time that the demand for police response to

A New Jersey State Police Detective on the New Jersey Homeland Security Task Force operates "Andros," a robot used to disarm weapons of mass destruction and bombs, at Lakehurst Naval Air Station in Lakehurst, New Jersey. World events have kept the New Jersey State Police Homeland Security unit busy since it was formed in the aftermath of 9/11. *(AP Photo/Tim Larsen)* public safety concerns and other expanding social problems continues to increase (p. 4). They also recognize that the "militarization of police" and the impact of technology will test "the balance between law enforcement and limitations on civil liberties" (2005:6). Emergent social, political, and economic dynamics will continue to affect priorities in policing, but the "lack of budgetary resources" will limit how law enforcement responds to the challenges (p. 8).

DISCUSSION: THE BALANCE

The successes of community policing—not only in confronting crime and bridging relations between police and community but also in promoting a different mission and vision of police—must be considered in the context of the image of police characterized by the militaristic mentality of the war model discussed in Chapter 1. At the same time that police are working with the community, they are becoming more aggressive and armed for the "war on crime." Kraska and Kappeler (1997) present convincing evidence that use of the war metaphor—especially in the continuing "drug war"—has paralleled an increase in the number of police paramilitary units (PPUs). This has intensified the warrior culture, justified the use of "militaristic equipment and technology," and reinforced "the cynical view that the most expedient route to solving social problems is through military-style force" (p. 12).

The media have also facilitated the popularization of this image of police. Special Weapons and Tactics (SWAT) teams and ninja-masked "techno-cops" have become popular themes not only in movies but also in news coverage of police raids and special operations (Kraska & Kappeler, 1997:3). The image of elite units of police appeals to the public and offers police the status and identity that some feel has been diminished by the rhetoric of community policing.

In a study of 548 police departments, Kraska and Kappeler found significant increases in the level of police paramilitary unit activity between 1986 and 1995. This was due to the "unprecedented number of search warrants" and reaction-oriented call-outs that coincided with the drug war in the late 1980s and early 1990s (p. 7). In addition, the authors noted that the militarism of the drug wars has also become "normalized" in routine patrol work, where "proactive policing" in some departments has become synonymous with military-style suppression (e.g., gang suppression) of "aggregate populations" in targeted areas (p. 12). The findings of a "heightened ethos of militarism" and "the normalization of paramilitary units into mainstream police work" (p. 12) suggest that there are unintended consequences of promoting the war metaphor as crime policy. As Kraska and Kappeler observed:

"Politicians, the media, and government officials joined in fueling drug war hysteria during the 1980s, leading Congress and two presidents to transform drug war discourse into tangible militarized action" (p. 1).

In this context, it is not surprising that stories of police brutality (Sigelman, Welch, Bledsoe & Combs, 1997) and abuse (Sontag & Barry, 1997) have become more salient issues. As discussed earlier, the tactics and motivations warranted by the war model sometimes result in excesses and allegations of police misconduct. It is also noted that with the war model and the accompanying increase in police paramilitary units, there has been a parallel increase in special elite units in corrections (e.g., Special Operations Response Team—SORT). These elite corrections officer teams are also part of the effort to control an "enemy" (i.e., the "prisoners of war").

While advanced technology and improved tactics are necessary for effective policing, the bifurcated images of police are reinforced: the PPU focused on reactive and proactive militarism, and the COP focused on preventive and problem-oriented policing. The images may seem contradictory; however, they are not incompatible. In fact, Kraska and Kappeler observed that they "are ideologically and pragmatically intertwined in an emerging form of policing" (1997:13):

1. The "war on crime and drugs" metaphor;

2. Community and problem-oriented policing ideology; and

3. The escalation and normalization of PPU activities.

The challenge is to avoid politics and ideological dogma that lead to extremism while at the same time achieving and maintaining balance among these elements of contemporary policing. After 9/11, this becomes even more difficult as law enforcement has engaged in a new war: the war on terrorism. Not surprising, the proposed federal budget for fiscal year 2006 eliminates funding for the COPS programs while increasing funding to the Department of Homeland Security and the FBI (counterterrorism and intelligence) (Budget of the United States Government, 2005). President Bush's "highest priority" for the Department of Justice is combating terrorism and, because the COPS grants were not determined to be effective in reducing crime, these programs are marked for elimination in fiscal year 2006 (Budget of the United States Government, 2005:201). In response, the position of the National Criminal Justice Association is that these funding eliminations "undermine criminal justice at the state and especially local levels" (2005:1).

DISCUSSION QUESTIONS

1. Discuss why images of police and policing are distorted. What can be done to create more balanced views of police?

2. Explain the cycles of police reform, and discuss the social and political dynamics that precipitated these reforms.

3. What are the consequences of viewing criminals as "evil enemies" in the war on crime?

4. Discuss why some observers are skeptical about community policing. What is the rhetoric versus the reality of this policing reform? What is your assessment of community-oriented policing?

5. Discuss how politics and political pressure affect police policies and practices. What examples can you identify?

6. What is "third-party policing"? How is it consistent with community policing initiatives? What are some unintended effects?

7. What are some reasons for the increase in police paramilitary units? Discuss some concerns surrounding this policing development.

8. Discuss the implications of dualistic views of police. What impact does this have for police recruits and the police subculture?

9. Examine the media's role in portraying crime and police. Discuss the consequences of a "law and order" image on the public's expectations and understanding of the police.

REFERENCES

Barry, Dan (1997). "Officers' Silence Still Thwarting Torture Inquiry." *New York Times* (September 5). *http://www.nytimes.com*

Bortner, M.A. (1988). *Delinquency and Justice: An Age of Crisis.* New York: McGraw-Hill.

Breci, Michael G., and Timothy E. Erickson (1998). "Community Policing: The Process of Transitional Change." *FBI Law Enforcement Bulletin* 67(6):16-21.

Broder, John M. (2005). "Man and Young Daughter Die in Shootout With Police." *New York Times* (July 12). *http://www.nytimes.com*

Budget of the United States Government (2005). *Fiscal Year 2006 Budget.* Washington, DC: U.S. Government Printing Office. *http://www.gpoaccess.gov/usbudget*

Buerger, Michael E., and Lorraine Green Mazerolle (1998). "Third-Party Policing: A Theoretical Analysis of an Emerging Trend." *Justice Quarterly* 15(2):301-327.

Butterfield, Fox (1998). "Possible Manipulation of Crime Data Worries Top Police." *New York Times* (August 3). *http://www.nytimes.com*

Carter, David L. (2004). "Law Enforcement Intelligence: A Guide for State, Local, and Tribal Law Enforcement Agencies." Washington, DC: U.S. Department of Justice, Office of Community Oriented Policing Services.

Cooper, Michael (1998). "As Number of Police Raids Increase, So Do Questions." *New York Times* (May 26). *http://www.nytimes.com*

Cordner, Gary, and Elizabeth Perkins Biebel (2005). "Problem-Oriented Policing in Practice." *Criminology and Public Policy* 4(2):155-180.

Davis, Lois M., K. Jack Riley, Greg Ridgeway, Jennifer E. Pace, Sarah K. Cotton, Paul Steinberg, Kelly Damphousse, and Brent L. Smith (2004). *When Terrorism Hits Home: How Prepared Are State and Local Law Enforcement?* Santa Monica, CA: RAND.

Dowler, Kenneth (2003). "Media Consumption and Public Attitudes Toward Crime and Justice: The Relationship Between Fear of Crime, Punitive Attitudes, and Perceived Police Effectiveness." *Journal of Criminal Justice and Popular Culture* 10(2):109-126. *http://www.albany.edu/scj/jcjpc/vol10is2/dowler.html*

Electronic Privacy Information Center (2005). "More Cities Deploy Camera Surveillance Systems with Federal Grant Money." (May). *http://www.epic.org/privacy/surveillance/spotlight/0505.html*

English, T.J. (1995). *Born to Kill*. New York: William Morrow.

Fairchild, Erika S., and Vincent J. Webb (eds.) (1985). *The Politics of Crime and Criminal Justice*. Thousand Oaks, CA: Sage.

Federal Bureau of Investigation (2004). "Law Enforcement Officers Killed and Assaulted, 2003" (November). Washington, DC: U.S. Department of Justice.

Finnegan, William (2005). "The Terrorism Beat: How is the N.Y.P.D. Defending the City?" *The New Yorker* (July 25):58-71.

Fried, Joseph (1998). "Louima Files Suit, Citing 'Blue Wall' of Silence." *New York Times* (August 7). *http://www.nytimes.com*

Fyfe, James J., Jack R. Greene, William F. Walsh, O.W. Wilson, and Roy Clinton McLaren (1997). *Police Administration*, 5th ed. New York: McGraw-Hill.

Glensor, Ronald W., and Kenneth Peak (1998). "Lasting Impact: Maintaining Neighborhood Order." *FBI Law Enforcement Bulletin* 67(3):1-7.

Goldberg, Jeffrey (1998). "Sore Winner." *The New York Times Magazine* (August 16):30-33.

Goldstein, Herman (1990). *Problem-Oriented Policing*. New York: McGraw-Hill.

Griffin, Catherine, and Jim Ruiz (1998). "The Sociopathic Police Personality: Is It a Product of the 'Rotten Apple' or the 'Rotten Barrel.'" Paper presented at the annual meeting of the Northeastern Association of Criminal Justice Sciences, Bristol, RI, June 11, 1998.

Harris, David A. (2005). *Good Cops: The Case for Preventive Policing*. New York: The New Press.

Innes, Martin (2005). "Reaction Essay: What's Your Problem? Signal Crimes and Citizen-Focused Problem Solving." *Criminology & Public Policy* 4(2):187-200.

Kershaw, Sarah (2005). "Suicide Bombings Bring Urgency to Police in U.S." *New York Times* (July 25). *http://www.nytimes.com*

Kinzer, Stephen (2004). "Chicago Moving to 'Smart' Surveillance Cameras." *New York Times* (September 21). *http://www.nytimes.com*

Kocieniewski, David (1997a). "Man Says Officers Tortured Him After Arrest." *New York Times* (August 13). *http://www.nytimes.com*

Kocieniewski, David (1997b). "Relatives, Not Officers, Were First to Complain." *New York Times* (August 14). *http://www.nytimes.com*

Kocieniewski, David (1997c). "Analysis: Drop in Crime Not So Easy to Explain." *New York Times* (October 28). *http://www.nytimes.com*

Kocieniewski, David (1998). "Panel is Said to Propose a New Class of Officers." *New York Times* (March 24). *http://www.nytimes.com*

Koper, Christopher K., Gretchen E. Moore, and Jeffrey A. Roth (2002). *Putting 100,000 Officers on the Street: A Survey-Based Assessment of the Federal COPS Program*. Washington, DC: The Urban Institute.

Kraska, Peter B., and Victor E. Kappeler (1997). "Militarizing American Police: The Rise and Normalization of Paramilitary Units." *Social Problems* 44(1):1-17.

Manning, Peter K. (2005). "Editorial Introduction: Problem Solving." *Criminology & Public Policy* 4(2):149-154.

Mastrofski, Stephen D., Roger B. Parks, and Albert J. Reiss, Jr. (1998). "Policing Neighborhoods: A Report from Indianapolis." *National Institute of Justice Research Preview* (July). Washington, DC: U.S. Department of Justice, Office of Justice Programs.

McAlary, Mike (1988). *Buddy Boys*. New York: G.P. Putnam's Sons.

Moore, Martha T. (2005). "Cities Opening More Video Surveillance Eyes." *USA Today* (July 17). *http://usatoday.com*

National Criminal Justice Association (2005). "The New Federal Budget and Its Impact on Crime and the Criminal Justice System." *http://www.ncja.org*

National Institute of Justice (1995a). "Community Policing in Chicago: Year Two." *Research Preview* (October). Washington, DC: U.S. Department of Justice, Office of Justice Programs.

National Institute of Justice (1995b). "Community Policing Strategies." *Research Preview* (November). Washington, DC: U.S. Department of Justice, Office of Justice Programs.

New York Times (1997). "The Police and Civil Liberties." (April 29). *http://www.nytimes.com*

Newsfront (1998). "DOC Initiates Disciplinary Proceedings at SCI Greene." 24(2):3, 13. Camp Hill, PA: Pennsylvania Department of Corrections.

Packer, Herbert L. (1968). *The Limits of the Criminal Sanction.* Stanford, CA: Stanford University Press.

Polk, O. Elmer, and David W. MacKenna (2005). "Dilemmas of the New Millennium: Policing in the 21st Century." *ACJS Today* 30(3):1,4-9.

Roth, Jeffrey A., and Joseph F. Ryan (2000). "The COPS Program After 4 Years—National Evaluation." *National Institute of Justice Research in Brief* (August). Washington, DC: U.S. Department of Justice, Office of Justice Programs.

Sasson, Theodore (1995). *Crime Talk: How Citizens Construct a Social Problem.* New York: Aldine de Gruyter.

Scheingold, Stuart A. (1991). *The Politics of Street Crime: Criminal Process and Cultural Obsession.* Philadelphia: Temple University Press.

Sherman, Lawrence W. (1997). "Policing for Crime Prevention." In Lawrence W. Sherman, Denise Gottfredson, Doris MacKenzie, John Eck, Peter Reuter, and Shawn Bushway, *Preventing Crime: What Works, What Doesn't, What's Promising,* pp. 8-1–8-58. Washington, DC: National Institute of Justice.

Sigelman, Lee, Susan Welch, Timothy Bledsoe, and Michael Combs (1997). "Police Brutality and Public Perceptions of Racial Discrimination: A Tale of Two Beatings." *Political Research Quarterly* (December) 50(4):777-791.

Skogan, Wesley G. (1997). "The Community's Role in Community Policing. In John J. Sullivan and Joseph L. Victor (eds.), *Criminal Justice 97/98*, pp. 93-95. Guilford, CT: Dushkin/McGraw-Hill.

Sontag, Deborah, and Dan Barry (1997). "Using Settlements to Measure Police Abuse." *New York Times* (September 17). *http://www.nytimes.com*

Staten, Clark (1992). "L.A. Insurrection Surpasses 1965 Watts Riots, 38 Dead, More Than 1,200 Injured." Emergencynet News Service (April). *http://www.emergency.com/la-riots.htm*

Taylor, Robert W., Eric J. Fritsch, and Tory J. Caeti (1998). "Core Challenges Facing Community Policing: The Emperor Still Has No Clothes." *ACJS Today* 17 (1):1, 3-5.

Thomas, Evan, and Peter Annin (1998). "A Loner's Odyssey." *Newsweek* (August 3):20-26.

U.S. General Accounting Office (1998). *Law Enforcement: Information on Drug-Related Police Corruption.* Washington, DC: U.S. General Accounting Office.

Verhovek, Sam Howe (1998). "Border Patrol is Criticized as Abusive." *New York Times* (May 21):A12.

Walker, Samuel (1998). *Sense and Nonsense About Crime and Drugs: A Policy Guide,* 4th ed. Belmont, CA: West/Wadsworth.

Warchol, Greg (1998). *Workplace Violence, 1992-1996.* Washington, DC: Bureau of Justice Statistics.

The Washington Post National Weekly Edition (1998). "Guardians at the Gate." (August 3):25.

Wilson, James Q. (1994). "What to Do About Crime." *Commentary* (September):25-35.

Weiss, Eric M. (2005). "D.C. Considering More Police Cameras: London Bombings Prompt New Debate on Surveillance of Public Places." *Washington Post* (July 14):B1

Weitzer, Ronald (2002). "Incidents of Police Misconduct and Public Opinion." *Journal of Criminal Justice* 30(5):397-408.

Wittmeyer, Alicia, and Richard Winton (2005). "Killing of Toddler Hostage in Shoot-Out Probed." *Los Angeles Times* (July 11). *http://www.latimes.com/news/local*

3

The Court Conundrum:
Confronting the Consequences of Policy

From the coverage of the Washington snipers' (John Allen Muham-mad and John Lee Malvo) murder trials, and the sexual abuse trials of the Catholic Church in Boston, to the conviction and sentencing of Den-nis Rader (the self-described "BTK" killer), it appears that society's pen-chant for crime news continues. Using content analysis, Yanich (2005) studied local television broadcasts in 20 markets in various parts of the country in the Spring of 1998. There were 2,002 crime news stories (26%) out of 7,667 total stories (Yanich, 2005:107). These news sto-ries typically led the broadcast, and they were accompanied by "the most dramatic pictures and words that were possible" (Yanich, 2005:130). In addition, the stories were presented as "episodes of human peril that were not connected to any other context" (Yanich, 2005:130). As a result, Yanich concluded that the ". . . viewers were left with the notion that they were all equally vulnerable to that peril regardless of their circumstances" (2005:130). Given these limita-tions, one might wonder how the public continues to consider local tele-vision news coverage as a primary source of information about crime and criminals.

CRIME NEWS, PUBLIC PERCEPTIONS, AND POLICY

When the media are confronted with a crime news story that is particularly heinous, more news time is devoted to the crime and, in some instances, a variety of crime experts are consulted. Even if the experts who are interviewed or quoted in high-profile cases are only capable of speculation, the media persist in soliciting their input. For example, in the Washington sniper case in 2002, television networks regularly offered profiles of the suspects from the crime experts. The experts had the same information on the suspects that the police made available to the public, but yet they were asked to describe the gender, race, age, residence, motivation, and social background of the unknown snipers. Incidentally, none of them predicted accurately, although they all agreed that they were men rather than women (Smolkin, 2002). According to Montgomery County State's Attorney, Douglas Gansler, the press increased the public's fear of the snipers. "The fear was such that everyone thought they were going to get shot" (Gansler quoted in Smolkin, 2002:31). Nonetheless, experts discuss and compare cases, speak authoritatively, and inform the public regularly when there is violent crime news.

Morning network news shows also appear to exert significant influence. According to Jeff Zucker, the president of NBC Universal Television Group, these shows "are driving network-television news divisions" (quoted in Auletta, 2005:68). The shows have shifted their focus to what Auletta categorizes as a "tabloid narrative." "On morning television, breaking news is usually less about Iraq and judicial nominations than about the tabloid narrative of the moment: the Michael Jackson trial, the disappearance of Jennifer Wilbanks (the 'runaway bride'), . . . a high school senior missing in Aruba" (Auletta, 2005:70). The networks are cognizant of the importance of these kinds of stories because they conduct minute-by-minute calculations of television viewers' reactions to stories, and according to Harry Smith (a veteran of television news programming), these tabulations indicate ". . . that the tabloid stuff bumps the numbers" (Smith quoted in Auletta, 2005:70).

Despite all the television coverage about crime, the average citizen does not appear to be very well informed regarding the reality of crime in the United States. From 1968 until 1990, and irregularly since then, the Gallup Organization has polled samples of the American population and asked, "Is there more crime in the U.S. than there was a year ago, or less?" (Pastore & Maguire, 2003). In each year until 1994, 80 percent or more of the respondents indicated that there was more crime (Tonry, 1998:13). It was not until 1996 and 1997 that those percentages began to decrease: in 1996, 71 percent responded "more," and in 1997, 64 percent responded that there was "more"

(Maguire & Pastore, 1997). Most recently, in 2002, 62 percent of the respondents indicated that there was "more" crime than the previous year. By contrast, 47 percent of the respondents in 2000 and 41 percent of the respondents in 2001 indicated that they thought there was more crime (Pastore & Maguire, 2003:129). The most recent data suggest that the public perceives that crime is increasing despite the decreases that are reported in official data.

If the average citizen is so ill-informed about the realities of crime, that might help to explain the impetus for the changes that have occurred in the area of criminal sentencing. The public's perception of crime appears to be enhanced by forces such as media coverage and politicians. In fact, Beckett's research illustrates that "both media coverage of and political initiatives on the crime issue were significantly associated with subsequent levels of public concern about crime, but the reported incidence of crime was not" (1997:9). In short, her findings suggest that rather than official statistics, it is the politicians' ability to focus the public's attention on crime that has greater impact on how the public evaluates the severity of the problem (Beckett, 1997:9).

The media portrayal of crime in the United States, then, is important in influencing public debate and public policy about criminal sentencing. The media have been extremely effective in promoting the demand for harsher sanctions in a variety of areas, from sexual offender legislation to parole. The extensive coverage directed at the Jessica Lunsford case and the earlier cases of Megan Kanka and Polly Klaas highlighted the danger that a "stranger" can pose to a child and the tragedy that can occur because of a parole decision to release an offender. A particularly heinous crime by one parole violator is enough to terminate parole for violent offenders in some states. It is with this premise that we examine the courts and sentencing in the United States.

There are many manifestations of the public's demand for more punitive sanctions. Perhaps the most obvious is the death penalty. Although the vast majority of the states (38 as of July 2005) and the federal government now have death penalty statutes (Death Penalty Information Center, 2005a), evidence demonstrates that Americans are somewhat equivocal in their support. For example, in their earlier research, Durham, Elrod, and Kinkade (1996) found that the Florida residents in their sample strongly supported capital punishment. Similarly, Gallup Poll data from the spring of 2005 indicate that 74 percent of Americans favor the death penalty (Death Penalty Information Center, 2005c). These data suggest that politicians know the American public overwhelmingly supports capital punishment and perceive no need to disabuse the public of the costs associated with its application or its likelihood of reducing crime (Durham, Elrod & Kinkade, 1996). Based upon their research, Durham and colleagues (1996) predicted that the death penalty would be used more frequently after 1996. According to the Death Penalty Information Center, the number of executions began to increase in 1997, reaching a high of 98 executions in 1999, and then 85 in 2000. However, in 2004, the number of executions had dropped to a low of 59 (Death Penalty Information Center, 2005a).

Research has also demonstrated that when respondents were presented with alternative sanctions, public support weakened. For example, in the same Gallup Poll in the spring of 2005, support for the death penalty declined to 56 percent when respondents were offered the alternative of life without possibility of parole in lieu of a death sentence. In 1997, when respondents were given the choice of a life sentence without possibility of parole instead of a death sentence, 61 percent of respondents chose this option. These data suggest that the public attitude toward the death penalty softens when there are alternative sanctions available. A sentence of life without possibility of parole (LWOP) is authorized in 37 states that had death penalty statutes in 2005 and in 11 states that do not have death penalty statutes (Death Penalty Information Center, 2005a).

There is still widespread belief that expenditures in the area of education and vocational training are more effective in addressing crime than prison construction (Cullen, 2005; Cullen et al., 1990, cited in Beckett, 1997:8). In short, while we do not speak with one voice when deciding how to deal with offenders, we clearly have embraced elements of a more punitive approach and, to a lesser extent, a more lenient approach for dealing with crime and criminals.

One of the consequences of a punitive stance on crime is the apparent disregard for the "costs" associated with it. The overreliance on incarceration is promoted with little concern for the costs of this public policy. We make little or no attempt to determine what the community's priorities are. For example, is the public willing to reduce education, health care, and community services such as trash collection, environmental protection policies, and road repair in exchange for incarcerating drug offenders or other nonviolent offenders?

Downing and Lynch (1997) suggest that when the "sentencer" (judge or jury) is asked to determine what an appropriate sentence for a particular offender should be, he or she should be given an actual estimate of what incarceration versus probation will cost the community. These estimates could be incorporated into the presentence investigation. If, for example, the recidivism rates for prison and probation are fairly similar, the judge might decide that probation is a more judicious way to spend the jurisdiction's limited resources. These economic statements are not intended to displace issues like public safety or justice, but Downing and Lynch contend that if the costs were calculated, the utilization of incarceration might be reduced and local communities would be included in any discussions about how their resources should be allocated (p. 188).

How is it that this relatively easy mathematical exercise is over-looked? One possible explanation is that we have become so sensitized to punishment, particularly incarceration, as the primary crime control strategy that we eschew discussions of alternatives. It is no coincidence that our indifference to the costs of crime control has made it possible for politicians to seize the crime issue and politicize criminal justice policy without concern for the ultimate costs—both economic and social—that such actions will cause. Oliver and Barlow (2005) examined federal crime-control legislation that was enacted by Congress between 1946-1996. They found that there is a cycle to the legislation, and that it tends to occur in the second year of a member of Congress's term (Oliver & Barlow, 2005:279). The timing of the legislation makes it possible for an elected official to communicate to his or her congressional district that he or she is doing a good job. Crime bills are particular favorites in this regard (Oliver & Barlow, 2005:279).

Although sentencing decisions today do not involve an assessment of the "costs" to the community, the judge and/or jury are no longer insulated from the personal accounts of the victims' families' testimony on the impact the crimes have had on their lives. Family members routinely testify or provide written statements about how their lives have changed due to the death of a loved one. For example, in the Oklahoma City Federal Building bombing, 168 people were killed and 500 others were injured. Prior to imposing the death sentence on Timothy McVeigh, the judge and the jury heard detailed accounts from the victims' families regarding the loss of loved ones. McVeigh appealed his death sentence, arguing that their testimony injected too much passion into the proceedings. In a rejection of McVeigh's appeal, the federal appeals court concluded that the jury's decision to impose the death penalty was done with careful consideration and not because of passionate family members' testimony (New York Times, 1998a:A13).

Similarly, in the sentencing phase of the Scott Peterson murder trial, Laci Peterson's parents and siblings spoke emotionally about her and her unborn son, Conner, and the loss they suffered. Laci's mother, Sharon Rocha, said that she was "haunted" by her daughter Laci's final hours. Rocha explained that she would never know the color of Conner's hair or eyes, whether he would have dimples, and how he would dress for Halloween (Ryan, 2005:4). Scott Peterson was sentenced to death by lethal injection; he is currently on death row at San Quentin (Ryan, 2005).

When we study the criminal justice system and its policies, we often tend to overlook the interrelatedness of the various components—the effects any particular policy, philosophical stance, or ideology has on the other parts of the system. In this book, we attempt to examine each part of the system to illustrate more clearly how no one part operates in a vacuum. This symbiotic relationship is perhaps most apparent in the courts. The decisions that are made in the courts, from formal charges to criminal sentencing, have a tremendous impact on all other parts of the system.

One of the more obvious areas in which ideology has had a dramatic effect is in the area of drug policy. The drug "crisis" that America experienced from 1986-1992 was largely generated by President Reagan and the media. Reagan's agenda included a "nationwide crusade against drugs." With the endorsement of the President, Congress enacted legislation in 1986, 1988, and 1992 that significantly increased the funding for the "war on drugs" (Berger, 1998). The media attention that was focused on the problem was not insignificant. In fact, Berger (1998) contends that it increased 20 times from the early 1980s to the late 1980s. There can be little doubt that the President's position, coupled with the media attention, not only facilitated the increased funding but also raised the public's consciousness about drugs. The proportion of Americans polled who regarded drug abuse as the "number one problem facing the country today" increased from between 2 and 3 percent in the early and mid-1980s to 64 percent in September of 1989 (Berger, 1998:22).

Some citizens are aware that overall violent crime is down in the United States. In fact, according to both the National Crime Victimization Survey and the *Uniform Crime Reports*, the victimization rates recorded in 2003 were the lowest ever recorded since the National Crime Victimization Survey (NCVS) began collecting data in 1973 (Bureau of Justice Statistics, 2005a). The incidences of murder, robbery, and rape were 25 percent lower in 2003 than in 1994 (Uniform Crime Reports, 2004).

If crime is down, one might expect that the actual number of people in prison would start to decrease rather than continuing to increase. However, this has not yet occurred. One of the oft-cited reasons for the continuing growth of the prison population is the imposition of longer sentences. Part of the increase is attributed to legislative changes in sentencing laws that require offenders to be in prison for a requisite number of years. The increasing prison population is partly explained by this mandatory incarceration, accompanied by: (1) the requirement that offenders serve longer portions of their sentences, (2) the reluctance to utilize probation as extensively as in previous years, (3) the reduced use of parole and the abolition of parole in some states, and (4) the return to prison of parole violators (Butterfield, 1998:14).

CONSEQUENCES OF FELONY CONVICTION

In 2002, approximately 1,051,000 adults were convicted of a felony in state courts (Durose & Langan, 2004:1). The majority (69%) of these felons were sentenced to confinement in either a prison or jail, 41 percent went to a state prison, and 28 percent went to a local jail. Approximately 31 percent of all felons were placed on probation and were not required to serve jail or prison time (Durose & Langan, 2004:1). The largest number of felony convictions was for drug offenses (possession, trafficking, or unspecified), followed by property offenses (burglary, larceny, and fraud), violent offenses, weapons offenses, and other nonviolent offenses such as vandalism or receiving stolen property (Durose & Langan, 2004:3).

A felony conviction can result in incarceration in a state prison. In 2002, 38 percent of those who were convicted of a single felony and 45 percent of those convicted of two felonies were sentenced to incarceration in a state prison (Durose & Langan, 2004:7). The percentage of offenders sentenced to prison in 2002 (41%) actually reflects a decrease from 1994, when 45 percent of felons were sentenced to a state prison. However, these decreases are offset by the fact that more offenders were sentenced to jail (28%) and probation (31%) in 2002 compared to 1994 (Durose & Langan, 2004:10).

The sentence to incarceration is particularly evident on the federal level. In 2002, there were 63,217 offenders sentenced; approximately 83 percent were incarcerated and 17 percent were placed on probation. These data illustrate the dramatic shift in the incarceration of federal offenders that has occurred since the first edition of this book. In 1995, 67 percent of federal felons were incarcerated, and 27 percent had been sentenced to probation (U.S. Department of Justice, 1998a:2). In fact, offenders convicted of a felony in a federal court are more likely to be incarcerated than offenders convicted in a state court in all offense categories except property offenses (Durose & Langan, 2004:3).

In 2002, the likelihood of being sentenced to a federal prison was equal for violent offenders and drug-trafficking offenders; approximately 92 percent of those convicted of crimes in these two categories were sentenced to prison. Among those convicted of felony public-order offenses, 82 percent were sentenced to prison while 59 percent of felony property offenders received prison sentences (Durose & Langan, 2004:3).

In addition to incarceration in a prison or jail or a sentence to probation, 36 percent of state offenders were required to pay victim restitution or a fine, to undergo treatment, to participate in community service, or to adhere to some other kind of sanction, such as routine drug tests or a period of house arrest (Durose & Langan, 2004:9). The imposition of fines appears to be the most common additional sanction for felons; in 25 percent of the felony sentences in 2002, judges ordered offenders to pay fines. The second most frequent additional sanction was restitution; it was required in 12 percent of the felony sentences in 2002 (Durose & Langan, 2004:10). These findings suggest that judges are incorporating additional penalties in their dispositions to a greater extent than they did in the past.

In some states, offenders are required to start to pay their fines and restitution while they are incarcerated. One example is Pennsylvania's Act 84, which was passed in 1998. Although the legislation has been challenged, the Pennsylvania Supreme Court has upheld the Department of Corrections' policy, which automatically deducts 20 percent for fines and/or restitution from the inmates' daily wages (which can range from 72 cents to 3 dollars a day) (Reed Ward, 2005:B-4). Adding more penalties to the offender's prison, jail, or probation sentence is one more manifestation of the movement toward a more conservative and punitive philosophy in dealing with offenders.

THE JUDICIARY, PROSECUTION, AND DEFENSE COUNSEL

There are three key actors in the courts that have an effect on the criminal justice system: (1) the prosecutor or district attorney, (2) the defense counsel, and (3) the judge. Even though their actions are circumscribed by legislation, court decisions, and the public, all have tremendous discretion and power in the criminal justice system.

In recent years, the appointment of judges has become increasingly politicized. Consider the recent nomination of Judge John G. Roberts for Chief Justice of the U.S. Supreme Court. Even before the confirmation hearings were conducted in the Senate, both the Republicans and the Democrats were deluged with supporters and opponents who were funding campaigns designed to either endorse or reject his nomination. During the Clinton Administration, judicial nominees like William A. Fletcher sometimes waited more than three years to be confirmed (Lewis, 1998:A19). Although the media and politicians focus on the potential contentious nominations process, most judicial nominees during the Bush Administration have been confirmed with relative ease.

In this politicized context, consider the prosecutor or district attorney. It is estimated that there are 2,341 chief prosecutors in the United States who try felonies (DeFrances, 2002:1). Most chief prosecutors (more than 95%) are elected to their positions (DeFrances & Steadman, 1998:1). In addition to processing felony cases, the prosecutors' offices that were surveyed by the 2001 National Survey of Prosecutors (NSP) (N=2,243) also indicated that they had authority to deal with misdemeanor cases (91%), traffic violations (84%), and child support enforcement (49%) as well as to represent the government in civil cases (54%) (DeFrances, 2002:5). In recent years, chief prosecutors increasingly have tackled cases involving computer-related crime ranging from child pornography to credit card fraud. In addition, they have used more technology in the courtroom. According to DeFrances, 68 percent of chief prosecutors used DNA evidence in their cases (2002:1). Clearly, chief prosecutors and district attorneys handle diverse cases, in terms of both the level of seriousness and complexity. Moreover, the prosecutors have a variety of cases and constituents. In order to enhance possibilities for election, the prosecutor must represent the philosophy of the local electorate.

Defense Attorneys

The public's image of the defense attorney is often based on high-profile cases such as the Scott Peterson, Michael Jackson, and Martha Stewart trials. Those images, however, do not reflect reality. The average defendant in a criminal proceeding is indigent and not capable of hiring the "best attorney money can buy." These defendants are assigned a public defender, a court-appointed attorney (also known as assigned counsel), or, in some jurisdictions, a contract attorney. Harlow found that 66 percent of federal felony defendants and 82 percent of court defendants in large states had either a public defender or court-assigned counsel by the end of their case (2000:1).

The assignment of counsel by the court has been found to affect the outcome of the proceedings. For example, there is evidence that black offenders are more likely than white offenders to be represented by a public defender rather than a private attorney (Harlow, 2000:9) and to be detained prior to court (Spohn, Gruhl & Welch, 1980-1981). Harlow found that while 79 percent of state defendants who had private counsel were released before trial, only 52.2 percent of those with publicly funded defense attorneys were released before trial (2000:5). The ability to post bond, live in the community, retain private counsel, maintain employment, and work on a defense are significant advantages. Spohn and colleagues (1980-1981) have found that these factors ultimately affect the severity of the sentence.

Although Harlow's research suggests that defendants represented by private counsel and those represented by public defenders or court-appointed counsel have similar conviction rates, those who had defense attorneys that were publicly financed (public defender or court-appointed) were more likely to be sentenced to prison than those who were represented by private counsel (2000:1). In the state courts, 71.3 percent of defendants represented by publicly funded counsel were sentenced to incarceration in jail or prison, and 53.9 percent of defendants who were represented by private counsel were subject to similar sanctions (Harlow, 2000:6).

Public defenders' caseloads are extraordinary due to their volume and complexity. They routinely handle murder, rape, robbery, burglary, larceny, fraud, and drug cases, and they manage large caseloads. These limitations affect their ability to meet with clients as frequently as private counsel. For example, Harlow found that 37 percent of inmates who were represented by appointed counsel spoke with their attorney during the first week after they were arrested. By contrast, 60 percent of state inmates who were able to hire private attorneys communicated with them during the first week after their arrest (2000:8). The frequency of these attorney–client contacts is also related to the type of representation a defendant has. For those state inmates with publicly financed counsel, about 26 percent of them indicated that they discussed their cases with their attorneys at least four times. Among inmates in state prisons who had private counsel, 58 percent spoke with their attorney at least four times about the charges (Harlow, 2000:8).

Guilty Pleas and Trials

The criminal justice system is dependent on offenders pleading guilty to crime. In fact, it is the plea-bargaining process that facilitates the daily functioning of the federal and state courts. In the federal courts in 1995, 91 percent of the felony convictions were the result of guilty pleas (U.S. Department of Justice, 1998a:2). Similarly, in 2002, 95 percent of those offenders who were sentenced in state courts had entered a plea of guilty to the felony they were charged with committing (Durose & Langan, 2004:9). There is some variation in the offenses for which defendants are likely to enter a guilty plea. For example, 96 percent of offenders charged with drug offenses in state courts entered guilty pleas, while approximately 68 percent of the defendants charged with murder entered a guilty plea (Durose & Langan, 2004:8). It is this heavy reliance on plea bargaining that explains the short period of time from arrest to sentencing; in 2002, the average was approximately six months (Durose & Langan, 2004:8). Approximately 78 percent of felons were convicted and sentenced within one year of their arrest (Durose & Langan, 2004:1).

There are a number of other findings from Durose and Langan's (2003) previous research conducted on felony sentences. In 2000, a higher percentage of individuals charged with murder or other violent offenses were most likely to opt for jury trials, followed by individuals charged with weapons offenses, other nonviolent offenses, drug offenses, and property offenses, respectively (Durose & Langan,

2003:8). In fact, murder convictions comprised approximately 11 percent of all jury trials in 2000, and 21 percent of all jury trials for violent offenses (Durose & Langan, 2003:8).

THE EVOLUTION FROM INDETERMINATE TO DETERMINATE SENTENCING

If you were asked to describe criminal sentencing in the United States, you would have difficulty doing so in clear, concise, and unambiguous terms. In fact, if you were to walk through a prison or jail and interview offenders or review their files, you would likely be astounded by the tremendous range in sentences. Variation occurs both between and within states, and often it is due to factors over which the offender has little or no control.

The federal and state governments employ a variety of sentencing strategies to deal with offenders. According to the U.S. Department of Justice, "the basic difference in sentencing systems is the apportioning of discretion between the judge and parole authorities" (1988:91). That apportionment has radically changed over the last 55 years. In the 1940s (after World War II), sentencing statutes predominantly authorized indeterminate sentences. In this model, the judge would impose a minimum sentence and a maximum sentence, but the actual time served was determined by someone other than a member or representative of the judiciary. Typically, it was the parole authority.

Another type of sentencing statute authorized the judge to set the maximum sentence (but not the minimum) that was to be served. In partially indeterminate sentencing, the decision to release the offender from prison was typically made by the state parole authority (U.S. Department of Justice, 1988:91). Both indeterminate and determinate sentences reflected the rehabilitative ideal; the offender was to receive some kind of treatment and rehabilitation while in prison and was to be released when it was determined that he or she had made sufficient progress and could be assumed to be ready to return to society. These kinds of indeterminate sentences were popular in the United States during the 1950s and the 1960s.

Indeterminate sentences faced criticism from both liberals and conservatives beginning in the 1970s. Liberals were convinced that the rights of offenders were being violated and that offenders were being treated differently depending on the judge handling the case (Goodstein & Hepburn, 1985:15). Conservatives criticized the lack of rehabilitation occurring in prisons and lobbied for tougher sentences and less judicial discretion (Goodstein & Hepburn, 1985:15; Wilson, 1975, cited in Tonry & Hamilton, 1995:3).

Determinate sentences appeared to satisfy both camps. They were believed to be less partial (thus, not influenced by who the offender was) and more likely to prevent further crime. The main feature of this type of sentence was a fixed period of time that the offender would serve in prison. Determinate sentences effectively ended parole discretion (U.S. Department of Justice, 1988:91). The offender was required to serve his or her entire sentence, less any good-time credits that were awarded. Advocates contended that determinate sentences could physically restrain offenders from participating in crime while simultaneously preventing them from future criminal tendencies.

Laws that require offenders to serve the time to which they are sentenced (less any circumscribed good-time credits) are referred to as "truth-in-sentencing" laws. Truth-in-sentencing legislation has been enacted in 30 states, and these laws require offenders to serve at least 85 percent of their sentences before release (The Sentencing Project, 2004). In 1995, Ohio ended its use of indeterminate prison sentences and introduced a new determinate sentencing model. Under the new legislation, the judge can augment the offender's sentence with an additional one to 10 years for a repeat violent offender. Additionally, the offender can no longer accrue good-time credits, and the parole authority no longer makes release decisions (Rauschenberg, 1997:10). Pennsylvania reviewed and revised its sentencing statutes in 1994 and again in 1997 (Kempinen, 1997:14). One of the rationales for the more recent changes was to provide harsher sentences than were stipulated in the 1994 legislation for violent offenders (Kempinen, 1997:14).

Indeterminate, partially indeterminate, and determinate sentences are the basic components of state and federal sentencing statutes. There are other sentencing options that can be incorporated into or included along with these kinds of sentences (U.S. Department of Justice, 1988:91). For example, mandatory sentencing laws exist in almost every state (U.S. Department of Justice, 1988:91). These sentencing laws require the judge to impose a specific fixed period of incarceration if the offender is convicted of any of a certain group of crimes. Such mandatory sentences, which significantly restrict judicial discretion, have been very popular.

CURRENT TRENDS IN SENTENCING IN THE UNITED STATES

There has been a great deal of legislative activity in the area of sentencing during the last 25 years. Part of this can be explained by focusing on the dominant role that has been afforded law enforcement officials, politicians, and official representatives of the criminal justice system. The media's reliance on these representatives to explain the incidence of crime and the various strategies to address it serves to shape our perceptions of crime causation and crime control.

In a content analysis of four major newspapers from 1992 to 1995, Welch, Fenwick, and Roberts (1998) found that there is a difference in the way crime news and crime control policies are presented. "Politicians and practitioners endorse strategies of hard control in dealing with crime; professors and nonacademic researchers overwhelmingly support soft control" (1998:232). For the most part, this view has focused on a reactive stance whereby the system promises to deliver harsher sentences or punishments to offenders who commit crime and disavow any relationship between societal conditions and crime (Welch, Fenwick & Roberts, 1998:239). Such a strategy entails enhancing the criminal justice system's ability to incarcerate or punish offenders for long periods of time. Sentencing revisions are an integral part of this approach.

One legislative initiative involves the abolition of parole for first-time violent offenders. Although parole has been abolished in a number of states, more recently it has been abolished for all violent offenders—including those who do not have a history of violent crime. For example, in 1998, the New York legislature enacted legislation that precludes all violent offenders from ever being considered for parole (*New York Times*, 1998b:A25).

Along with determinate sentencing, the states and the federal government have utilized presumptive sentencing statutes, sentencing guidelines, and sentence enhancements. Presumptive sentencing statutes instruct a judge to impose a specified period of incarceration for offenders who have been convicted of certain offenses. There is some latitude for the judge to deviate from the terms established by the legislature, but only if there are mitigating or extenuating circumstances. Even then, the judge cannot ignore the boundaries that have been established by the legislature. Any time the judge strays from the statute, he or she is required to stipulate in writing the rationale that was utilized in changing the sentence that was authorized by the legislature (Holten & Handberg, 1994:222; U.S. Department of Justice, 1988:91).

Sentencing Guidelines

Far more popular than presumptive sentencing laws in recent years are sentencing guidelines and sentence enhancements. Sentencing guidelines are usually prepared by a separate commission rather than the legislature. Typically, the guidelines are either advisory, in which case they provide the sentencing judge with some information but do not require him or her to impose a specific sentence, or they can be prescriptive, in which case they instruct the judge to impose a particular prison sentence (U.S. Department of Justice, 1988:92). The degree to which the guidelines are mandated varies from state to state. In some states, a judge who departs from the guidelines may be asked to explain his or her rationale for the decision and may experience some informal disapproval. In other states, a failure to follow the guidelines can facilitate an appeal to a higher court to overturn a disposition that did not adhere to the established guidelines (Wright, 1998:11). Guidelines are either used selectively by the federal government and the states or they can be included in the legislation (U.S. Department of Justice, 1988:91).

Congress enacted the Comprehensive Crime Control Act of 1984, which included the Sentencing Reform Act of 1984 (Kennedy, 1985:113). One of the provisions of the legislation established the U.S. Sentencing Commission. The Commission was to be comprised of seven voting members appointed by then-President Ronald Reagan. Of the seven members, at least three had to be federal judges and two were to be nonvoting *ex officio* members (Wohl, 1992:37).

The Commission's work culminated in the creation of federal sentencing guidelines, which provided federal court judges with a strict set of standards to adhere to in sentencing federal offenders. These guidelines were intended to reduce judicial discretion and to quell the allegations of disparate treatment. Under the previous system, two defendants might receive widely different sentences for their involvement in the same or similar activities, depending on such factors as the victim's or offender's race or gender, socioeconomic status, or geographical area of residence (Merlo, 1997; Wohl, 1992:37). The guidelines were designed to ensure fair and equal treatment for all offenders. No one could deny the importance of having equal treatment for all in the federal system.

The guidelines incorporate the minimums established by statute and then augment them with aggravating and mitigating factors. The judges have the opportunity to depart from the guidelines and sentence an offender to more or less time (Wohl, 1992:40). The guidelines abolished parole and mandated that offenders could only accrue good-time credits not to exceed 15 percent of their total sentence or 54 days per year (Kennedy, 1985:119; Langan, Perkins & Chaiken, 1994:8). In the federal system, this law applied to offenders who committed crimes after November 1, 1987 (Langan, Perkins & Chaiken, 1994:8).

The Reality of the Federal Sentencing Guidelines

In the years since the federal sentencing guidelines were implemented, there is little evidence that they have achieved the expected equal treatment for all defendants and reduction in disparity. Although the idea of an independent commission making sentencing policy is laudable in theory, the political process has seized control of the guidelines and demonstrated the Commission's unimportance. For example, Congress enacted legislation in 2003 that required the Commission to enact new policies limiting discretion in sentencing, and provided for the acquisition of data on individual judges' sentencing practices (Greenhouse, 2003:A17). In a follow-up to the legislation, the then–Attorney General, John Ashcroft, mandated that prosecutors had to notify the Justice Department every time a federal judge gave a sentence that was a downward departure from the range set in the guidelines (Greenhouse, 2003:A17). The Judicial Conference of the United States is comprised of 27 judges who make policy for the federal courts and are led by the Chief Justice of the Supreme Court. The judges voted unanimously to ask Congress to repeal the law, noting that it was an unnecessary; there was no evidence to suggest that the federal judges were regularly disregarding the sentencing guidelines (Greenhouse, 2003:A17).

In 2004, the federal sentencing guidelines were challenged by two defendants, Freddie Booker and Ducan Fanfan. In *U.S. v. Booker* (124 S. Ct. 738 [2005]), the United States Supreme Court determined that the sentencing guidelines that authorized judges to impose sentence enhancements based on aggravating factors that had not been proven beyond a reasonable doubt at trial violated the defendant's Sixth Amendment rights. In addition, the justices determined that the guidelines are now to be advisory rather than mandatory (*U.S. v. Booker* (124 S. Ct. 738 [2005]). The long-term effect of the recent decision is not yet known. (See Chapter 6 for a discussion.)

One of the most glaring problems with the guidelines has to do with the sentencing of drug offenders. In 2002, drug defendants accounted for the largest percentage (41%) of convictions in the federal courts, surpassing public order offenses (which accounted for 26%), property offenses (which accounted for 20%), weapons offenses (which accounted for 8%), and violent crimes (which accounted for 4%) of all federal con-

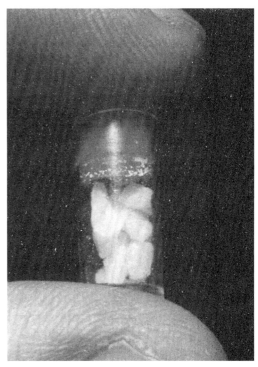

A plastic container of crack, the smokable, purified form of cocaine, is displayed at a Boston news conference. The 100:1 ratio for powder and crack cocaine means that someone trafficking in juts five grams of crack cocaine will receive the same penalty as someone trafficking in 500 grams of powder cocaine. *(AP Photo)*

victions (Durose & Langan, 2004:3). Offenders who were sentenced to federal prison in 2002 were sentenced to 58 months (slightly less than five years) on average. However, drug offenders received an average 76-month sentence (slightly more than six years), which was slightly less than that for violent offenders, whose average sentence was 89 months (approximately seven years) (Durose & Langan, 2004:3).

Discrepancies in the sentencing process, particularly for the penalty of crack cocaine versus powder cocaine, are the most obvious. The 100:1 ratio for powder and crack cocaine means that an offender who traffics in 500 grams of powder is required to serve a five-year prison term, and that same five-year term is required for offenders who traffic just five grams of crack cocaine (Yellen, 1997:6). As discussed in Chapter 4, African Americans are more likely to be convicted of crack cocaine offenses, while whites are more likely to be convicted of powder cocaine offenses. This crime category alone helps to explain the disproportionate representation of African Americans in the federal prison system. (See Table 3.1.)

When the Commission evaluated the penalties required for drug offenders in the 1990s, it decided that the penalties were too disparate, given the lack of pharmacological differences between crack cocaine and powder cocaine. As a result, it proposed eliminating the differences in the penalties imposed and requiring the same penalties for offenders convicted of powder cocaine and crack cocaine offenses. The Commission's recommendations were opposed by the Justice Department and the Congress. In fact, for the first time since the Commission was established, Congress refused to act on the Commission's proposals for amendments to the guidelines and instead created legislation that overturned the Commission's sentencing guideline amendments for cocaine (Yellen, 1997:6).

This incident highlights the futility of the sentencing commission. According to Yellen (1997:6), Congress is in the habit of changing the guidelines by statute. Instead of relying on a neutral and detached panel of experts to determine sentencing guidelines for judges in the federal system, we are in the unenviable position of having sentencing guidelines amended by statutes that more clearly reflect the politics of a punitive criminal justice policy than the consideration of an appropriate sanction for crimes (Yellen, 1997:6).

Critics of the sentencing guidelines include Supreme Court Justice Stephen Breyer, who not only helped secure the passage of the Sentencing Reform Act of 1984 but also served on the United States Sentencing Commission for four years (Greenhouse, 1998a:A10). Justice Breyer and the six other Commission members were responsible for helping to determine the formula for sanctions for 700 federal offenses (Greenhouse, 1998a:A10). In the intervening years since the guidelines were created, Congress has established mandatory minimum sentences that have significantly altered the original intentions of the guidelines.

Table 3.1

Facts Leading the Sentencing Commission to Recommend Equivalent Base Sentences for Crack and Powder Cocaine

1. The Commission's guidelines provide for severe punishment for those trafficking in powder cocaine. There have been few if any complaints about the leniency of those guidelines.

2. Powder and crack cocaine have the same active ingredient—the cocaine alkaloid—and both produce the same type of physiological and psychological effects.

3. While smoking crack cocaine can lead to addiction in a greater number of cases than can snorting powder, injecting powder cocaine is as dangerous as or more dangerous than smoking crack. In light of the fact that crack cocaine can be easily produced from powder cocaine, the form of cocaine is simply not a reasonable proxy for dangerousness associated with use.

4. Any quantity ratio greater than equivalency will lead to the unfair result that more sophisticated, higher-level powder distributors will be sentenced relatively less severely than some of the retailers they supply.

5. The present system results in obvious punishment inequities by providing the same penalty for 500 grams of powder (1/2 kilo)—yielding between 1,000 and 5,000 doses and costing up to $75,000—as for five grams of crack cocaine—yielding between 10 and 50 doses and costing up to $750.

6. Any quantity ratio higher than equivalency will impact almost entirely on minority defendants.

The Commission commented:

> When the Commission began studying cocaine sentencing policy, it found that the picture of crack painted by the media bore little resemblance to the reality portrayed by scientific research on the subject. What the Commission learned was that there really is not much of a distinction, at least pharmacologically, between powder and crack cocaine, and that wherever crack is distributed, inevitably powder cocaine is somewhere nearby. After all, crack cocaine is actually powder cocaine converted through a very simple process. Experience suggests that most drug distributors traffic in multiple drugs, and that crack cocaine distributions frequently involve powder as well. To target crack cocaine for dramatically higher penalties ignores the reality of these polydrug distributions and the risks associated with the other drugs present in a "crack cocaine" distribution. On the other hand, the Commission has learned that the purveyors of crack cocaine have found a way to get the drug to the people on the lowest rungs of the economic ladder in our country and into the hands of children, because the drug is cheap and easy to use.

Source: Excerpted from Update on the Activities of the United States Sentencing Commission, Part Two, Majority and Minority Opinions on Crack and Powder Cocaine, September 1995.

It is the politicization of the sentencing guideline process that belies any hope that the creation of a sentencing commission would result in fairer and more appropriate punishments for offenders convicted in the federal courts. The guidelines were designed to reduce the judicial disparity that had occurred in the federal system; instead, the guidelines resulted in unnecessarily harsh sanctions and new problems associated with prosecutorial decisionmaking (Yellen, 1997:8). There are tremendous differences in the way in which prosecutors determine who will be charged and with which specific offenses. It is these decisions that ultimately impact the plea negotiations, trials, and sentences that are imposed.

Sentencing Commissions and Politics

One of the consequences of sentencing commissions and the guidelines they have drafted is that the members do not have to rely on constituents for re-election. In short, there is no need to fashion policies that will have sound-bite appeal in future elections. There are no media events to convince the public of the commission's stance on crime because the commission is comprised of individuals who theoretically have no political stake in the outcome of their recommendations. It is this very facet of the guidelines that some elected officials find most annoying. Crime policy is a political issue, and elected officials continue to demonstrate their willingness to resist any attempt to remove it from the political spectrum.

Sentence Enhancements: "Three Strikes and You're Out"

Sentence enhancements are also very popular today. These kinds of sentencing statutes permit judges to impose longer prison sentences and to remove the opportunity for parole for chronic offenders (U.S. Department of Justice, 1988:91). One of the most publicized examples of such initiatives is the "three strikes and you're out" legislation in the United States. Most of the three-strikes laws were enacted from 1993 to 1995, when the federal government and 24 states relied on that term for their new legislation (Clark, Austin & Henry, 1997:1).

The popularity of three-strikes laws is impressive. There are a number of factors that contribute to their widespread appeal. First, three-strikes legislation aptly reflects the public's get-tough attitude toward crime. Second, it suggests that criminals will no longer be on the streets and that the citizenry will be protected from future victimization. Third, it is a phrase that has sound-bite appeal: its meaning is clear and it is easily communicated because of the baseball metaphor. Fourth, it continues to be perceived as an effective strategy to deter crime. For example, when California voters had a chance to revise their three-strikes law in November of 2004, more than 52 percent of the voters chose to continue the legislation as it was originally drafted (Institute of Governmental Studies, 2004).

It was through a citizens' group ballot initiative in Washington in 1993 that the first piece of three-strikes legislation was enacted by the voters (Van Wagenen, 1997:6). They were successful in getting the first three-strikes law in the country enacted; their activism in this area persists. In 1995, the same group drafted another proposal, which the legislature adopted, known as "hard time for armed crime" that required enhanced penalties ranging from six months to 10 years for felonies when the offender carried a weapon (Van Wagenen, 1997:6).

In March of 1994, California became the second state to enact three-strikes legislation. California's legislation differs from Washington's by authorizing enhanced penalties for a second strike and requiring offenders on the third strike to do a minimum of 25 years with the possibility of parole (Clark, Austin & Henry, 1997:2-3). Eligibility for parole occurs after the offender has served 80 percent of the sentence (Ehlers, Schiraldi & Ziedenberg, 2004:3).

Although not uniform, the legislation adopted by other states and the federal government does have certain characteristics in common. Clark, Austin, and Henry (1997:12-13) highlight these similarities:

1. All either permit or require longer periods of incarceration when an offender has been convicted of a violent crime. Ironically, all but one of the 24 states that enacted three-strikes legislation already had legislation aimed at violent offenders and requiring enhanced penalties.

2. All significantly reduce or restrict the judge's discretion in sentencing.

3. The speed with which such laws were enacted by the Congress and state legislatures suggests that there was a perception that previous legislation was not satisfactorily protecting the public either in its application and/or outcome, that the laws could not address the egregious acts that were being committed, or that the laws were not being adequately enforced due to extraneous factors such as overcrowded institutions.

4. Although it is still early to make a full assessment, these new laws appear to have had only a minor impact on states' prison populations. Because chronic violent offender legislation has been in existence for some time, offenders were already serving longer sentences. Any impact on correctional systems will more likely be felt by the creation of the two-strike statutes.

The sentencing legislative initiatives that states have enacted have been prompted, in part, by financial assistance from the federal government. As an incentive to create legislation that authorized longer sentences for violent offenders and with assurances that offenders would serve at least 85 percent of the sentence imposed, states and local correctional systems were given Violent Offender Incarceration and Truth-in-Sentencing Incentive (VOI/TIS) Grants in the 1990s (U.S. Department of Justice, 1998b:1). These grants were earmarked for new or renovated institutional construction, either private or public, for violent and nonviolent offenders (U.S. Department of Justice, 1998b:1). Most states (41) and the District of Columbia did institute some TIS policy by the end of the 1990s. However, research conducted on the 28 states and the District of Columbia that received the federal grants suggests that the grant money might not always have been related to the changes that occurred in the sentencing statutes. Of the 28 states, 13 received the funding due to previously established TIS practices. Nine of the states indicated that the funding was influential in their decision to change their laws, and among the seven states that made major reforms, only one state indicated that the grant money was a significant consideration (Rosich & Kane, 2005:19).

Three-Strikes Legislation Litigation

In the 20 years since California's three-strikes law has been in existence, there has been some litigation surrounding its application. Most recently, in March of 2003, the U.S. Supreme Court upheld California's three-strikes legislation in the case of *Ewing v. California* (538 U.S. 11 [2003]). Ewing had been convicted of grand theft for stealing three golf clubs. By a 5–4 decision, the majority of the justices determined that the statute that authorizes a sentence of 25 years to life for a third strike does not violate the Eighth Amendment ban on cruel and unusual punishment; specifically, it determined that the sentence is not disproportionate. In addition, the justices found that this law served the state's goal of deterring and incapacitating repeat offenders (*Ewing v. California*, 538 U.S.11 [2003]).

In 2003, the U.S. Supreme Court reversed the Ninth Circuit's ruling in *Lockyer v. Andrade* (538 U.S. 63 [2003]). Andrade had been sentenced to two consecutive terms of 25 years to life after he was convicted of stealing approximately $150 worth of videotapes from two different stores. Each of the thefts constituted a separate strike. On appeal, the California Court of Appeals ruled that the three-strikes sentences Andrade received did not violate the Eighth Amendment ban on cruel and unusual punishment. The Ninth Circuit Court of Appeals reviewed Andrade's case and determined that the sentence was a violation of the federal law. However, the U.S. Supreme Court determined that the Ninth Circuit had erred in that ruling (*Lockyer v. Andrade* (538 U.S. 63 [2003]:2).

Previously, the justices of the Supreme Court upheld the California Supreme Court decision in *Monge v. California* (118 S.Ct. 2246 [1998]). The case dealt with the Fifth Amendment's protection against double jeopardy as applied to criminal sentencing. Under California law, an offender is able to have a jury trial to decide if an earlier conviction would count as a "strike" (Greenhouse, 1998b:A10). In order for a previous conviction to count as a "strike," it had to have been a serious felony (Greenhouse, 1998b:A10). In *Monge*, when the judge decided that there was insufficient evidence to allow the previous conviction to count, the prosecutor proceeded to appeal. The California Court of Appeal determined that the case constituted double jeopardy. However, the California Supreme Court ruled that the double-jeopardy provisions of the Fifth Amendment do not apply to sentencing and, therefore, the judge's decision could be appealed (Greenhouse, 1998b:A10). In a 5–4 ruling, the Supreme Court determined that prosecutors are permitted to "retry defendants on whether they used dangerous weapons in previous crimes in order to apply the three strikes law" (Dickey & Hollenhorst, 1998a:20).

The California Supreme Court in *People v. Superior Court (Romero)* (917 P.2d 628 [1996]) authorized judges to disregard a prior conviction when a 25-year sentence would be too extreme. This decision has had the effect of softening the impact of the legislation by restoring some judicial discretion in the sentencing process. However, the application of the decision has not been consistent in the various counties of California (Dickey & Hollenhorst, 1998b:7). Additionally, in 1998, the California Supreme Court *in People v. Williams* (948 P.2d 429 Ca., [1998]) appears to have limited the effects of the *Romero* decision by precluding the judge from disregarding a prior conviction when the offender's previous conduct falls within "the spirit of the three strikes law" (*People v. Williams*, cited in Dickey & Hollenhurst, 1998a:20). In *Williams,* the California Supreme Court further required judges to state the reasons for not considering a prior conviction as a strike and determined that the judges' decisions are subject to review (Dickey & Hollenhorst, 1998a:20).

The Effect of Three-Strikes Legislation

Despite the fact that three-strikes legislation exists in 23 states and the federal system, recent research suggests that this legislation has had its greatest impact in California, where more than 42,000 offenders or one in every four California inmates is serving a doubled or 25-years-to-life term. Another state relying on three-strikes legislation is Georgia, where in June of 2002 more than 5,800 inmates (approximately 12.5 percent of the inmate population) were incarcerated under Georgia's law. The other states do not have significant numbers of offenders convicted under these kinds of laws (Ehlers, Schiraldi & Ziedenberg, 2004).

The California data illustrate the effect that one piece of legislation can have on a prison population. As a result of the three-strikes legislation, the number of second- and third-strike offenders in the California prison system increased dramatically from 4,408 in 1994 to 42,445 in September of 2003 (Ehlers, Schiarldi & Ziedenberg, 2004:5). In addition, the California law has resulted in the long-term incarceration of nonviolent offenders who have been sentenced under its provisions. For example, according to Ehlers, Schiraldi, and Ziedenburg (2004:8), almost two-thirds of offenders who were convicted of second or third strikes were in prison for nonviolent offenses, which include petty theft and drug possession.

However, these data also indicate that the law has not yet impacted the prison population in the way that was predicted earlier. According to Ehlers, Schiraldi, and Ziedenberg (2004), there are at least two reasons for California prisons not experiencing the kind of overcrowding that was originally anticipated. First, the law has not been implemented to its full extent; and second, the voters enacted Proposition 36, the Substance Abuse and Crime Prevention Act in 2000, which stipulates that any offender who is apprehended for possession of drugs, including those offenders who previously had a three-strikes conviction but have been out of prison for five years, are eligible for drug treatment rather than incarceration (2004:4).

Although get-tough strategies, which include three-strikes legislation, are often credited with reducing crime in the United States, there is little empirical support for that position. Kovandzic, Sloan, and Vieraitis (2004) studied 188 cities with a population of 100,000 or more for 20 years (1980 to 2000) to assess the effect of these kinds of laws. Their findings indicate that there is no statistical evidence that the enactment of three-strikes legislation reduces crime through deterrence or through the incapacitation of repeat offenders (Kovandzic, Sloan & Vieraitis, 2004:234). Similarly, Sorensen and Stemen (2002) studied state sentencing policies and found that it is drug offenders rather than violent offenders who have been affected by three-strikes legislation. "In fact, states with three strikes laws do not admit more offenders per arrest for violent offenses than states without such laws" (Sorensen & Stemen 2002:469). In short, three-strikes laws add to the prison population by increasing the number of drug offenders rather than violent offenders.

Race and Sentencing:
Disproportionate Representation of Blacks

There is overwhelming evidence that African Americans are disproportionately represented in prisons and jails in the United States. For example, in 2002, African Americans comprised 12 percent of the adult population in the United States, but accounted for 37 percent of convicted felons and 39 percent of the felons who were convicted of a violent crime in state courts (Durose & Langan, 2004:6). By contrast, 82 percent of the adult population was white, and white offenders comprised 60 percent of those convicted of a felony and 57 percent of those convicted of a violent felony in state courts (Durose & Langan, 2004:6).

The percentage of blacks convicted of felonies in state courts has been particularly high in certain crime categories. However, part of the increase in African-American convictions can be explained by the large number of blacks who were convicted of drug trafficking (47%) in 2002 (Durose & Langan, 2004:6). Although earlier research by Durose and Langan (2003) illustrates that the percent of convictions for drug trafficking decreased from 1992 to 2000, it is not clear if African-American offenders have experienced the effects of that decline in the same way as white offenders.

With respect to the federal courts, the situation is even worse. When the United States Sentencing Commission released its findings of a 15-year review of the sentencing guideline system in 2004, the Commission concluded that there was evidence of racial disparity in the guidelines. The researchers found that African-American defendants generally received harsher punishments than white offenders (*New York Times*, 2004:A11). Prior to the implementation of the guidelines, the majority of federal offenders had been white, but now it is minorities who are most prevalent in the system. In addition, the Commission found that their sentences are longer. For defendants convicted of crack cocaine charges, who are more frequently lower-income African-American offenders, the average penalty is 115 months (9.5 years), whereas defendants who have been convicted of powder cocaine charges, who are more likely to be suburban white offenders, faced an average of 77 months (approximately 6 years) (Fields, 2004:A4).

In fact, the Department of Justice estimated in 1997 that almost 29 percent of all black men "can expect to serve a state or prison sentences in their lifetimes" (Proband, 1997:1). For white men, the chances of going to prison are approximately 4 percent, while 16 percent of Hispanic men can expect to go to prison in their lifetime (Proband, 1997:1). Additionally, there is some evidence that three-strikes legislation disproportionately affects black offenders. In California, blacks comprised approximately 7 percent of the state's population in 2000, but 21.7 percent of those arrested for committing a felony, almost 30 percent of all state inmates, and 45 percent of those offenders who were incarcerated for a third strike (Ehlers, Shiraldi & Lotke 2004:2). The data indicate that in 2000, African Americans accounted for 36 percent of those convicted of a second strike and 45 percent of those convicted of a third strike (Ehlers, Schiraldi & Lotke, 2004:2).

Although there have been a number of studies that have sought to identify factors that might help us understand or explain why this phenomenon occurs, there is no clear-cut answer. In fact, there is no unanimity regarding racial discrimination in sentencing; some research suggests that discrimination occurs, other research has found that there are no significant differences in the way that blacks and whites are treated, and still other research suggests that blacks may be treated more leniently (Walker, Spohn & DeLone, 1998:363). For example, Joseph, Henriques, and Ekeh (2003) discuss the racial double standard that is observed in drug sentencing decisions. They found ". . . that judges have a tendency to recommend medical and rehabilitation services for white drug users and prison for African-American drug users (2003:109).

Research on departures from the established sentencing guidelines in states suggests that race and ethnicity do make a difference. In examining departures from the sentencing guidelines in Pennsylvania over a three-year period (1996-1998), Johnson (2003) found when compared to white defendants, African-American and Hispanic defendants ". . . have a decreased likelihood of receiving downward departures and an increased likelihood of receiving upward departures" (2003:482). In short, both African Americans and Hispanics in Pennsylvania courtrooms were not only more likely to be sentenced above the guideline recommendations than white defendants, but also less likely to be sentenced below the guidelines than were whites (2003:468). Engen, Gainey, Crutchfield, and Weis (2003) studied departures from the sentencing guidelines in Washington state. Although they found that judges there were more likely to sentence offenders below the range than above the range, African-American and Hispanic offenders were not likely to benefit. "The odds of African-American or Hispanic defendants receiving downward departures, respectively, are about 32 percent less and 55 percent less than the odds of non-Hispanic white defendants" (Engen, Gainey, Crutchfield & Weis, 2003:116-117).

In subsequent research, Johnson (2005) examined departures from the sentencing guidelines in Pennsylvania to determine if there was a relationship between these departures and the social context of the courts. His findings indicate that downward departures for Hispanic offenders were less likely to occur ". . . as the percent of Hispanics in the community increased . . ." (Johnson, 2005:786). Hispanics who lived in communities with larger Hispanic populations were significantly less likely to have their sentence reflect a downward departure from the guidelines, and significantly more likely to see their sentence reflect an upward departure (Johnson, 2005:789). These findings suggest that even with sentencing guidelines, other contextual social factors affect the length of sentence.

However, current research is beginning to focus on some variables that may help us understand the sentencing process as it affects both African-American and white offenders. Spohn and Henderson (2000) examined 6,638 felony sentencing decisions in Chicago, Illinois; Miami, Florida; and Kansas City, Missouri. They found that in two of the cities, Miami and Chicago, the race/ethnicity of the defendant along with his or her age "is a more powerful predictor of sentence severity than either variable individually, and in Kansas City, age matters more than race" (Spohn & Holleran, 2000:301). For Kansas City defendants, younger defendants of all races seem to have a greater likelihood of incarceration than middle-aged white men (Spohn & Holleran, 2000:301). However, a combination of factors: being young, African-American or Hispanic, male, and unemployed were related to being sentenced to incarceration. When unemployed African-American men were compared to white employed defendants, they were 16.9 percent more likely to be sentenced to incarceration, and unemployed Hispanic men were 23.5 percent more likely to be sentenced to incarceration (Spohn & Holleran, 2000:298). Spohn and Holleran's research suggests that it is the combination of these factors rather than any one specific factor like race or ethnicity that is related to incarceration (2000:301).

Previous research has also examined the defendant's employment status as a predictor of sentence severity. In their study of Kansas City and Chicago sentencing decisions, Nobiling, Spohn, and DeLone found that unemployed black and Hispanic males had a greater likelihood of being sentenced to a period of incarceration than white males (1998:482). It is unclear why judges would determine that unemployed black males pose a greater danger to society than unemployed white males. The judge's decision may be based upon the high unemployment rate of black males versus white males and the perception by the sentencing judge that the white males are only temporarily unemployed and will soon change that status. Conversely, the judge may view black males as likely to remain unemployed for the foreseeable future and conclude that their unemployment and resulting economic marginalization place them at a greater risk of reoffending (Nobiling, Spohn & DeLone, 1998:483).

Researchers have also explored the effects of the seriousness of the crime and the race of the victim and attempted to determine if those factors are related to harsher sentences for blacks (Walker, Spohn & DeLone, 1998:359). In earlier research, Spohn studied sentences of offenders convicted of violent crime in Detroit and found that the race of the offender and the victim were important in two kinds of cases: murder and sexual assault. Blacks who were convicted of sexually assaulting or murdering white victims received harsher sentences than blacks who were convicted of sexually assaulting or murdering black victims or than whites who were convicted of sexual assaulting and/or murdering white victims. In short, blacks who were convicted of these two violent crimes (sexual assault and murder) receive the harshest sanctions when the victim is white and the most lenient penalty when the victim is black (Walker, Spohn & DeLone, 1998:361). These findings suggest that racial discrimination in sentencing ". . . is not universal but rather is confined to certain types of cases, certain types of settings, and certain types of defendants" (Walker, Spohn & DeLone, 1998:363).

In his research, Crank (2003) discusses the systemic cumulative disadvantage that African-American and minority defendants confront. Rather than focusing on a specific process in the system like arrest or sentencing, he notes that police and prosecutorial discretion has ". . . led to a systemic shift: from discriminatory practices that are contextual based to practices today that are systemic" (Crank, 2003:241). This cumulative disadvantage adversely affects minority groups (Crank, 2003:240). Kappeler and Potter also note that, "Research has suggested that the small effects of race and class may not be statistically significant at any one point, but the cumulative effects throughout the process from arrest to sentencing can be significant" (2005:271). For example, the defendant's employment status is one variable that affects a variety of the criminal justice system processes—from posting bail to hiring private counsel. It may be the case that employment is but one indicator of economic stability that may be significantly related to decision outcomes of the criminal justice system.

Overcoming attitudes that place a greater value on the victimization of whites versus blacks—and penalizes blacks more harshly than whites for these victimizations—is not something that occurs overnight. The media play a role in enabling our fears and prejudices. This myth has resulted in perpetrators convincing authorities that African-American men were responsible for crimes that they themselves committed (Kappeler & Potter, 2005:271).

Consider the story concocted by Susan Smith, a woman who allegedly had been the victim of a carjacking. Smith contended that she had been forced to get out of the car, but then a black assailant reportedly drove off with her two young sons. The sensational national news coverage of the crime was instantaneous. The possibility that a white woman could be forced to abandon her two helpless children while a black offender drove off with them shocked and saddened the public. The mother of the boys, however, ultimately confessed that there was no carjacker—she drove the car into a lake with her two sons in it.

Although these kinds of stories might have been just as tragic and compelling if the alleged perpetrator had been a white person, the fact that the offender chose to use the African-American male as the "fantasy offender" suggests that she was playing on the public's sentiments that victimization by a black is somehow more terrifying and dangerous than other crimes—and that would explain her inability to prevent the tragedy from occurring. It may also suggest that when black males kill or kidnap white victims, people behave as if it is a greater loss than if the victims were also black or if the offenders were white.

SENTENCING IN THE 2000s

Capital Punishment

There can be no more severe sanction than death. In the United States in 2005, there were 3,452 people in federal and state prison systems who had been sentenced to die (Death Penalty Information Center, 2005a:2). Demographically, there were 1,572 white offenders, 1,440 African-American offenders, and 359 Hispanic offenders on death row (Death Penalty Information Center, 2005a:2). The death penalty is now sanctioned in 38 states (Death Penalty Information Center, 2005a:1).

Recent evidence illustrates that there is some ambivalence about the application of the death penalty. For example, an Alabama survey conducted in July of 2005, found that less than 50 percent of those surveyed think that Alabama's death penalty is applied fairly; and 57 percent of respondents in the statewide poll thought that there should be a halt to the executions there until "questions about fairness and reliability are studied" (Death Penalty Information Center, 2005d:1). However, there is little likelihood that the death penalty will cease to be imposed completely in the near future.

The states of California, Texas, Florida, and Pennsylvania have the largest number of offenders on death row. In fact, these four states house 49 percent of the entire death row population in the country (Death Penalty Information Center, 2005a:2). With 313 executions since 1977, Texas stands alone as the state that has administered capital punishment the most frequently (Bonczar & Snell, 2004:9). With respect to women on death row, four states (California, Texas, Pennsylvania, and North Carolina) have two-thirds of the women on death row in the United States in their population (Bonczar & Snell, 2004:7). The methods of execution utilized are lethal injection (37 states and the federal government) and electrocution (one state). In some states, lethal injection is authorized, but inmates can choose an alternative method, which may include lethal gas or electrocution. A couple of states permit the firing squad or hanging if lethal injection cannot be administered (Bonczar & Snell, 2004:4; Death Penalty Information Center, 2005b:1-4). However, lethal injection accounted for 98 percent of the executions in 2003 and all but one of the 58 executions in 2004 (Bonczar & Snell, 2004:1, 11).

When reviewing the death penalty in the United States, researchers frequently focus on the demographic profile of those who have been sentenced to death. It was not until the U.S. Supreme Court reviewed the revised state statutes authorizing the death penalty in 1976 that the imposition of the death penalty began to occur more often. During the period from 1976 to 2005, there were 974 executions in the United States (Death Penalty Information Center, 2005a:1). Fifty-eight percent of those executed were white, 34 percent were African-American, 6 percent were Hispanic, and 2 percent were classified as other races (Death Penalty Information Center, 2005a:1).

Other preliminary data suggest that fewer executions are occurring every year. In 1999, 98 inmates were executed. This was the largest number of executions carried out since 1955, when 76 inmates were executed (Bonczar & Snell, 2004:10; Snell, 1997:12). However, the number of executions has fallen since 1999, and there appears to be greater reluctance to impose the death sentence in state courts. It is difficult to predict how this trend will change in the foreseeable future. At this time there is conflicting evidence suggesting both support for and a disinclination to apply the death penalty with the same frequency as in the past (Bonczar & Snell, 2004). For example, the highest court in New York State declared the death penalty statute unconstitutional in 2004, and legislators there seem disinclined to revise it. At the same time, Governor Mitt Romney, has endorsed enacting a capital punishment statute in Massachusetts, but has not yet succeeded in persuading the legislature to draft and deliver one for his signature (Yardley, 2004:32).

One of the more troubling aspects of society's willingness to impose capital punishment is the widespread endorsement of this sanction despite the lack of evidence that it is effective in deterring crime, reducing crime, or eliminating the costs associated with long-term incarceration (see Durham, Elrod & Kinkade, 1996). Perhaps more than any other sanction, the death penalty illustrates the public's willingness to support crime-control policies based on what the politicians and the media contend rather than what the empirical evidence demonstrates: not deterrence but revenge.

As Cook (1998) notes, it is the harshness of the sanction that appeals to the public. The punitive philosophy helps explain a variety of actions taken during the 1990s: "three strikes and you're out" legislation, welfare reform, and the elimination of various programs in prison (Cook, 1998:342). She contends that abolishing the death penalty "will require the convincing, more punitive argument that life without parole in fact may be harsher and more severe than execution. After all, putting a convict to death ends his or her suffering on death row" (1998:343).

This is a significant problem with capital punishment and the acceptance of it by politicians and the public. It is not enough to document that a particular punishment is expensive, ineffective in deterring or reducing crime, and inhumane. Instead, the abolition of the death penalty has to be presented to the public as being too soft on criminals or as immoral. Such a "marketing" strategy and accompanying changes in the application of the death penalty may occur, but slowly, in the foreseeable future. Therefore, capital punishment will continue to be one component of our arsenal of crime-control strategies.

Prison and Jail Sentences

The popularity of prisons and jails cannot be underestimated. There were more than 2 million individuals incarcerated at midyear 2004 (Harrison & Beck, 2005:1). Approximately two-thirds of all inmates are incarcerated in federal and state prisons, and one-third of them are incarcerated in jails (Harrison & Beck, 2005:1). Although the growth appears to have slowed slightly in the last two years, there is every indication that we will continue to utilize imprisonment frequently in the next five years. In fact, at the end of 2003, one in every 32 adults in this country was in a state or federal prison, local jail, or on probation or parole (Glaze & Palla, 2004:2). Previously, Bonczar and Beck (1997) contended that if the trend continues, "1 of every 20 persons in the United States will serve time in a prison during their [sic] lifetime" (1997:1).

Men, as compared to women, are more than eight times more likely to go to prison in their lifetimes (Bonczar & Beck, 1997:1). However, the number of women being sentenced to prison is increasing; and in midyear 2004, women comprised 7 percent (103,310) of all inmates in federal and state prison systems (Harrison & Beck, 2005:5). There is little doubt that the "war on drugs" has affected the incarceration rates of women offenders as well as men offenders. A more detailed discussion of these trends is provided in Chapter 4.

There are some differences in the prison populations at the federal and state levels. However, the growth in the state prison population can be attributed to judges' reliance on prisons for the sentencing of violent offenders (52%), drug offenders (39%), property offenders (38%), weapons offense offenders (45%), and nonviolent offenders like vandals and those convicted of receiving stolen property (35%) to prison in 2002 (Durose & Langan, 2004:2). There were some demographic differences: other than murder, robbery, and weapons offenses for which a larger percentage of African Americans were sentenced to state prisons in 2002 when compared to white offenders, a higher percentage of white offenders was sentenced to prison for every other crime. This shift accounted for the large increase in white offenders in state prisons (Durose & Langan, 2004:6).

On the federal level, drug offenders largely accounted for the increase in the prison population. In 2003, 55 percent of federal inmates were incarcerated for a drug offense (The Sentencing Project, 2005). Previously, in 1995, drug offenders comprised 60 percent of the inmates incarcerated in federal prisons. Although the percentage of violent offenders has decreased in the federal system since 1985, there has been a dramatic increase in the number of federal inmates. Recently, a larger number of offenders in the federal system has been sentenced to prison, and more than 70 percent of them are nonviolent offenders with no prior violent history. Some of these are first-time, nonviolent offenders including white-collar offenders (The Sentencing Project, 2005:1).

One other trend worth noting is the increase both in the number of inmates admitted and released from prison in 2003. This increase in offender releases occurred on the state and federal levels. For example, 634,149 offenders (an increase of 7.5% over 2002) were released from state institutions; and 52,288 (an increase of 25.2% over 2002) were released from federal prisons (Harrison & Beck, 2005:6). However, the number of inmates who were admitted to both state and federal prisons in 2003 also increased when compared to 2002. In both systems, the number of inmates admitted to the prison in 2003 exceeded the number of inmates released. In the state system, more than 21,000 more inmates were admitted compared to those released; and in the federal system, more than 8,000 more inmates were admitted than released (Harrison & Beck, 2004:6).

There are also some interesting changes in inmates released from prison. More than 50 percent of the offenders released from prison and paroled in 2003 were mandatory releases compared to 1995 when 45 percent of inmates paroled were mandatory releases (Glaze & Palla, 2004:1). Inmates in state prisons who were paroled in 1994 served, on average, about one-third of the sentence that the courts stipulated. In 2002, inmates were paroled after having completed slightly more than one-half of the sentence imposed by the courts (Durose & Langan, 2004:10). These data illustrate the effect of the sentencing initiatives drafted in the late 1980s and the 1990s that require offenders to serve longer sentences and to serve longer portions of their sentences in order to be released.

In the 1990s and the first five years of the 2000s, the criminal justice system has been heavily dependent on prison and jail sentences to deter and control crime. Rather than wait to determine if such an expensive strategy (both short-term and long-term) merits such an elevated status, society has enthusiastically endorsed legislation that requires offenders to serve longer sentences and to remain in prison long after their "crime-prone years" have ended. There are no rational explanations or objective data that support such sanctions. Rather, the politicization of criminal justice policy and the compartmentalization of crime as an isolated condition led to the assumption that it will help to simply remove individual offenders who engage in these activities from the rest of society.

Sex Offender Sentencing and Notification Statutes

One of the most publicized practices of the criminal courts involves the sentencing of sexual offenders. Although sexual offenders may be sentenced to prison, it is their eventual release and reintegration into the community that has caused the greatest public concern. In 1996, it was estimated that there were about 234,000 sex offenders in the care and custody of the various correctional agencies of the states, and that approximately 60 percent of them were living in the community under some kind of supervision program (Greenfield, cited by Pearson, 1998:45). Currently, it is estimated that there are 500,000 registered sex offenders in the United States (Schofield, 2005:1).

Part of the public's concern was heightened by the sexual victimization and murder of Megan Kanka by a sexual offender, Jesse Timmendequas, who had been paroled and was living in her neighborhood. The media attention and public outrage surrounding Megan Kanka's death has significantly changed the system's response to sexual offenders. In fact, the legislation in New Jersey is specifically called "Megan's Law." So pervasive is the effect of Kanka's victimization and death that the term, "Megan's Law," is routinely used to refer to any type of sexual offender registration legislation anywhere in the United States.

Legislation in all states now requires community registration (Pearson, 1998:45). These kinds of legislative initiatives have been in existence since 1947, when California enacted its first sex offender registry requirement (Pearson, 1998:45; Welchans, 2005). A more recent development is the creation of community notification legislation. Specifically, the legislation mandates that the community in which the offender plans to reside be informed that he or she will be living there. Statutes vary regarding when the notification is to occur, the kind of information included, to whom the information is to be distributed, and the length of time registration is required (Finn, 1997:3). With respect to the latter, registration is typically required for more than 10 years, but 16 states require lifetime registration in all or specific instances (Finn, 1997:2).

Recently, the state of Florida enacted the Jessica Lunsford Act which requires offenders who have victimized children under the age of 12 to be sentenced to at least 25 years in prison, and to be monitored for the rest of their lives ("America's Most Wanted," 2005). In July of 2005, the Justice Department initiated the National Sex Offender Public Registry (NSOPR), a web site that links state and territory public registries. This web site provides anyone with web access information on sex offenders, including photographs and specific information. Although NSOPR now links 22 states, the Justice Department plans to enable it to list all states in 2006 (Schofield, 2005:1).

According to Finn (1997), the most frequently stated objectives of such legislation are to augment public safety and to help law enforcement officers with their investigations of sex offenders (Finn, 1997:16). There is also a widespread belief that such notification legislation has the ability to prevent future criminality by the offender. However, there is no empirical evidence to date to suggest that these objectives have been accomplished. The empirical analysis that was conducted (only one study) found that the notification legislation has "no impact on recidivism" (Finn, 1997:16).

Despite the lack of evidence to support continuing community notification procedures, most criminal justice professionals support the utilization of such statutes. They contend that these statutes assist them in managing and supervising sexual offenders and that the legislation is an impetus to educating the public about sexual offenders (Finn, 1997:16). Perhaps one of the most important dimensions to consider involves the community education that can occur as a result of the public's heightened awareness. One of the difficulties confronted by law enforcement officials involves apprehending those offenders who victimize family members (Finn, 1997:16). Offenders whose actions are not reported by (and are sometimes facilitated by) family members may go undetected because family or friends may be aware of the victimization but are unable or unwilling to share the information with the authorities. If the victims of sexual offenders in those settings can benefit from the notification legislation, then such legislation will have performed a valuable, albeit unintended, community service.

Lastly, the reliance on notification legislation as the panacea for preventing sexual offending is without empirical and anecdotal support. Welchans (2005) reviewed 12 studies that had been conducted on sex offender registration and community notification mandated under Megan's Law. Her research indicates that although sexual abuse therapists are opposed to the legislation, most of the sex offenders are comfortable with the policy. However, not all sex offenders share these sentiments (Welchans, 2005:131). Most importantly, when looking at child sexual victimization, Welchans's review of the published research found that those involved in the treatment of offenders see the legislation's ability to provide protection as illusory: it does not reduce the likelihood of child sexual victimization. Finally, the two studies that examined the effect of Megan's Law on recidivism found that the policy does not work (Welchans, 2005:135). In his research, Finn (1997:16) found that the respondents reiterated that notification is but one part of the process in preventing sexual offender victimization. Practitioners contend that in order to be successful, the process should involve a treatment program, close monitoring and supervision of the offender, polygraph testing, and effective communication and educational programs designed to teach the community how to respond in a constructive manner to suspicious offender behavior (Finn, 1997:16).

Probation

The dramatic changes in sentencing have required offenders to serve longer prison sentences and to complete a greater portion of their sentence prior to being released. However, a large number of offenders are still sentenced to probation. In 2003, there were 4 million offenders on probation; they accounted for 59 percent of all adults under some form of correctional supervision (Glaze & Palla, 2004:1). Although probation is frequently imposed in the United States, its use has been steadily decreasing since 1990, when 61.4 percent of all adults under correctional supervision were on probation (Mumola & Bonczar, 1998:2). In 2002 and 2003, the number of offenders placed on probation increased after dropping in 2001 (Glaze & Palla, 2004:3). Approximately one in every 53 adults was on probation in the United States at the end of 2003 (Glaze & Palla, 2004:3).

As previously noted, it is no longer the case that an offender is simply sentenced to prison, jail, or probation without additional sanctions or stipulations. This trend is particularly evident in probation. Of those offenders (both felons and misdemeanants) sentenced to probation in 2003, 54 percent of them received a direct sentence to probation, 25 percent were sentenced to incarceration but that sentence was suspended, 8 percent received a "split sentence" (a sentence that involves a period of incarceration in a prison or jail and then probation), and 13 percent began their probation before their cases had been resolved by the court (Glaze & Palla, 2004:4). Probation is also just part of the sanction for offenders. For example, all probationers in Georgia must pay 23 or 29 dollars each month for supervision (Georgia Department of Corrections, 2005). On the national level, Bonczar and Beck (1997:6) found that 61 percent were ordered to pay fees for their supervision, 56 percent were ordered to pay a fine, and 55 percent were ordered to pay court costs. Additionally, restitution to the victim(s) of crime was required in about one-third of the cases, and one of every four probationers had to perform community service.

These preliminary conditions of probation are not the only ones to which offenders must adhere in order to successfully complete their probation status. Conditions typically include the requirement to obtain and retain employment, attend alcohol or other drug treatment programs, participate in a special counseling program, submit to drug testing, wear electronic monitoring devices, complete a period of house arrest, and/or report at specified times to the probation officer (Bonczar & Beck, 1997). Failure to comply with any of these conditions can result in the probation officer asking the judge to revoke the probation. In 2003, 16 percent of probationers were discharged from probation and incarcerated either for violating the terms of their probation or for the commission of a new offense. In addition, 13 percent had their probation revoked, but were not sentenced to jail or prison (Glaze & Palla, 2004:4).

Research overwhelmingly demonstrates that African Americans report more negative feelings toward the criminal justice system than whites, that they perceive that African Americans are treated more harshly by the system, and that racism is prevalent among law enforcement (Wood & May, 2003:606). In addition, Wood and May (2003) found that 20-25 percent of the African Americans in their sample chose prison over alternatives like local jail sentence, boot camp, electronic monitoring, day reporting, intensive supervision probation, or intermittent incarceration. African Americans "are approximately two to four times as likely as whites to choose prison rather than participate in a given alternative sanction" (Wood & May, 2003:627). These data indicate that African-American and white offenders perceive the deterrent effect of a sentence to prison differently, and that the attractiveness of alternative sanctions may depend on the demographic characteristics of the offender (Wood & May, 2003:628). Greater research is necessary to explore these differences and to make the system more responsive to the needs of all offenders.

Although the importance of offender accountability cannot be overestimated, there appears to have been little thought given to the concomitant staffing and resource needs mandated by these additional conditions. There is no evidence to suggest that the probation departments have significantly expanded their staff. The lack of resources that has historically characterized the courts has not changed. If anything, probation officers have been asked to take on more responsibilities with the assumption that corresponding additional resources will not be required. In their research, Purkiss, Kifer, Hemmens, and Burton (2003) found that when compared to 1992, probation officers in 2002 were more likely to be required by state statute to perform more tasks. Simultaneously, probation officers must refute the barrage of criticism that probation is nothing more than "a slap on the wrist" and that it is ineffective in reducing or deterring crime.

Probation data suggest that significant involvement with alcohol and other drugs is reported by probationers. In fact, drug violation offenders represented the largest percentage of probationers (25%) in 2003 (Glaze & Palla, 2004:4). Previous research found that approximately two-thirds of probationers indicated that they had been involved in alcohol or other drug abuse during the time that led up to their current offense (Mumola & Bonczar, 1998:7).

These data would suggest a need for drug testing and treatment for the vast majority of probationers. However, this is not the case. Although almost one-half of all probationers reported that they were tested for drug use during their probation, Mumola and Bonczar found that between 26 and 45 percent of probationers who reported prior drug use did not report being tested for drugs, and two-fifths of intravenous drug users reported that they had not received any drug treatment during the course of their sentence (1998:7).

These findings are consistent with the White House's 1998 National Drug Control Strategy, which found that drug treatment is available for only 52 percent of Americans who are in immediate need of it (Wren, 1998:A14). This is despite the fact that evidence from a study of more than 1,700 people five years after they had participated in drug abuse treatment programs in 1989 and 1990 found that addicts were less likely to use drugs and engage in crime after undergoing treatment. The study was conducted by the Substance Abuse and Mental Health Services Administration of the Department of Health and Human Services (Wren, 1998:A14).

Part of the difficulty lies in determining which programs exist in the criminal justice system. The National Institute on Drug Abuse is undertaking the National Criminal Justice Treatment Practices Survey. It is designed to assess the availability, scope, use, and types of treatment available for substance abusers in the criminal justice system (Taxman, Beard & Delany, 2004:1). The respondent groups include state administrators, state budget directors for clinical programs, local authorities like chief probation officers and sheriffs, and institutional and community treatment program line staff (Taxman, Beard & Delany, 2004:2). The survey is designed to describe the current state of drug treatment as well as the climate in which it is offered (Taxman, Beard & Delany, 2004).

The lack of funding for and low priority of drug treatment programs in the United States are further examples of the criminal justice system's failure to adequately address a significant social problem. One of the more troubling issues is the disproportionate funding ratios for efforts like drug interdiction, arrest, and incarceration versus treatment. The National Drug Control budget for fiscal years 2004-2006 illustrates the long-standing emphasis on enforcement over treatment (The White House, 2005:61). These priorities in funding allocations persist. According to Taxman, Beard, and Delany, "It is estimated that 70 to 85 percent of the more than 6.6 million adults currently incarcerated or on probation or parole in the United States have some type of substance abuse problem, and nearly half require treatment" (2004:1). Although the federal government has increased its spending for drug treatment since 1992, there is little public demand for treatment programs and little or no accountability of enforcement expenditures and policies (Wren, 1998:A14).

Drug and alcohol treatment programs can be costly, but they are no more costly than long-term incarceration. By that standard, they are a bargain. If the available data indicate that probationers report involvement with alcohol or other drugs, it would be an effective policy to require that they participate in treatment programs while they are on probation. Treatment will increase the likelihood that these offenders refrain from future crime and lead law-abiding, productive lives.

Despite the fact that judges utilize probation quite frequently, there is little attention directed toward its effectiveness in reducing recidivism as measured by empirical evidence, or to the strategies that could be implemented to make it function more efficiently. Probation in the United States is yet another manifestation of correctional policy driven primarily by politics and rhetoric versus reality.

DISCUSSION: PROMISING APPROACHES IN THE COURTS

Two promising developments that have the potential to transform the courts and the judicial process include an innovative court model and an alternative philosophical-conceptual model for criminal justice.

Specialty Courts

As will be discussed in the final chapter of this text, one of the problems with the criminal justice system—and the courts—is that decisions about cases and offenders are often conceptualized as "either/or" options (e.g., probation or prison, jail or bail, guilty or innocent). For example, regarding juveniles and the recent legislative activity to transfer more adolescents to criminal court (see Chapter 5), Butts and Harrell observe that (1998:9):

> In the current "all-or-nothing" system, most complex issues are resolved with a simple question, "should the case be tried in juvenile court or adult court?" The answer has often been too simple.

In response, the authors discuss "new, alternative court models" that are providing greater "flexibility to choose different ways of responding to different offenders" (p. 9). The model is a "specialty courts" approach that presents the court system with choices and a full range of alternatives. The model includes gun courts, drug courts, community-based courts, teen courts, mental health courts, domestic violence courts, and even reentry drug courts. Four characteristics are described by Butts and Harrell (p. 12):

1. Treatment and rehabilitation programs are individually matched to offender characteristics.

2. Judges personally negotiate written treatment agreements with offenders and monitor their compliance.

3. The court process involves a combination of immediate penalties and rewards that are contingent on offender behavior.

4. The court relies heavily on community-based programs for delivering both services and sanctions.

Essentially, this gives judges more control over cases, a wider array of dispositional options, and a model to use the court's authority in monitoring, supervising, and sanctioning offenders. Judicial discretion to meet the needs of the offender and to maintain public safety signals a more balanced approach for the courts and a shift away from deterministic sentencing policies.

There are more than 1,600 drug courts operating in the United States, and President George W. Bush has indicated that he is willing to increase funding to $70.1 million for fiscal year 2006 (Walters, 2005:32). Research on the effectiveness of drug courts suggests that they do make a difference. A National Institute of Justice study compared the rearrest data from a sample of 17,000 offenders who had successfully participated in drug court programs versus those who had been imprisoned for drug offenses. The findings indicate that 16.4 percent of the drug court graduates versus 43.5 percent of the prison releases were rearrested and charged with a serious offense in the first year after completion of the sentence, and these differences persisted in the second year (27.5% rearrested compared to 58.6% rearrested after prison) (Roman, Townsend & Bhati, 2003:2; Walters, 2005:31).

Increasingly, we are aware of the relationship between mental illness and criminal justice. When President Bush signed the Mentally Ill Offender Treatment and Crime Reduction Act into law in October of 2004, attention was focused on the opportunity to provide federal funds for jail diversion, treatment for offenders in prison with mental illnesses, community reentry assistance, and training programs (Honberg & Gruttadaro, 2005:24). Although it is too soon to know how effective this legislation will be in providing for the delivery of treatment to juvenile and adult offenders, it appears to recognize the immediacy of the problem.

Prior to the legislation, mental health courts had been established. Currently, mental health courts operate in more than 100 communities in the United States. They service offenders who have mental illnesses and who are charged with nonviolent felonies or misdemeanors. Through the collaboration of dedicated judges, prosecutors, defense attorneys, and mental health professionals, and with the voluntary participation of offenders, these courts are intended to provide treatment with supervision in lieu of incarceration (Honberg & Gruttadaro, 2005:23-23).

Sentencing Reform

Similar to the flexibility available in specialty courts, Mauer (1998) discusses the need to move away from the "three strikes and you're out" sentencing system reviewed earlier in this chapter that has had detrimental consequences on corrections systems. Mauer proposes three steps to develop a more effective sentencing system (pp. 137-140):

1. Create a more individualized sentencing process.

2. Repeal mandatory minimum sentencing laws and other overly restrictive sentencing policies.

3. Reconsider the appropriate balance of resources between the criminal justice system and other institutions.

He identifies some promising indicators that this type of thinking about criminal justice and related strategies for responding to crime and criminals is already occurring (p. 141):

> Fortunately, there are signs that some leaders within the criminal justice system are beginning to reassess their roles and are considering new paradigms for their work. These include such efforts as community policing, or "problem-oriented" policing, where police departments emphasize the resolu-

tion of conflict rather than making arrests; victim-offender reconciliation programs to achieve healing for victims and appropriate sentencing for offenders; drug courts that restore the goal of rehabilitation as one of the functions of sentencing; and efforts such as those of the Vermont and Minnesota Departments of Corrections to promote "restorative justice" through sentencing and other programs.

Evidence that these strategies are gaining a foothold can be found in Kansas, Texas, Michigan, and Washington, where legislatures have reduced the mandatory minimums for minor drug offenders (DiMascio, 2003:3). In California, Proposition 36 provides for the diversion of low-level drug offenders into treatment programs. In 2004, the Pennsylvania legislature enacted Title 37. It establishes an intermediate punishment program for drug-related offenders and includes an individualized drug offender treatment program (*The Pennsylvania Bulletin*, 2005:1).

There are also changes occurring in the use of parole. In several states, the number of inmates granted parole has increased in the last couple of years (The Sentencing Project, 2004:2). Overall, more offenders were released on parole in 2003 (23,654) than in each of the previous nine years (Glaze & Palla, 2004:5). The largest percentage of parole releases from prison continues to be drug offenders. Special pre-release treatment programs and follow-up are essential to facilitate the reintegration and successful reentry of these offenders into the community (Hughes, Wilson & Beck, 2002).

Other states, such as North Carolina, continue to support the Criminal Justice Partnership Program (CJPP), which was established in 1994 to provide community supervision for less serious offenders. In order to alleviate prison overcrowding and reduce the costs associated with incarceration, CJPP is available for probation offenders (Bartlett & Walker, 2004:114). With 80 different programs in the state, CJPP offers pretrial programs, day reporting centers, satellite substance abuse treatment programs through public or private providers, and resource centers (Bartlett & Walker, 2004:115).

Restorative Justice

Mauer's discussion is consistent with the restorative justice perspective, which recognizes that crime is more than just a violation of the law—crime is also a violation of victims and communities, and it disrupts peace and order. Punishment by itself does not restore order or accomplish the more elusive goal of justice. Van Ness and Strong discuss the development of restorative justice thinking. They identify three principles of the model (2002:38-43):

> Justice requires that we work to restore victims, offenders and communities who have been injured by crime.
>
> Victims, offenders and communities should have opportunities for active involvement in the restorative justice process as early and as fully possible.
>
> In promoting justice, government is responsible for preserving order and the community for establishing peace.

The model presents an alternative to the conservative, get-tough policies that focus on punishment, incapacitation, and deterrence. By seeking to respond to the needs of the victim, offender, and community, restorative justice operates from a substantive principle as opposed to the formal, procedural mechanisms of the determinate sentencing models. The court has opportunities to individualize dispositions and to seek a balance among the goals of criminal justice. In the context of these principles, an example of an initiative that seeks to resolve problems rather than to simply punish is the Dispute Settlement Center in Durham, North Carolina.

The Center not only provides mediation services for minor criminal cases but also for "family and divorce mediation, school conflict resolution programs, and corporate workplace training" (McGillis, 1998:2). The programs target the causes of conflict and attempt to keep problems or minor crimes from escalating to serious incidents. In his review of the program, McGillis concludes that (p. 13):

> Mediation provides disputants with the opportunity to communicate face to face, enables disputants to see each other as human beings rather than abstract opponents, and provides opportunities to identify common ground that can lead to resolution of conflict.

Another restorative justice model can be found in the Vermont Reparative Probation Program. It is ". . . the only U.S. state-wide effort to institutionalize the citizen role in restorative decision making" (Karp, Bazemore & Chesire, 2004:502). The task of the volunteers is to meet both the victim(s) and the offender(s) and try to reach a restorative justice contract (2004:491). The offenders must abide by the conditions of the contract, which can range from letters of apology to community service (2004:491). These citizen volunteers (N=292) indicate that they are satisfied with their involvement, that they work cooperatively with the justice system, and that they are actively involved. Their participation reflects the partnership between community and offender that criminal justice practitioners and policymakers prefer (Karp, Bazemore & Chesire, 2004).

These strategies—specialty courts, sentencing reform, and initiatives based on the principles of restorative justice—are indications that courts can become involved in transforming the business of criminal justice. With flexibility to focus on the problems rather than to administer procedures and protocols, judges can use their authority to invoke services and sanctions to hold the offender accountable to the victim and the community.

Clearly, there are alternatives to the current crisis in the courts. However, their success depends, in part, on providing judges and court staff with the discretion to employ creative and flexible approaches in dealing with offenders. Particularly in the federal system but also in the state systems, judges may not have any alternative dispositions available to them. Although the legislative goal of reducing judicial disparity in sentencing is commendable, the current situation in the courts demonstrates that these policies have not transformed the sentencing of offenders into an objective and impartial procedure. Rather, they appear to have exacerbated the disproportionate representation of minorities in the system, discouraged judges from participating in sentencing, and sanctioned relatively minor offenders with long prison sentences. If we are to reverse this trend, new strategies have to be explored, embraced, and expeditiously implemented. The media, the politicization of criminal justice policy, and conservative ideology have had a profound impact on sentencing in the United States. In the next chapter, we examine how these phenomena have affected corrections.

DISCUSSION QUESTIONS

1. Why does a large segment of the public still believe that crime is increasing? What are the implications of this perception on sentencing policies? What can be done to improve the general public's knowledge about crime trends and crime information?

2. Explain how public defenders affect a defendant's experiences and court proceedings. What can be done to improve the equity of defendant representation?

3. Critique the rationales for determinate and indeterminate sentencing policies. What factors have emphasized the use of the determinate model?

4. Discuss why recommendations by the U.S. Sentencing Commission—especially regarding drug sentences—have been opposed by Congress.

5. What is the rationale of three-strikes sentencing legislation? What are the politics of this legislation?

6. Discuss the issue of race, crime, and sentencing. What attitudes and perceptions affect the public's understanding of this issue?

7. Why are sex offender notification statutes popular? What does the research suggest about their effectiveness? What does this suggest about the nature of sentencing legislation?

8. Critique the specialty courts model. What do you think would be the public's response to this model? What can be done to gain legislative and public support for this approach to the courts?

9. What are the goals of the restorative justice model? How does this model affect sentencing policy? Develop an argument in support of restorative justice. What are some obstacles to implementing this model?

REFERENCES

America's Most Wanted (2005). "Lunsford Act Signed Into Law."

Auletta, Ken (2005). "The Dawn Patrol." *The New Yorker* (August 8-15):68-77. *http://www.amw.com/features/feature_story_detail.cfm?id=426&mid=0*

Bartlett, Marie, and Pamela Walker (2004). "Making a Difference in North Carolina." *Corrections Today* 66(6) (October):114-116.

Beckett, Katherine (1997). "Political Preoccupation with Crime Leads, Not Follows, Public Opinion." *Overcrowded Times* 8(5):1, 8-11.

Berger, Peter L. (1998). "The Culture of Liberty: An Agenda." *Society* 35(2):407-415.

Bonczar, Thomas P., and Allen J. Beck (1997). "Lifetime Likelihood of Going to State or Federal Prison." *Bureau of Justice Statistics Special Report.* Washington, DC: U.S. Department of Justice, Office of Justice Programs.

Bonczar, Thomas P., and Tracy L. Snell (2004). "Capital Punishment, 2003." *Bureau of Justice Statistics Bulletin.* Washington, DC: U.S. Department of Justice, Office of Justice Programs.

Britt, Chester L. (1998). "Race, Religion, and Support for the Death Penalty: A Research Note." *Justice Quarterly* 15(1):175-191.

Brown, Jodi M., Patrick A. Langan, and David J. Levin (1999). "Felony Sentences in State Courts, 1996." *Bureau of Justice Statistics Bulletin.* Washington, DC: U.S. Department of Justice, Office of Justice Programs.

Bureau of Justice Statistics (2005a). "Crime and Victims Statistics." Washington, DC: U.S. Department of Justice, Office of Justice Programs. *http://www.ojp.usdoj.gov/bjs/cvict.htm*

Butterfield, Fox (1998). "Prison Population Growing Although Crime Rate Drops." *New York Times* (August 9):14.

Butts, Jeffrey A., and Adele V. Harrell (1998). *Crime Policy Report: Delinquents or Criminals?: Policy Options for Young Offenders.* Washington, DC: The Urban Institute.

Clark, John, James Austin, and D. Alan Henry (1997). "Three Strikes and You're Out: A Review of State Legislation." *National Institute of Justice Research in Brief.* Washington, DC: U.S. Department of Justice, Office of Justice Programs.

Cook, Kimberly J. (1998). "A Passion to Punish: Abortion Opponents Who Favor the Death Penalty." *Justice Quarterly* 15(2):329-346.

Crank, John P. (2003). *Imagining Justice.* Cincinnati: Anderson.

Crawford, Charles (2000). "Gender, Race, and Habitual Offender Sentencing in Florida." *Criminology* 38(1):263-280.

Criminal Justice Newsletter (1994). "State Chief Justices Oppose Senate Crime Bill Provisions."(February 15):1-3.

Cullen, Francis T. (2005). "The Twelve People Who Saved Rehabilitation: How the Science of Criminology Made a Difference." *Criminology* 43(1):1-42.

Death Penalty Information Center (2005a). "Facts about the Death Penalty." Washington, DC: Death Penalty Information Center. *http://www.deathpenaltyinfo. org/FactSheet.pdf*

Death Penalty Information Center (2005b). "Methods of Execution." Washington, DC: Death Penalty Information Center. *http://www.deathpenaltyinfo.org/article. php?scid=8&did=245*

Death Penalty Information Center (2005c). "New Polls on the Death Penalty." Washington, DC: Death Penalty Information Center. *http:// www.deathpenaltyinfo.org/ article.php?did=1452*

Death Penalty Information Center (2005d). "Public Opinion: Majority in Alabama Supports a Temporary Halt to Executions." Washington, DC: Death Penalty Information Center. *http:// www.deathpenaltyinfo.org/article.php?did=1522&scid=64*

DeFrances, Carol J. (2002). "Prosecutors in State Courts, 2001." *Bureau of Justice Statistics Bulletin.* Washington, DC: U.S. Department of Justice, Office of Justice Programs.

DeFrances, Carol J., and Greg W. Steadman (1998). "Prosecutors in State Courts, 1996." *Bureau of Justice Statistics Bulletin.* Washington, DC: U.S. Department of Justice.

Dickey, Walter, and Pam Stiebs Hollenhorst (1998a). "'Three Strikes': Five Years Later." *Public Policy Reports.* Washington, DC: Campaign for an Effective Crime Policy.

Dickey, Walter, and Pam Stiebs Hollenhorst (1998b). "Three Strikes Laws: Massive Impact in California and Georgia, Little Elsewhere." *Overcrowded Times* 9(6):2-8.

DiMascio, William (2003). "Dilemma." *Correctional Forum* (September):2-3.

Downing, Kevin, and Richard Lynch (1997). "Pre-Sentence Reports: Does Quality Matter?" *Social Policy and Administration* 31(2):173-190.

Durham, Alexis M., H. Preston Elrod, and Patrick T. Kinkade (1996). "Public Support for the Death Penalty: Beyond Gallup." *Justice Quarterly* 13(4):705-736.

Durose, Matthew R., and Patrick A. Langan (2003). "Felony Sentences in State Courts, 2000." *Bureau of Justice Statistics Bulletin.* Washington, DC: U.S. Department of Justice, Office of Justice Programs.

Durose, Matthew R., and Patrick A. Langan (2004). "Felony Sentences in State Courts, 2002." *Bureau of Justice Statistics Bulletin*. Washington, DC: U.S. Department of Justice, Office of Justice Programs.

Eaton, Judge O.H., Jr. (1997). "Florida Sentencing Laws in Ferment." *Overcrowded Times* 8(3):7-9.

Ehlers, Scott, Vincent Schiraldi, and Eric Lotke (2004). "Three Strikes and You're Out: An Examination of the Impact of Strikes Laws 10 Years after Their Enactment." Washington, DC: Justice Policy Institute.

Ehlers, Scott, Vincent Schiraldi, and Jason Ziedenberg (2004). "Still Striking Out: Ten Years of California's Three Strikes Law." Washington, DC: Justice Policy Institute.

Engen, Rodney L., Randy R. Gainey, Robert T. Crutchfield, and Joseph G. Weis (2003). "Discretion and Disparity under Sentencing Guidelines: The Role of Departures and Structured Sentencing Alternatives." *Criminology* 41(1):99-130.

Fields, Gary (2004). "Commission Finds Racial Disparity in Jail Sentences." *The Wall Street Journal* (November 24):A4.

Finder, Alan (1999). "New York's Death Penalty: Most Defendants Are White, From Upstate." *New York Times* (January 21):A23.

Finn, Peter (1997). "Sex Offender Community Notification." *National Institute of Justice Research in Action*. Washington, DC: U.S. Department of Justice, Office of Justice Programs.

Georgia Department of Corrections (2005). "FY03 Field Collections." *http://www.dcor.state.ga.us/CORR/ProbationSupervision/FieldOperations.Collect.html*

Gilliard, Darrell K., and Allen J. Beck (1998a). "Prison and Jail Inmates at Midyear 1997." *Bureau of Justice Statistics Bulletin*. Washington, DC: U.S. Department of Justice, Office of Justice Programs.

Gilliard, Darrell K., and Allen J. Beck (1998b). "Prisoners in 1997." *Bureau of Justice Statistics Bulletin*. Washington, DC: U.S. Department of Justice, Office of Justice Programs.

Glaze, Lauren E., and Seri Palla (2004). "Probation and Parole in the United States, 2003." *Bureau of Justice Statistics Bulletin*. Washington, DC: U.S. Department of Justice, Office of Justice Programs.

Goodstein, Lynne, and John Hepburn (1985). *Determinate Sentencing and Imprisonment*. Cincinnati: Anderson.

Greenhouse, Linda (1998a). "Federal Sentencing Guidelines Criticized by a Key Supporter." *New York Times* (November 21):A10.

Greenhouse, Linda (1998b). "In Sentencing Under '3 Strikes' Laws, Deciding Whether Crime Is Strike Isn't Double Jeopardy." *New York Times* (June 27): A10.

Greenhouse, Linda (1999). "Three Strikes Challenge Fails, but Others Are Invited." *New York Times* (January 20):A12.

Greenhouse, Linda (2003). "Judges Seek Repeal of Law on Sentencing." *New York Times* (September 24): A17.

Harlow, Caroline Wolf (2000). "Defense Counsel in Criminal Cases." *Bureau of Justice Statistics Special Report*. Washington, DC: U.S. Department of Justice, Office of Justice Programs.

Harrison, Paige M. and Allen J. Beck (2005). "Prison and Jail Inmates at Midyear 2004." *Bureau of Justice Statistics Bulletin.* Washington, DC: U.S. Department of Justice.

Holten, N. Gary, and Roger Handberg (1994). "Determinate Sentencing." In Albert R. Roberts (ed.), *Critical Issues in Crime and Justice*, pp. 217-231. Thousand Oaks, CA: Sage.

Honberg, Ron, and Darcy Gruttadaro (2005). "Flawed Mental Health Policies and the Tragedy of Criminalization." *Corrections Today* 67(1):22-24, 27.

Hughes, Timothy A., Doris James Wilson, and Alan J. Beck (2002). "Trends in State Parole: The More Things Change, the More They Stay the Same." In Joanne Naughton and Joseph L. Victor (eds.), *Annual Editions: Criminal Justice, 2005/2006*, pp. 183-190. Dubuque, IA: McGraw-Hill/Dushkin.

Institute of Governmental Studies (2004). "Proposition 66: Limitation on 'Three Strikes' Laws." Berkeley, CA: Institute of Governmental Studies, University of California. *http://igs.berkeley.edu/library/htThreeStrikesProp66.htm*

Johnson, Brian D. (2003). "Racial and Ethnic Disparities in Sentencing Departures Across Modes of Conviction." *Criminology* 41(2):449-490.

Johnson, Brian D. (2005). "Contextual Disparities in Guideline Departures: Courtroom Social Contexts, Guidelines Compliance, and Extralegal Disparities in Criminal Sentencing." *Criminology* 43(3):761-796.

Joseph, Janice, Zelma Watson Henriques, and Kaylene Richards Ekeh (2003). "Get Tough Policies and the Incarceration of African Americans." In Janice Joseph and Dorothy Taylor (eds.), *With Justice for All: Minorities and Women in Criminal Justice*, pp. 105-119. Upper Saddle River, NJ: Prentice Hall.

Kappeler, Victor E., and Gary W. Potter (2005). *The Mythology of Crime and Criminal Justice*, 4th ed. Long Grove, IL: Waveland.

Karp, David R., Gordon Bazemore, and J.D. Chesire (2004). "The Role and Attitudes of Restorative Board Members: A Case Study of Volunteers in Community Justice." *Crime & Delinquency* 50(4):487-515.

Kennedy, Edward M. (1985). "Prison Overcrowding: The Law's Dilemma." *The Annals of the American Academy of Political and Social Science* 478:113-122.

Kempinen, Cynthia (1997). "Pennsylvania Revises Sentencing Guidelines." *Overcrowded Times* 8(4):1, 14-18.

Kovandzic, Tomislav V., John J. Sloan III, and Lynne M. Vieraitis (2004). "'Striking Out' as Crime Reduction Policy: The Impact of the 'Three Strikes' Laws on Crime Rates in U.S. Cities." *Justice Quarterly* 21(2):207-239.

Kurki, Leena (1998). "U.S. Crime Rate Continues to Fall." *Overcrowded Times* 9(1):4-8.

Langan, Patrick A., and Jodi M. Brown (1997). "Felony Sentences in State Courts, 1994." *Bureau of Justice Statistics Bulletin.* Washington, DC: U.S. Department of Justice, Office of Justice Programs.

Langan, Patrick A., Craig A. Perkins, and Jan M. Chaiken (1994). "Felony Sentences in the United States, 1990." *Bureau of Justice Statistics Bulletin.* Washington, DC: U.S. Department of Justice, Office of Justice Programs.

Lewis, Anthony (1998). "Moving the Judges." *New York Times* (April 27):A19.

Maguire, Kathleen, and Ann L. Pastore (1997). *Sourcebook of Criminal Justice Statistics*. Washington, DC: U.S. Department of Justice, Bureau of Justice Statistics.

Mauer, Marc (1998). "Sentencing and the Practice of Peacemaking." *The Justice Professional* 11(1-2):133-141.

McGillis, Daniel (1998). *Resolving Community Conflict: The Dispute Settlement Center of Durham, North Carolina*. Washington, DC: National Institute of Justice.

Merlo, Alida V. (1997). "The Crisis and Consequences of Prison Overcrowding" In Joycelyn M. Pollock (ed.), *Prisons: Today and Tomorrow*, pp. 55-83. Gaithersburg, MD: Aspen.

Mumola, Christopher J., and Allen J. Beck (1997). "Prisoners in 1996." *Bureau of Justice Statistics Bulletin*. Washington, DC: U.S. Department of Justice, Office of Justice Programs.

Mumola, Christopher J., and Thomas P. Bonczar (1998). "Substance Abuse and Treatment of Adults on Probation, 1995." *Bureau of Justice Statistics Special Report*. Washington, DC: U.S. Department of Justice, Office of Justice Programs.

New York Times (2004). "Sentencing—Guideline Study Finds Continuing Disparities." (November 27):A11.

New York Times (1998a). "Court Upholds Death Penalty for McVeigh." (September 9):A13.

New York Times (1998b). "In Reversal, Lawmaker Agrees to Curtail Parole." (June 4):A25.

New York Times (1999). "Violent Crime Falls 7 Percent, to Lowest Level in Decades." (July 19):A10.

Nobiling, Tracy, Cassia Spohn, and Miriam DeLone (1998). "A Tale of Two Counties: Unemployment and Sentence Severity." *Justice Quarterly* 15(8):459-485.

Office of National Drug Control Policy (2005). *Drug Data Summary, March 2003*. Washington, DC: Executive Office of the President. *http://www.whitehousedrug policy.gov/publications/factsht/drugdata/index.html*

Overcrowded Times (1998). "Crime Regains Top Spot in Television News Coverage in 1997." 9(2):4. Reprinted from Media Monitor, January/February 1998.

Oliver, Willard M., and David E. Barlow (2005). "Following the Leader? Presidential Influence over Congress in the Passage of Federal Crime Control Policy." *Criminal Justice Policy Review* 16(3):267-286.

Pastore, Ann L., and Kathleen Maguire (2003). *Sourcebook of Criminal Justice Statistics, 2003* [online]. *http://www.albany.edu/sourcebook/*

Pearson, Elizabeth A. (1998). "Status and Latest Developments in Sex Offender Registration and Notification Laws." National Conference on Sex Offender Registries 45 (U.S. Department of Justice). Washington, DC: U.S. Government Printing Office.

The Pennsylvania Bulletin (2005). "Statements of Policy, Title 37-Law." *http://www. pabulletin.com/secure/data/vol35/35-21/992.html*

Proband, Stan (1997). "Black Men Face 29 Percent Lifetime Chance of Prison." *Overcrowded Times* 8(1):1, 22.

Purkiss, Marcus, Misty Kifer, Craig Hemmens, and Velmer Burton, Jr. (2003). "Probation Officer Functions: A Statutory Analysis." *Federal Probation* 67(1):12-23.

Rauschenberg, Fritz (1997). "Ohio Guidelines Take Effect." *Overcrowded Times* 8(4):10-11.

Reed Ward, Paula (2005). "Victims Get Prisoner Payments Despite Suits." *Pittsburgh Post-Gazette* (August 1):B-4.

Roman, John, Wendy Townsend, and Avinash Singh Bhati (2003). *Recidivism Rates for Drug Court Graduates: Nationally Based Estimates, Final Report*. Washington, DC: U.S. Department of Justice.

Rosich, Katherine J., and Kamala Mallik Kane (2005). "Truth in Sentencing and State Sentencing Practices." *NIJ Journal* 252:18-21.

Ryan, Harriet (2005). "Judge Sentences Scott Peterson to Death for Killing His Wife and Unborn Son." CourtTV.com (March 16). *http://www.courttv.com/trials/peterson/031605_ctv.html*

Schofield, Regina B. (2005). *The National Sex Offender Public Registry*. Washington, DC: U.S. Department of Justice, Office of Justice Programs.

The Sentencing Project (1999). "Facts About Prisons and Prisoners." Washington, DC: The Sentencing Project.

The Sentencing Project (2004). "New Incarceration Figures: Growth in Population Continues." Washington, DC: The Sentencing Project. *http://www.sentencingproject.org*

The Sentencing Project (2005). "The Federal Prison Population: A Statistical Anaysis." Washington, DC: The Sentencing Project. *http://www.sentencingproject.org*

Smolkin, Rachel (2002). "Off Target." *American Journalism Review* (24) 10:26-32.

Snell, Tracy L. (1997). "Capital Punishment 1996." *Bureau of Justice Statistics Bulletin*. Washington, DC: U.S. Department of Justice, Office of Justice Programs.

Sorensen, Jon, and Don Stemen (2002). "The Effect of State Sentencing Policies on Incarceration Rates." *Crime & Delinquency* 48(3):456-475.

Spohn, Cassia, John Gruhl, and Susan Welch (1980-1981). "The Effect of Race on Sentencing: A Re-Examination of an Unsettled Question." *Law & Society Review* 16:71-88.

Spohn, Cassia, and David Holleran (2000). "The Imprisonment Penalty Paid by Young, Unemployed Black and Hispanic Male Offenders." *Criminology* 38(1):281-306.

Taxman, Faye S., Courtney Beard, and Peter Delany (2004). "The National Criminal Justice Treatment Practices Survey: Understanding How Services Are Provided to Offenders." *On the Line* 27(3):1-3.

Tonry, Michael (1998). "Crime and Punishment in America, 1971-1996." *Overcrowded Times* 9(2):1, 12-20.

Tonry, Michael, and Kate Hamilton (1995). *Intermediate Sanctions in Overcrowded Times*. Boston: Northeastern University Press.

Uniform Crime Reports (2004). *Crime in the United States 2003*. Washington, DC: U.S. Government Printing Office.

U.S. Department of Justice (1988). *Report to the Nation on Crime and Justice-Sentencing and Corrections*, 2nd ed. Washington, DC: Bureau of Justice Statistics.

U.S. Department of Justice (1998a). *Compendium of Federal Justice Statistics, 1995*. Executive Summary. Washington, DC: Bureau of Justice Statistics.

U.S. Department of Justice (1998b). *National Institute of Justice Solicitation for Research and Evaluation on Corrections and Sentencing 1998*. Washington, DC: U.S. Department of Justice, Office of Justice Programs.

Van Ness, Daniel, and Karen Heetderks Strong (2002). *Restoring Justice*, 2nd ed. Cincinnati: Anderson.

Van Wagenen, Richard D. (1997). Washington State Sentencing Changes 1994-97." *Overcrowded Times* 8(6):1, 6-8.

Walker, Samuel, Cassia Spohn, and Miriam DeLone (1998). "Race and Sentencing." In George F. Cole and Marc G. Gertz (eds.), *The Criminal Justice System: Politics and Policies*, 7th ed., pp. 352-365. Belmont, CA: Wadsworth.

Walters, John (2005). *National Drug Control Strategy*. Washington, DC: The White House.

Welch, Michael, Melissa Fenwick, and Meredith Roberts (1998). "State Managers, Intellectuals, and the Media: A Content Analysis of Ideology in Experts' Quotes in Feature Newspaper Articles on Crime." *Justice Quarterly* 15(2):219-241.

Welchans, Sarah (2005). "Megan's Law: Evaluations of Sexual Offender Registries." *Criminal Justice Policy Review* 16(2):123-140.

The White House (February, 2005). *National Drug Control Strategy: Update*. Washington, DC: Office of National Drug Control Policy.

Wohl, Alexander (1992). "The Calculus of Rationality." *American Bar Association Journal* 78:37-40.

Wood, Peter B., and David C. May (2003). "Racial Differences in Perceptions of the Severity of Sanctions: A Comparison of Prison with Alternatives." *Justice Quarterly* 20(3):605-631.

Wren, Christopher S. (1998). "Study Finds Treatment Aids Addicts." *New York Times* (September 12):A14.

Wright, Ronald F. (1998). "Flexibility in North Carolina Sentencing Structure, 1995-1997." *Overcrowded Times* 9(6):1, 11-15.

Yanich, Danilo (2005). "Kids, Crime, and Local Television News." *Crime & Delinquency* 51(1):103-132.

Yardley, William (2004). "Where Execution Feels Like Relic, Death Looms." *New York Times* (November 21):A1-32.

Yellen, David (1997). "Little Progress in Federal Sentencing After Ten Years of Guidelines." *Overcrowded Times* 8(3):1, 4-7.

CASES

Ewing v. California, 538 U.S. 11 (2003).

Lockyer v. Andrade, 538 U.S. 63 (2003).

Monge v. California, 118 S.Ct. 2246 (1998).

People v. Superior Court (Romero), 917 P.2d 628 (1996). See also *People v. Superior Court (Alvarez)*, 928 P.2d 1171 (1997).

United States v. Booker, 124 S. Ct. 738 (2005).

4

Punishment and Prisons:
Correctional Policy in Crisis

In spite of nine years of decreasing crime rates, incarceration continues to be a major crime control strategy for dealing with crime and criminals. Beginning in 1790 with the Walnut Street Jail in Pennsylvania, policymakers have steadfastly demonstrated enthusiasm for expanding, renovating, and relying on prisons to deal with offenders. In the last two decades, the United States has made an even greater commitment to constructing prisons and increasing the nation's inmate population. This chapter will critically examine the ideology, the media's role in correctional policy initiatives, some alternative approaches, and future directions.

There are numerous factors that account for America's penchant for incarceration. They include: the media sensationalism of crime, the politicization of crime, the enactment of new laws designed to mandate incarceration and extend confinement for certain categories of offenders, statutory changes that require longer terms of incarceration, the "war on drugs," and an increase in offenders being returned to prison as parole violators.

Even though there have been nine years of decreasing crime in the United States, Americans have not seen a proportional decrease in crime news (Dreier, 2005:194). On the contrary, Dreier contends that ". . . the media give their audience of readers and viewers little reason for optimism that ordinary people working together effectively can make a difference, that solutions are within reach, and that public policies can make a significant difference" (2005:199). These negative feelings have consequences, and more punitive policies are one manifestation of them.

The policymakers' decision to develop punitive crime control policies is not without its costs. The financial commitments include the construction and maintenance of facilities, the care of elderly inmates who will age and eventually die in prisons, and the policies, programs, and services that will be marginalized or eliminated as governments try to cope with the exorbitant costs of incarceration. Additionally, these policies reflect the pervasive influence that ideology, the media, and politics have in shaping the perception of and response to crime and crime control strategies.

PRISONS AND INCARCERATION IN THE 1990S AND 2000S

The Prison Boom

The good news is that there is no shortage of jobs. In American corrections, unlike most other segments of business, down-sizing, facility closings, and retrenchment are unlikely to occur any time in the foreseeable future. As Adams aptly noted, it is a "tremendous bull market" in corrections (1996:461). Unfortunately, the fact that institutions are in demand does not bode well for society. There are now more than 2 million offenders in federal, state, and local institutions in the United States, and the numbers continue to increase (Harrison & Beck, 2005:1).

During the period from December 31, 1995, to June 30, 2004, the number of offenders in state and federal prisons increased from 1,585,586 to 2,131,180 (Harrison & Beck, 2005:2). Each year, the annual average increase has been 3.5 percent. The rate of incarceration in June of 2004 was 486 inmates for every 100,000 residents of the United States. On June 30, 2004, one out of every 138 residents of the United States was in prison or jail (Harrison & Beck, 2005:2). The state with the highest incarceration rate was Louisiana, which had 814 inmates for every 100,000 residents; the state with the lowest incarceration rate was Maine, which had 149 inmates for every 100,000 residents on June 30, 2004 (Harrison & Beck, 2005:4). The rate of incarceration is much higher for men than women. In June of 2004, there were 923 male inmates for every 100,000 men, and 63 female inmates for every 100,000 women. Men were almost 15 times more likely than women to be imprisoned on June 30, 2004 (Harrison & Beck, 2005:5).

Several reasons have been cited to explain the increase in prison populations and the concomitant overcrowding that has characterized some state institutions. An earlier survey of correctional administrators in all 50 states by Vaughn found four factors that 44 administrators listed as particularly important in understanding why prisons were over-crowded: (1) increased sentence length, (2) the drug problem, (3) the public's desire to get tough on crime, and (4) the legislative response to that demand (Vaughn, 1993:15-16). In their examination of incar-ceration trends, Clear and Cole also recognize these factors but iden-tify demographic shifts, increased arrest rates, higher probabilities of incarceration, and the availability of more prison cells resulting from prison construction as additional explanations for escalating prison populations (1997:481-488).

The increase in the length of sentences is partially due to the pub-lic's desire to get tough on crime and the legislative response to that demand. Beginning in the 1990s, policymakers applied a baseball metaphor to correctional policy. Although chronic-offender legislation had been in existence in most states for a long time (habitual offender legislation was enacted in New York in the 1700s; by 1968, 23 states had statutes authorizing life imprisonment for chronic offenders), those statutes did not have the same cachet as "three strikes and you're out" laws (Turner, Sundt, Applegate & Cullen, 1995:17). After all, why use an old statute when you can push a new one with a catchy sound bite?

State legislatures were particularly adept at drafting legislation that would be politically powerful and that would send a message to prospective offenders that crime is serious business and that it will be countered with serious sanctions. Washington became the first state to step up to the plate by enacting the first three-strikes legislation in 1993 (Dickey, 1996:2). Not to be "out-legislated" by the states, in the Fall of 1994, Congress enacted and President Clinton signed the Violent Crime Control and Law Enforcement Act of 1994. Typically, federal and state laws mandate life imprisonment for offenders who have been previously convicted of one or two violent or drug crimes. In some states, such as Washington, a third conviction for specified offenses can result in life imprisonment without possibility of parole. Under Geor-gia law, an offender who has twice been convicted of specified violent offenses can be imprisoned for life without possibility of parole, par-don, or early release (Benekos & Merlo, 1995).

Pete Wilson, the former Governor of California, even recom-mended "one strike and you're out" legislation. His ideas, although well publicized, were not reflected in California's legislation. Since 1994, California requires judges to impose an indeterminate sentence of 25 years to life or triple the normal sentence, whichever is greater, for offenders who are convicted of certain felonies who have two previ-ous convictions for any felony (Benekos & Merlo, 1995). California's law has received a great deal of media attention, partly because more than 500 offenses are felonies in California, including such activities as larceny and betting on an office pool.

Beginning in January 1998, California also applied this strict mandatory sentencing model to felonies committed with guns. "The law requires an additional 10 years in prison for carrying a gun while committing a serious violent felony," 20 years if the gun is fired, and an additional 25 years to life "if a shooting results in a serious injury to a victim" (*Criminal Justice Newsletter*, 1997b:1). Referred to as the "10-20-LIFE" penalties, this legislation indicates that get-tough policies show no sign of waning in California.

It was an ingenious strategy to utilize the imagery of "America's favorite pastime" in correctional policy. Perhaps it was coincidental that the shibboleth, "three strikes and you're out," became so popular when major-league baseball players were on strike in 1994. The most shocking thing about this mandatory legislation is the belief by the public that these kinds of initiatives are actually doing something about crime. These sentiments persist over time. In 2004, California voters had the opportunity to revise the three-strikes legislation through Proposition 66. However, more than 52 percent of the voters chose to continue the legislation as it was drafted (Institute of Governmental Studies, 2004). Based on their review of three-strikes legislation, Clark, Austin, and Henry concluded (1997:13):

> The rapid expansion of three-strikes laws, regardless of how they are defined, reflects the perceptions that existing laws did not adequately protect public safety in their application and/or outcome, that exceptional incidents had occurred that the new laws would address, or that the intent of current laws was being frustrated by other factors such as prison crowding.

A recent study by Kovandzic, Sloan, and Vieraitis (2004) found that there is no statistical evidence that three-strikes legislation reduces crime either through deterrence or the incapacitation of repeat offenders (2004:234). In their analysis, Schiraldi, Colburn, and Lotke (2004) found that those counties in California that had higher rates of sentencing offenders to prison under the three-strikes law did not report any greater reductions in their crime rates than counties that utilized the three-strikes legislation less often (2004:7). These studies suggest that the "three strikes and you're out" rallying cry propelled state legislatures to enact new legislation that may not have been necessary.

Not long after the law was enacted, Joseph Sandoval (1996), the Secretary of California Youth and Adult Correctional Agency, argued that the declining crime rates in California provided support that the legislation was in fact working. In spite of the increased costs and prison crowding, he concluded that the longer sentences were "a sound investment" in long-term crime reduction (p. 22).

The Politics of Corrections

The politicization of crime is not new. Nationally, it was Barry Goldwater who first promoted the theme of "law and order." In an attempt to portray Johnson's "war on poverty" as a softheaded response to crime and disorder, Goldwater succeeded in placing the country's focus on crime. Johnson was elected, but the "nationalization" of the crime issue was established, and the federal government began "a new era of involvement in crime control" (*Congressional Digest*, 1994:162; see also Benekos & Merlo, 1995). As a result, "in recent years, it has become fashionable for just about every candidate for public office to have a position on crime, and the only position worth having is appearing to be tougher than your opponent" (Greenwood, 1998:138).

As reviewed in Chapter 1, this was clearly demonstrated in the 1988 Presidential election when then–Vice President George Bush successfully challenged Governor Michael Dukakis's correctional policies, which had allowed Willie Horton to be granted a furlough in Massachusetts. Willie Horton became the poster child of Republicans and served as a constant reminder that appearing to be soft on crime was politically incorrect (Benekos & Merlo, 1995).

Other cases have also captured the public's attention and fueled the public's perception that violent crime is increasing, that we are too soft on criminals, and that offenders are released from prison after serving only a small part of their sentences. The abduction and tragic murder of Polly Klaas in California, and the kidnappings, sexual assaults, and murders of Jessica Lunsford in Florida and Megan Kanka in New Jersey are but three examples. As noted earlier, these celebrated cases served to draw media and political attention to how and when offenders (especially violent offenders) are released from prison. As a result, the get-tough climate has generated political support for truth-in-sentencing laws that have toughened parole policies and contributed to prison crowding. As an incentive to states to require violent offenders to serve more time (at least 85% of their sentences), the Violent Crime Control and Law Enforcement Act of 1994 authorized the Department of Justice to "award" grants to those states that enacted truth-in-sentencing legislation. In 1996, 25 states were awarded a total of $195.8 million in truth-in-sentencing grants; in 1997, 27 states received $234.9 million (U.S. General Accounting Office, 1998:2-3).

The fact that violent crime (as recorded and reported by the FBI) is down for the ninth consecutive year (Uniform Crime Reports, 2004) seems to provide no solace to the public. Butterfield (1997a:1) sees these kinds of tragedies as symbolic of the grip that violent crime has on our country. The public fears crime. Any politician who can convince the public that he or she is tough on crime—and that the opponent or incumbent is soft on crime and allows criminals out of prison—has an effective election strategy. As a result of this politicization, candidates have become effective in manipulating the public's fear of victimization and in justifying an expansion of incarceration policies (Fabelo, 1996).

The role of the media is also a crucial component in this distortion of crime policy. Fabelo describes how the "personalization and dramatization of crimes"—which is conveyed primarily by television—helps to create a "virtual reality" in which crime across the country is perceived as crime across the street (1996:477). Consequently, the public does not feel safe and is inclined to support and expect tougher responses to crime. In his assessment of public opinion on crime and punishment, Warr (1995) identified some prevailing trends that help explain the public's anger and punitiveness. For example, in addition to the passionate and emotional responses generated by crime, he found a "relative constancy" in the public's fear of crime over the last two decades and a parallel view that the courts are too lenient in dealing with criminals (1995:297). This creates a condition easily manipulated by politicians to expand control over offenders and use more incarceration as public policy.

In her study of public views of youth crime in Ontario, Sprott (1996) found that most respondents perceived that there were high levels of violent crime and that court dispositions were "too lenient." Again, the "public's main source of information" (and the basis of understanding crime) is the mass media. Sprott concluded that respondents generally have "inaccurate knowledge" and "lack of information" and that, therefore, they have distorted perceptions and little understanding of crime and court dispositions (p. 288). This characteristic applies to United States citizens as well as Canadians.

In response to the emotionally charged and ill-informed public, and partly due to an "escalation of toughness" mentality, states have enacted civil commitment statutes for sex offenders (Matson & Lieb, 1997). This initiative in incarceration policy provides for involuntary confinement of designated sexual offenders and has been upheld by the Supreme Court as a "protection" to society, not as a double-jeopardy punishment of offenders (*Criminal Justice Newsletter*, 1997b; Matson & Lieb, 1997). As discussed in Chapter 1, the Kansas legislation, referred to as "Stephanie's Law" and the Florida legislation referred to as "Jessica's Law" illustrate the politicized, emotional nature of crime policy when laws are named after victims and become a personal, reactive basis for developing public policy.

The costs associated with harsher sanctions such as three-strikes laws and civil commitment statutes are exorbitant. In 1994, the National Council on Crime and Delinquency (NCCD) estimated that if the other states followed the lead of the federal government, California, and Washington, the inmate population in American prisons would rise to a minimum of 2.26 million by 2004 (*Corrections Digest*, 1994:1). From all indications, they have followed that lead. Data from the Bureau of Justice Statistics indicate that on June 30, 2004, there were 2.13 million inmates (close to 2.26 million) in prison and jail in the United States (Harrison & Beck, 2005:1). These data indicate that NCCD's projection was pretty accurate.

A more recent assessment of the impact of three-strikes legislation is more optimistic about the number of offenders affected by these new sentencing laws (Schiraldi, Colburn & Lotke, 2004). Based on data from 21 states, Schiraldi and colleagues (2004) found that each had less than 100 offenders sentenced under three-strikes provisions. The notable exceptions were California, Florida, and Georgia (Schiraldi, Colburn & Lotke, 2004:4). One explanation for the lesser consequences for the prison population is that states already had provisions for serious, repeat offenders. Thus, the three-strikes legislation (with evidence of variations among the states) was more likely a political response for the public and not a substantive crime policy initiative. As a result, these specific laws alone do not account for prison overcrowding in most of the states.

Nonetheless, inmate populations have increased over the last 15 years and, by all indications, will continue to do so for the foreseeable future. Increased sentence lengths, the public's concerns with getting tough on crime (and legislative responses), and one other factor appear to have contributed to the prison population escalation: the increase in the number of released offenders who return to prison due to violation of one or more conditions of their release. According to Harrison and Beck (2005), the number of parole-violation admissions rose from 133,870 (29% of all admissions) in 1990 to 209,753 (33% of all admissions) in 2003 (2005:6). Even though the number of parole violators returning to prison has risen, the increase in new court commitments has played a more dominant role in prison admission data (Harrison & Beck, 2005:6).

While the number of parole violators and readmissions has increased, the number of discretionary parole releases has decreased (Glaze & Palla, 2004:6). In 1995, parole boards released 50 percent of prison inmates; in 2003, this decreased to 39 percent. However, the percent of mandatory releases increased from 45 percent in 1995 to 51 percent in 2003 (Glaze & Palla, 2004:6). There may be no apparent association between the decrease in discretionary parole releases and the increase in prison readmissions but the get-tough attitudes and policies that have contributed to curtailed parole discretion may be having the unintended effect of increasing recidivism. While arguments both for and against abolishing parole have been offered (see Clear & Cole, 1997), trends reveal that as a result of prison crowding and fiscal restraints, discretionary release may be experiencing a "rebirth" because community supervision on parole is "far less costly than incarceration" (Clear & Cole, 1997:433). The most recent parole data indicate that there was a 3.1 percent increase in the use of parole in 2003; this represents the largest increase in the parole population from 1995 to 2003 (Glaze & Palla, 2004:5).

PRISONER DEMOGRAPHICS

Elderly Inmates

Longer sentences mean that institutions will have to prepare for long-term inmates, some of whom will enter the institution when they are quite young. Inmates who are serving life sentences without possibility of parole will age and ultimately die while in prison. In 2003, one of every 11 inmates (127,677 inmates) in state or federal prison was serving a life sentence (Mauer, King & Young, 2004:1). Of those lifers, one in four was sentenced to life in prison without the possibility of parole. In some states, like Pennsylvania, all sentences to life in prison are sentences to life without possibility of parole (Mauer, King & Young, 2004:1).

In 2002, there were 121,000 inmates who were age 50 or older (*USA Today*, 2004). Comparatively, on January 1, 1998, there were more than 83,667 inmates age 50 or older in state and federal prisons in the United States (Camp & Camp, 1998:24). According to John Mills, of the Centers for Disease Control and Prevention, for inmates more than 60 years of age, the annual cost of incarceration is $70,000—almost three times the average cost for inmates (*USA Today*, 2004).

Not only will the costs of incarcerating so many offenders be high, but the offenders' special needs will also be significant. Prison administrators will not be able to incarcerate younger offenders and older offenders in the same cellblock. In fact, 16 states now have separate buildings to incarcerate older offenders (*USA Today*, 2004). Correctional administrators will have to recruit and train correctional officers to work in these geriatric units.

Medical costs for inmates are expected to increase dramatically in order to accommodate older inmates. Maruschak and Beck (2001) found that among inmates who were 45 or older, 48 percent of state inmates and 39 percent of federal inmates indicated that they had a physical impairment or mental condition (p. 4). Older offenders who suffer from arthritis, heart disease, Alzheimer's disease, depression, cataracts, and other age-related illnesses will need special medical units, services, and care. State appropriations for preventive health and medical services will have to take these populations into consideration. Already, predictions for the State of California indicate that it will cost $740 million a year to care for elderly inmates in 2030 (Auerhahn, 2002).

Elderly inmates cannot be expected to keep up with younger inmates and to move quickly for the morning count and breakfast. Some of them will need walkers, wheelchairs, or canes to assist them in walking. Some of the cells will have to be redesigned to make them wheel chair–accessible, with wider door openings, special beds, and special showers. A number of these inmates will need heart surgery and other kinds of medical interventions that are common among older people. For example, Dennis Whitney, a Florida inmate for the last 44 years, has had to undergo two angioplasties for which the state had to pay almost $9,000, and he needs to have another one (*USA Today*, 2004).

The increase in the number of elderly inmates will necessitate special programming to meet their needs. They will routinely require flu shots, pneumonia vaccines, vitamin supplements, and an array of special diets. Their recreational, educational, and work programs will necessitate sensitizing staff to recognize their impaired hearing, slower reflexes, lack of visual acuity, and memory loss. Based on Pennsylvania's experience, Harland noted this "changing face of prisoners" and the "creation of a special facility—a sort of old-folks home with

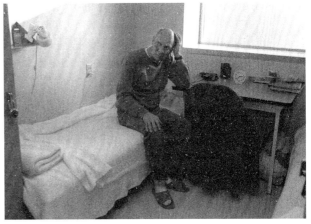

razor wire—to house geriatric inmates" (1996:381). Additional geriatric facilities will be needed, and the "cost of care and confinement is projected to be far higher than even the costs of maximum security imprisonment" (Harland, 1996:381). In at least one state, an aging lifer prison population has led to the creation of a hospice program. It is estimated that 7 percent of the prison population in Iowa is 51 years of age or older. The Fort Madison prison in that state started a hospice program for their inmates,

An inmate serving a 20-year sentence for second-degree murder sits on a bed in the Ahtanum View Assisted Living Facility. To serve the needs of elderly and disabled prisoners and save money on bed space, the state correction facility houses elderly, medically challenged, and disabled prisoners in a minimum-security environment. *(AP Photo/Jackie Johnston)*

reflecting a realization that these inmates may be afflicted with diseases for which there are no cures or communities to respond (DiMascio, 2005b:3).

Ironically, older inmates pose the least threat to society. They rarely are the burglars, thieves, assailants, and drug users and sellers that they once were. Yet, these sentencing policies will mandate their continued incarceration long past their crime-prone years. In California, the projections suggest that 9 percent of the prison operating budget in 2030 will be used for 4 percent of the population (Auerhahn, 2002). As Shichor has noted, the incarceration of the elderly "is an inefficient use of limited criminal justice resources" (1997:481).

Consequences of Drug Policy

As introduced in Chapter 1, other demographic changes have occurred in prisons. For instance, ethnic and racial disparities worsened during the 1990s. Two groups especially affected are women and minorities, particularly blacks. A black male in the United States in 2003 had a one in three chance of going to prison in his lifetime, a Hispanic male had a one in six chance, and a white male had a one in 17 chance of spending time in prison (Bonczar, 2003:1). In 2001, approximately 17 percent of adult black men were current or prior inmates in the state or federal system (Bonczar, 2003:5). On June 30, 2004, approximately 13 percent of black men between the ages of 25 to 29 were in prison or jail (Harrison & Beck, 2005:11). In 1999-2000, more African-American males were incarcerated in prison and jail (791,600) than were enrolled in institutions of higher education (603,000) (Ziedenberg & Schiraldi, 2002:3).

Even though their numbers are lower than those of men, black women are also more likely to be incarcerated than white or Hispanic women. Across all age groups, black women were almost 4.5 times as likely to be incarcerated in a prison or jail than white women, and 2.5 times more likely to be incarcerated than Hispanic women (Harrison & Beck, 2005:11).

The war on drugs has affected black men in America significantly. The Sentencing Project attributes part of the disparity to mandatory minimum sentences, plea bargaining, and departures based upon the substantial assistance that the defendant can provide (2005:1). The 100:1 powder to crack cocaine sentencing ratio translated into an average sentence of 123 months for a crack cocaine conviction in 2003, which was 50 percent higher than the average sentence for powder cocaine (The Sentencing Project, 2005:2). In terms of the race of the offenders involved in these offenses, 81 percent of those convicted of a crack cocaine offense in 2003 were African-American, and judges were compelled to impose long-term mandatory sentences in these cases (The Sentencing Project, 2005:2). Further complicating the process is the length of time that federal offenders serve before they are eligible to be released. In 2000, federal inmates served an average of 91 percent of their sentence before they were released (Durose & Langan, 2003:3). These policies help to explain why there are so many African Americans incarcerated for drug offenses (The Sentencing Project, 2005:2).

In Texas, African-American and Latino inmates comprise more than 70 percent of the prison population, even though they are approximately 40 percent of the general population (Justice Policy Institute, 2005:1). In terms of prison admissions for drug offenses, prison admissions of African Americans increased between 1986 and 1999, while the number of white drug offender admissions decreased during that time (Justice Policy Institute, 2005:2). Latino offenders in Texas are also considerably less likely to be found in drug courts. For example, in Dallas, only 14 percent of drug court participants were Latino, compared to 49 percent of the participants who were white and 35 percent who were African-American (Justice Policy Institute, 2005:2).

Women have also been targets of the "war on drugs." According to Pollock, "There is clear evidence to indicate that women are more heavily affected by federal and state drug sentencing that reduces judicial discretion and imposes mandatory sanctions on users as well as distributors" (Pollock, 2004:42). There is also some research to suggest that female drug use has increased, and it is related to women's involvement in criminal behavior (Davis, Merlo & Pollock, 2006). Unfortunately, less than 15 percent of female inmates are in drug treatment programs (Pollock, 2004:203).

The research suggests that African-American women may be especially vulnerable. Crawford (2000) examined 1,103 female offenders admitted to the Department of Corrections in the 1992-1993 fiscal year who were eligible to be sentenced under the habitual offender legislation in Florida. His findings indicate that African-American women who were convicted of ". . . drug-related offenses were more than nine times as likely to be sentenced as habitual offenders than white women . . ." (Crawford, 2000:277).

How are these demographic trends explained? Looking at national trends (which may or may not be the same as individual state trends), there are two observations that help to explain the changes:

1. States and the federal government have increased the length of sentences for offenders convicted of violent crimes. As previously mentioned, these kinds of legislative initiatives were encouraged by the 1994 crime legislation and the accompanying funding that it allocated to states for prison construction if the states were to adopt truth-in-sentencing legislation and policies designed to incarcerate violent offenders for longer periods of time (Mauer, 1997:10).

2. The "war on drugs," which began in the 1980s, has had a significant impact on the number of offenders being sentenced to prison and the length of their sentences. In 1994, 31 states had sentencing laws that mandated prison terms for specific drug offenses. There are probably even more states that have subsequently changed their statutes and now require such sentences (Mauer, 1997:10).

A closer look at prison data indicates that the majority of the increases in prison populations can be attributed to two categories of offenders: violent offenders and drug offenders. These increases are the result of more stringent sanctions for violent offenders and the greater likelihood of arrest and a sentence of incarceration for drug offenders (Durose & Langan, 2003; King & Mauer, 2005; Mauer, 1997:10; The Sentencing Project, 2005). In 2000, blacks comprised 53 percent of the drug offense convictions in the state courts (Durose & Langan, 2003:6). In addition to the disparity between sentences for crack cocaine versus those for powder cocaine, King and Mauer (2005) found that black males were disproportionately affected by marijuana arrests. For example, although black males comprise 14 percent of the marijuana users in the general population, they represent 30 percent of the arrests for marijuana violations (King & Mauer, 2005:2). Their research indicates that one-third of offenders who were convicted for a marijuana felony in state courts between 1990 and 2002 were sentenced to prison (p. 2).

Chiricos, Welch, and Gertz (2004) contend that ". . . the equation of race and crime is a significant sponsor of the punitive attitudes that are given material substance in the extraordinary rates of incarceration now found in this county" (2004:380). When crime is typified as an African-American phenomenon, it is related to increased support for punitive crime control strategies, which would include more incarceration (Chiricos, Welch & Gertz, 2004:380).

RESPONSES TO PRISON CROWDING

Construction

The federal and state governments have employed a variety of strategies to deal with overcrowding in prisons. In a survey, Vaughn found that states' responses to overcrowding included increasing the size of existing institutions through expansion projects, double-bunking, increased reliance on community-based correctional services, and new construction. Of these, the most prevalent response is new construction (Vaughn, 1993:16-18).

In 2000, there were 1,668 adult correctional institutions operating in the United States. This represents a 14 percent increase since June of 1995. There were seven federal institutions, 43 state institutions, and 154 private facilities added between 1995 and 2000 (Stephan & Karberg, 2003:iv). This trend of building new prisons is not new. In 1995, more new institutions began operations (70) than in each of the previous six years. Cumulatively, the 1990s witnessed the opening of 374 new institutions (Camp & Camp, 1998:74). The vast majority of these institutions were state institutions.

Although new construction has not surpassed the 1995 peak, prison construction projects continue. When comparing 1995 to 2000, more than 200 adult correctional facilities were added (Stephan & Karberg, 2003:iv). According to Stephan, state prison capital expenditures in fiscal year 2001 actually decreased from fiscal year 1996 ($1.5 billion to $1.1 billion) when adjusted for inflation. However, construction remains a large part of the capital expenditures, accounting for more than $860 million in fiscal year 2001 (Stephan, 2004:5).

Most of the institutions that were constructed between 1995 and 2000 appear to have been designed to house larger inmate populations. For example, the number of institutions that housed 2,500 or more inmates grew from 55 in 1995 to 65 in 2000, and the number of institutions that housed 1,500-2,499 inmates grew from 100 in 1995 to 176 in 2000. By contrast, those institutions designed to incarcerate 100-249 inmates decreased from 290 in 1995 to 289 in 2000 (Stephan & Karberg, 2003:iv).

Not only were states and the federal government involved in prison construction in the 1990s, but they were also adjusting the role of county jails. In fact, in some states, the sheriffs agreed to house state inmates, and the states entered into contracts for these services. When the states finished their new prison construction and jail space was no longer necessary, local officials began to advertise their jails to other states for their inmates. The result is that an offender from Hawaii may be in a Texas jail, or an offender from Indiana in jail in Louisiana. These geographical distances pose significant hardships for inmates and their families (Pollock, 2004:22).

Privatization

Another response to prison crowding and the increased costs of running prisons has been to turn the prisoners and prisons over to private companies. The trend toward privatization of corrections and the growth of the private-sector, for-profit prison industry are indicative of "a very lucrative market" (Burright, 1990:4). The first modern state contract with a private corporation occurred in 1985, and since then the growth has been exponential (White, 2001). In 1995, the average number of inmates held in private facilities was 16,426. By contrast, in June 2004, 98,971 adult prisoners were confined in private correctional facilities (Harrison & Beck, 2005:1) This represents a 500 percent increase in the use of private institutions for offenders in less than 10 years. There are now more than 100 private institutions operating (Stephan & Karberg, 2003:16). The federal system, Texas, Oklahoma, and Tennessee had the largest number of offenders incarcerated in private facilities in June of 2004. Five western states had at least 25 percent of their inmates in private facilities (Harrison & Beck, 2005:4). Based upon their research, Austin and Coventry (2001) concluded that private prisons are ". . . aggressively pursuing a share of the multibillion-dollar prison and jail industrial complex" (2001:38).

While prisons for profit are not new in the history of prisons, Smith has identified three trends that converged in the mid-1980s to provide momentum to this new era of privatization in corrections (1993):

1. The ideological imperatives of the free market.
2. The huge increase in the number of prisoners.
3. The concomitant increase in imprisonment costs.

The argument advanced by get-tough politicians and free-market ideologues of the Reagan era was that the private sector could run prisons "more cheaply and more efficiently" than government entities could (Smith, 1993:2). With concern about growing prison budgets, the appeal of saving money by contracting with private industry quieted concerns about the propriety of delegating government authority to confine and control prisoners. In addition to the issue of placing profit motives ahead of public interest, Logan (1990) reviewed other arguments surrounding correctional privatization, including: (1) whether minimizing costs would reduce the quality of services and personnel, (2) whether the private-sector training and supervision would lead to potential for abuse of authority, and (3) whether financial markets would increase the opportunities for corruption.

Studies have provided mixed evaluations of the efficiency and effectiveness of private prisons. Gaes contends that most of the earlier research on private prisons, which focused on ". . . the cost and the performance analyses, has been less than stellar" (Gaes, 2005:87). The National Center for Policy Analysis (1996) reported that private management saves 5 to 15 percent in expenses and that private construction saves as much as 20 percent in costs. The United States General Accounting Office (1996), however, did not find that private prisons could demonstrate lower operational costs than public prisons (p. 3), nor did they demonstrate better quality (p. 9). Recognizing the diffi-culties of comparing different facilities, the General Accounting Office's conclusions were cautious: it did not find "substantial evidence that savings had occurred," but at the same time it could not conclude "that privatization of correctional facilities will not save money" (p. 3).

More recently, Austin and Coventry (2001) found no definitive evi-dence that private facilities are less costly than public institutions or that their services are significantly better than public institutions (2001:38). Previously, in a matched-sample study comparing recidivism of inmates released from private and public prisons, Lanza-Kaduce and Parker (1998) found less short-term recidivism (i.e., 12 months) from prisoners released from the private prisons: 10 percent rearrest from the private facility versus 19 percent from the public institution. How-ever, subsequently, Bales, Bedard, and Quinn (2005) examined 81,737 inmates who were released from Florida prisons between 1995 and 2001 to compare differences in recidivism between public and private institutions. Their study indicated that there is no empirical evidence to suggest that private prisons are more effective than public institu-tions in reducing recidivism (Bales, Bedard & Quinn, 2005:78).

These studies suggest some of the concerns that have been and con-tinue to be investigated. However, much more research needs to be conducted. The continuing growth of private-sector prisons indicates that ethical and moral questions about punishment and profit are over-shadowed by get-tough policies, growing prison populations, and bud-get constraints. Smith also raises the concern that private enterprise and profit motives may influence policy decisions about corrections (1993:6):

> The most worrisome aspect of prison privatization is the inevitable emergence of a private "prison lobby" concerned not with social welfare but with increasing its dividends, not with doing good, but with doing well. . . . Unlike most other public policy arenas, criminal justice policy is largely determined not by the realities of crime but by its perception. That the fear of crime is exploited by politicians and "real-ity television" programming is a truism; but imagine a full-fledged corporate public relations campaign designed to whip up crime hysteria in order to increase profits.

In addition to the impact of media, politicians, and ideology on crim-inal justice, Smith suggests that private enterprise may also become a dimension of public policy and further distort perceptions of crime and the criminal justice system. Recall the question raised by Butterfield (1998; see Chapter 1) as to whether prison populations seem to have a dynamic that is independent of crime.

Consider the private prison in Youngstown, Ohio, operated by Corrections Corporation of America (CCA). The Northeast Ohio Correctional Center opened in 1997. Within 15 months, 20 inmates were stabbed, two were killed, and six escaped (Tatge, 1998:A1). Corrections officers complained that they were undertrained and that the institution was understaffed. Ohio state corrections officers received seven weeks of classroom and on-the-job training (and were paid $12.49 per hour), whereas CCA guards received three to four weeks of classroom and on-the-job training (and were paid $11.84 per hour) (p. A1). In addition, CCA officers were not trained or certified to use firearms, even though some officers were assigned perimeter security and were issued firearms. The private officers claimed the reason that CCA "did not train its employees to use firearms was the cost of state certification, which can run upwards of about $3,000 a person" (Tatge, 1998:A18). The reduced training and lower pay are consistent with how "private prisons save money: By hiring fewer people and paying them less" (p. A18).

While public prisons also experience management and staff problems, Tatge notes a pattern of problems at other private prisons, including inmates obtaining keys, employees having sexual contact with female inmates, and allegations of use of excessive force against inmates (p. A18). The theme of this report regarding Northeast Ohio Correctional Center is that cutting costs by understaffing, undertraining, and underpaying officers creates potential for abuse and mismanagement of inmates (see also Ogle, 1999). Interestingly, when these problems were being documented, the legislature was considering the privatization of all new prisons in Ohio. At the time of the report, two new prisons

Members of Corrections USA demonstrate in front of Wackenhut Headquarters in West Palm Beach, Florida, to protest the privatization of prison correctional officers. Prison privatization has surged in the past decade as governments seek ways to cut costs while handling burgeoning inmate populations. (*AP Photo/Gary I. Rothstein*)

under construction were intended to be operated by private companies. As Tatge observed, "Conservative Republicans see privatization as a way to save money" (p. A18).

According to Gaes (2005) and Thomas (2005), high-quality research is essential to the debate on private versus public prisons. Other jurisdictions that have contracted with private providers can inform this debate, particularly chronological outcomes. Ultimately, the research can help both public and private prison service providers become more accountable (Gaes, 2005:87).

Alternative Strategies

Prison construction, public or private, is not the only response to prison overcrowding that is currently being employed by states and the federal government. They have begun to increasingly rely on front-end strategies such as probation and other kinds of intermediate sanctions, including intensive probation, house arrest, electronic monitoring, and shock probation or split sentences (Clark, 1994:105). There were more than 4 million offenders on probation on December 31, 2003 (Glaze & Palla, 2004:1). One of the primary motivations for seeking alternative strategies is the exorbitant costs associated with building and expansion.

Despite their recent popularity, these alternative sanctions are not necessarily new. Georgia began to utilize intensive supervision probation in the early 1980s, and New Jersey began to publicize its intensive supervision parole program at the same time. These programs were developed in every state. House arrest and electronic monitoring were also touted in the 1980s and continue to be more widely utilized, along with shock probation and split sentences, for dealing with offenders (Tonry & Hamilton, 1995:4-5).

There are also some promising new strategies. Mauer reports that Wisconsin has developed "neighborhood probation." With this approach, probation officers are assigned to a particular neighborhood and urged to solicit the support of a number of agencies and institutions in the local community to help provide services and supervision (Mauer, 1996a). A number of other communities are experimenting with different forms of "restorative justice," by which the victim, offender, and the community are brought together to determine what the appropriate disposition should be (Mauer, 1996a).

Vermont has established "reparative probation." In this model, the community boards decide how a probationer will make amends to the community (Mauer, 1996a). The selected probationers tend to be first-time offenders who were involved in relatively minor property crimes, who have been carefully screened, and who do not pose a risk to the community.

These kinds of community-based alternatives are designed to deal with nonviolent offenders, including drug offenders. Employing alternative sanctions along with drug treatment and community service might perform the dual function of satisfying the public's demand for tougher sanctions and saving money for other public service projects. In fact, Petersilia and Deschenes (1994) found that approximately one-third of nonviolent offenders in Marion County, Oregon, chose prison instead of intensive supervision probation. Intermediate sanctions and intensive supervision probation do not seem to be perceived as lenient treatment by offenders.

Wyoming is attempting to deal with probation and parole revocations with a new "revocation center" located within a medium-security prison. Typically, inmates will remain in the center from three to nine months, with a six-month stay as the average. While they are there, offenders will participate in intensive treatment for substance abuse as well as education programs to enhance their work skills. The revocation center is intended to serve as a therapeutic community, with offenders helping and holding each other accountable. Ideally, offenders will successfully complete their probation or parole and will return to the community better equipped to address their substance abuse and other related problems (St. Gerard, 2005:2).

States have also employed back-end strategies to cope with overcrowding. Typically, these involve greater reliance on early release procedures or parole (Clark, 1994:105). On December 31, 2003, there were 774,588 adult parolees in the United States (Glaze & Palla, 2004:5). Parole practices vary from state to state. In 2003, California reported the largest number of parolees (113,185), and Maine reported the smallest (32) (Glaze & Palla, 2004:5). As previously mentioned, fewer eligible inmates were paroled in recent years than in the early 1990s, but more inmates were paroled in 2003 than in 1995 (Glaze & Palla, 2004:5). The increase in the number of parolees in 2003 may reflect legislative change as well as states' willingness to control the costs of incarceration.

There is a great deal of media coverage and controversy generated by these kinds of early release procedures. Perhaps one of the worst examples of an early release failure was Richard Allen Davis, the parolee who abducted and killed Polly Klaas after having served eight years of a 16-year sentence for kidnapping and who had previous kidnapping, assault, and robbery convictions (Benekos & Merlo, 1995; *New York Times*, 1993). The media attention garnered by such offenders may continue to preclude widespread adoption of many of these back-end strategies.

More commonly, states exercise emergency release procedures when they are under some form of consent decree. Sometimes a court can determine an institutional "cap," but more often it is the legislature that makes the determination (Durham, 1994:52). In 2000, 145 correctional facilities were under a court order to limit their population (Stephan & Karberg, 2003:9). In terms of court orders or a consent decree, the most common problem in 2000 was inmate crowding (Stephan & Karberg, 2003:9).

CHAPTER 4 • PUNISHMENT AND PRISONS: CORRECTIONAL POLICY IN CRISIS   129

One of the difficulties with these strategies is the lack of research that has been conducted to determine their effectiveness. The National Council on Crime and Delinquency evaluated an early release program that was utilized by Illinois. That study found that the program did not increase crime or jeopardize the public's safety. Additionally, the early release policy saved the state millions of dollars by preventing prison overcrowding and all its consequences (Lane, 1986:403). Even small reductions in sentences could translate into states saving millions of dollars each year. For example, the Justice Policy Institute (2005) found that if the average sentence of 4.5 years were reduced to 4 years, the State of Texas would save $114 million a year, and the inmate population would be reduced by 18,000 inmates (p. 2).

In seeking other cost-effective, safe, and punitive alternatives, Fabelo discusses the use of new technology such as "continuous electronic monitoring" and the potential to create "walking prisons" (1996:480). As prison costs continue to increase, more cost-effective alternatives may help to reduce prison populations and "prisons may become institutions to house only the most violent predators for a long time" (Fabelo, 1996:482). This post-industrial technology is cheaper than bricks and mortar but also presents the possibility of widening the control net. As more alternatives and interventions are developed, it becomes likely that more offenders will be placed under correctional control and surveillance. If prison populations continue to increase while alternatives also are expanded, the net widens and the "justice juggernaut" continues to expand (Gordon, 1990).

The Impact of Three-Strikes Legislation

Three-strikes legislation has not been uniformly enforced throughout the United States for a variety of reasons. Perhaps the most commonly cited reason has to do with the fact that state legislators hurriedly enacted these statutes without considering that judges already employed existing legislation that requires lengthy sentences to sanction violent offenders. In short, the judges have already removed serious violent offenders from the streets without utilizing new legislation. Several states also have habitual offender legislation to deal with repeat chronic offenders. Lastly, some of the state legislatures have been selective in deciding which crimes constituted a "strike," resulting in some offenders not qualifying for the sentence (Dickey, 1996:3). Schiraldi and colleagues (2004) analyzed three-strikes laws and concluded that they ". . . have had a negligible impact on states' imprisoned populations since their enactment, with the notable exceptions of California, Florida, and Georgia" (2004:4).

Although there are states in which relatively small numbers of offenders have been sentenced under these kinds of laws, California is not one of them. California has admitted more than 42,000 offenders into its prison system who are now serving a doubled or 25-years-to-life sentence. These "strikers" constitute more than one in four inmates (27.2%) in the California system (Ehlers, Schiraldi & Ziedenberg, 2004:6). For a second strike, California law mandates a doubling of the prison term normally imposed; for a third strike, a sentence of 25 years to life (or triple the normal sentence) is required. California's dominant position can be attributed to the fact that there are more than 500 crimes that constitute a third strike there. In fact, more than 57 percent of the felons who have been sentenced under the California law were convicted of a nonviolent third-strike offense, and 64.5 percent of second-strike offenders were incarcerated for a nonviolent offense (Ehlers, Schiraldi & Ziedenberg, 2004:8). More people have been sentenced for drug possession than for second-degree murder, rape, and assault with a deadly weapon combined (Ehlers, Schiraldi & Ziedenberg, 2004:8).

The costs associated with three-strikes policies are phenomenal. Inmates incarcerated in the California prison system between March of 1994 and September of 2003 have cost or will cost Californians an additional $10.5 billion in terms of prison and jail costs. Included in that figure is the $6.2 billion that is the result of extended prison sentences for offenders who committed nonviolent three-strikes offenses. In terms of length of incarceration, offenders currently incarcerated under the three-strikes law will serve an additional 164,314 years in prison than they would have prior to the legislation (Ehlers, Schiraldi & Ziedenberg, 2004:23).

One of the more distressing aspects of the three-strikes legislation is the disproportionate representation of minorities—particularly African Americans—who are affected by its application. Recent data from California indicate that African Americans have an incarceration rate that is 12 times higher than whites for a third strike, and when second- and third-strike African-American offenders are compared to whites, their rate of incarceration is more than 10 times higher than that for whites (Ehlers, Schiraldi & Ziedenberg, 2004:9). Three-strikes legislation has also had an impact on Latinos in California. Their incarceration rate for a third strike is 45 percent higher than that of white defendants (Ehlers, Schiraldi & Ziedenberg, 2004:9). Just as the "war on drugs" has contributed to the disproportionate incarceration of minorities, there is concern that these kinds of laws will continue to have a similar effect (Mauer, 1994:23).

CONSEQUENCES OF LONG-TERM INCARCERATION

A serious consequence of continued reliance on long-term incarceration is the commitment of vast sums of money without convincing evidence that such expenditures will pay off in the long run. There are, however, plenty of opportunity costs associated with these strategies. To build and maintain more prisons, the federal government and the states have to secure the revenue from public funds while foregoing other programs. Long after the prisons are built, staffed, and filled with inmates, the public is still required to pay for them at the expense of other services.

State correctional agency budget allocations vary considerably. The cost of maintaining adult state correctional facilities in fiscal year 2001 was $29.5 billion (Stephan, 2004:1). In California, the prison system budget is $5.3 billion a year (Institute of Governmental Affairs at the University of California, 2004). The total correctional agency budget for all the states for fiscal year 2001 was more than $38 billion (Stephan, 2004:1). In both the state and federal institutions, the cost for each inmate was approximately $22,600 per year (Stephan, 2004:1).

Zimbardo estimates the opportunity costs associated with prison construction by illustrating that one new prison in California is equal to 8,833 new teachers who could have been hired to teach the state's school children or equal to 89,660 children who could be supported to enroll in Head Start programs (1994:7). Similarly, for what the state of California will spend to incarcerate one third-strike burglar for 40 years, it could have provided two-year community college educations to 200 students (Baum & Bedrick, 1994:5).

The imbalance between state funding for prisons versus higher education shows no signs of abating. In their national study, Ziedenberg and Schiraldi (2002) found that corrections spending doubled (in 25 states) or tripled (in 10 states) between 1985 and 2000. With respect to higher education spending in real dollars, only one state (Nevada) had doubled its spending (Ziedenberg & Schiraldi, 2002). Jamison (2003) examined expenditures in Maryland on prison construction versus higher education, and concluded that when these expenditures are compared, ". . . it is clear that prison growth has come at the expense of Maryland's system of higher education" (p. 1). During the 1980s, California's higher-education budget was two and one-half times as much as that of corrections. In 1994, the state corrections budget of $3.8 billion was equal to the entire budget allocation for higher education (Baum & Bedrick, 1994:2; Skolnick, 1995:4; Zimbardo, 1994:7-8).

Perhaps one of the most disturbing aspects of the impetus to incarcerate more offenders and for increasingly longer periods of time is that policymakers convince the public that these are effective crime control strategies. Although some maintain that the current drop in violent crime is related to "locking up" more offenders for longer periods of time, no empirical evidence supports such a claim. As previously noted, Ehlers, Schiraldi, and Ziedenberg (2004) examined county-by-county data in California to see if there was any relationship between the crime rates of counties that used three-strikes laws and the rates of those counties that did not use the law so heavily between 1993 and 2002. Their findings indicated that those ". . . counties that used the Three Strikes law at a higher rate did not experience greater reductions in crime than counties that used the law less frequently" (Ehlers, Schiraldi & Ziedenberg, 2004:13). Earlier data reviewed by Mauer suggested that crime rates were already declining prior to get-tough sentencing policies (1996b).

As noted earlier, states without three-strikes legislation experienced the greatest crime rate reductions (*Criminal Justice Newsletter*, 1997a). In New York, which does not have a three-strikes provision, the decrease in Index crimes as well as violent crime was larger than that of California (Ehlers, Schiraldi & Ziedenberg, 2004:18). However, the momentum of get-tough, punitive politics seems resistant to rational analysis of the causes of crime and the consequences of retributive punishment.

Finally, one might ask at "what cost" we have embarked on these kinds of strategies. Auerhahn (2002) notes that

> [b]etween 1980 and 2000, the proportion of violent offenders in California's prisons declined more than 30 percent while the proportion of drug offenders tripled. These facts should arouse skepticism . . . regarding the claims made about the relationship between growing prison populations and public safety. California has indeed gotten tough on crime, seemingly for little gain, at a heavy price (par. 6).

Three-strikes policies are successful at making the public feel as though something is being done about the crime problem. Unfortunately, they camouflage the real issues regarding the antecedents and correlates of crime (Benekos & Merlo, 1995:8). They are one more manifestation of a "quick fix" for a complicated societal problem. It will take more than the reactive application of baseball metaphors to address crime in America (Merlo, 1997a).

One of the reasons cited for the drop in crime has to do with demographics. There are fewer people in their late teens and early twenties than there have been in recent years. The baby-boom generation has grown out of the crime-prone decades of the life course. Other reasons include the improvements in the economy in the mid- and late 1990s, when there were job opportunities and increased wages. In addition, the crack trade of the 1980s has stabilized, and law enforcement techniques and technology have been enhanced in the last 15 years (Schiraldi, Colburn & Lotke, 2004:11). However, America's honeymoon with decreasing crime rates may not last forever.

The desire to control and incarcerate offenders will cost all Americans. Unfortunately, prison costs are expected to increase dramatically. It is estimated that health care costs account for 10-20 percent of the state prison operating budget, and they represent the area that is growing the fastest (Auerhahn, 2002). For example, in Alabama, state authorities contracted with Prison Health Services in November of 2003 at a cost of $142.7 million for a three-year agreement (vonZielbauer, 2005:A11). In fiscal year 2001, states spent $3.3 billion on medical care for inmates (Stephan, 2004:1). Maruschak and Beck (2001) contend that almost 6 percent of inmates entering state prisons will have to have surgery while they are incarcerated, and approximately 16 percent will have some other medical problem excluding injury, colds, virus, or flu while they are incarcerated (p. 7). Drug injection and alcohol use prior to admission to prison are related to increased medical problems in prison (Maruschak & Beck, 2001:10). With respect to injuries sustained while incarcerated, it is projected that 22 percent of inmates will be injured while they are incarcerated at a state prison (Maruschak & Beck, 2001:6).

At jeopardy are early education programs like Head Start, medical services for the poor, and college education. The building of prisons will necessitate curtailment of road construction, repair and expansion projects, health care, literacy, drug prevention and treatment, and immunization programs (Merlo, 1997a).

In examining many state expenditures during the last 15 years, a common thread emerges. While unprecedented allocations have occurred for corrections, the allocations for the other departments have not kept pace. According to Stephan (2004), in fiscal year 2001, increases in states' costs of adult incarceration were greater than those of health care, education, and natural resources (p. 2). As the costs associated with current correctional policies continue to escalate, Americans will have to forfeit a great deal.

Post-Modern Punishment

After passing tougher, longer sentences and increasing the reliance on imprisonment, what do politicians and policymakers present to the public to demonstrate and maintain the commitment to punitive ideology? After contributing to an "ethos of vindictiveness and retribution" (Johnson, Bennett & Flanagan, 1997:25) and to "simplistic ideas about crime and its control" (Irwin, 1996:490), how do legislators raise the deterrent bar of punishment and distract the public from the high costs of imprisonment? Feeley and Simon (1992) have observed that a "new penology" has evolved that focuses on identifying and controlling populations or aggregates of offenders and managing them through rational processes. This includes "low-frills, no-services control centers" with new forms of control based on "risk assessment" (p. 457).

As a continued shift away from "humane treatment of prisoners and the rehabilitative ideal," Johnson and colleagues also perceive a "no-frills prison movement," which suggests that prison conditions may continue to worsen. Evidence that courts are becoming more tolerant of violations of prisoners' rights (Johnson, Bennett & Flanagan, 1997) and that lawmakers are reducing and removing "amenities, privileges, activities and opportunities" for prisoners (Toch, 1996:496) supports Feeley and Simon's (1992) proposition of a shift in focus for criminal justice.

When offenders are depicted as evil persons who are a threat to safety and social order, it becomes easier for a society to tolerate more punitive, retributive, and even inhumane conditions of confinement. Prisoners, in effect, are banished, lose their citizenship, and are not deemed worthy of having the same rights or privileges provided to law-abiding citizens. This motive is recognized in the principle of least eligibility, which is "the doctrine that prisoners ought to receive no goods or services in excess of those available to persons who have lived within the law" (Clear & Cole, 1997:359). This is one of the concerns cited by Cullen and Gilbert (1982) for reaffirming rehabilitation. They maintain that the goal of rehabilitation as a justification for incarceration obligates the state to care for the offender. In the absence of a humane motive or rationale, brutality and repression easily fill the void.

Historically, sexual assault, specifically rape, is an institutional derogation. Sexual assault is widely recognized as an underreported crime among inmate victims, and, as such, its prevalence is not fully known. Some research suggests that more than 20 percent of male inmates have been raped or coerced into sexual activity while incarcerated (Pollock, 2004:108). In 2003, the Prison Rape Elimination Act was enacted by Congress. The legislation mandates the Bureau of Justice Statistics to devise a data collection method to measure the extent of sexual assault in prisons and jails (Bureau of Justice Statistics, 2004:1). The Bureau of Justice Statistics examined incidents of sexual violence that had been reported to corrections officials in 2004 and found that more than 8,000 allegations of sexual violence had been reported (Beck, 2005:1). Victimization was perpetrated by both staff members and inmates (Beck, 2005:1).

Inmate suicides continue to occur and are even increasing in some prisons. During the first eight months of 2005, five Ohio inmates killed themselves (Welsh-Huggins, 2005). The suicide rate is generally higher in prisons and jails than in the general population, and inmate suicides in 2002 accounted for about 5 percent of the inmates who died. Inmates who are most at risk for suicide are new inmates, inmates with mental health problems, and those inmates who are in a segregation cell where no recreation or personal belongings are permitted (Associated Press, 2005:par. 12).

Derogations for offenders also include restrictions on their ability to participate in the electoral process. Pennsylvania legislators in the House of Representatives enacted HB 1318 in 2005. This legislation would preclude anyone who has been convicted of a felony from voting until the completion of his or her sentence. Currently, 33 states prohibit offenders who are on probation or parole from voting, and 13 states prohibit voting for the rest of the offender's life (Collis, 2005:14). These kinds of laws specifically disenfranchise African-American men in our society. According to Jake Wheatley, a legislator in Pennsylvania, on a national level, 30 percent of the offenders who are unable to vote because of these kinds of laws are African-American men (Collis, 2005:14). Proponents of the legislation point to the intention of the law as protecting the voting process rather than imposing additional punishment on offenders (Collis, 2005:14).

Medical care is another deprivation in prison systems. In New York, a female inmate repeatedly asked to see a doctor, but was refused permission. She died a couple of weeks after her request (at the age of 32) with congestive heart failure (Slevin, 2005:A03). One of the most notorious examples is Alabama's Limestone Correctional Facility. Alabama segregates its male HIV-positive and AIDS inmates at Limestone. Between 1999 and 2002, 36 inmates died there. When the inmates sued, Alabama fired the private health care provider and contracted with Prison Health Services, the largest private provider of health care for inmates (vonZielbauer, 2005:1). Prison Health Services hired one physician to care for the 230 men at Limestone as well as the 1,800 other inmates. In 2005, the "rat-infested" institution had no place to quarantine inmates when they contracted tuberculosis or hepatitis C. After three months on the staff, the lone physician at Limestone resigned (vonZielbauer, 2005:A1, A11).

This new wave of offender-prisoner derogation is also consistent with efforts (or the perception of efforts) to contain the tremendous costs of imprisonment. Adams (1996) cites containment of medical care (e.g., outsourcing, copayments), amenities (e.g., television, weightlifting equipment), and food services (e.g., VitaProTM—a soybean-based meat extender; foodloaf—a mix of the day's rations prepared as a loaf and baked). In addition, the increasing market share and profits of private corrections companies suggest that prisons and prisoners have become a "business" that requires efficient cost-management techniques. For example, Shichor (1997) has applied Ritzer's "McDonaldization" thesis (see Ritzer, 2004) to demonstrate this rational, businesslike approach to managing prisons. This is consistent with the "new penology," which incorporates probability and risk, new and efficient techniques of control, smooth delivery of services, and commitment to the principles of incapacitation (Merlo & Benekos, 1998). In other words, as a result of the "imprisonment binge," Irwin concludes that we are now "left to face the mess we have created" (1996:493). As with the get-tough ideology and policies of the 1980s and 1990s, the post-modern penology is likely to generate its own dysfunctions.

DISCUSSION: REVISING CORRECTIONAL POLICY

The continued reliance on incarceration as a prevailing strategy to reduce crime in America is contraindicative. The opportunity costs and human costs associated with these policies are too high. Allocating additional money into reactive policies masks the real issues. A successful comprehensive crime control strategy depends on realizing that there is no quick fix to the crime problem.

As Kappeler, Blumberg, and Potter have discussed, presenting simple explanations and quick solutions is part of the crime mythology perpetrated on the public (1996). By focusing on sensational, celebrated cases—usually of the "most bizarre and gruesome" nature—the media are giving "false impressions of order and magnitude to criminal events" (Kappeler, Blumberg & Potter, 1996:5). The resulting distortion and frenzy generated by media coverage serves to exacerbate fears of victimization (p. 10). As a result, isolated incidents can become social issues, and, over time, politicized, these emerge as crime problems (Kappeler & Potter, 2005:7). With an audience emotionally prepared for the worst and an industry focused on instant and dramatic coverage of crime stories, it is not surprising that (as Blumstein noted) crime and punishment have captivated public attention (1998). In spite of declining crime rates, "the continual demands for harsher sentencing, reductions in good-time credits required by truth-in-sentencing statutes, and stricter handling of parole violators all continue to push state prison populations to even higher levels" (Greenwood, 1998:136).

Get-Tough Politics

There is plenty of get-tough rhetoric in regard to criminal justice policies. For example, the House of Representatives passed the Gang Deterrence and Community Protection ("Gangbusters") Act in May of 2005. This legislation mandates sentences from 10 years to life and is viewed, in part, as a reaction to the U.S. Supreme Court decision in *U.S. v. Booker* (125 S. Ct. 738 [2005]). In *Booker*, the Court determined that federal judges were not required to adhere to the sentencing guidelines, and that sentence enhancements violated the defendant's Sixth Amendment rights (see Chapter 3). Although it is unclear whether the legislation will successfully pass in the Senate, it is estimated that it will add 900 inmates a year to the federal prison system and cost $62 million in the first four years (Allen, 2005). In addition, some members of Congress have responded to the Court's ruling by threatening to enact mandatory sentences that will be even harsher than the sentencing guidelines.

Legislatures also continue to focus on tougher sex offender notification/registration provisions in legislation. In September of 2005, the House passed the Children's Safety Act of 2005. The names of 11 prior victims of sexual assault and/or murder are listed along with brief details of their victimization in the legislation's purpose section (GovTrack, 2005). Although the Senate has not passed its version of the legislation, some of the provisions in the House bill would strengthen the sex offender registry laws by making it a crime for offenders who fail to keep their registrations current or fail to register. These violations would constitute a new crime with a mandatory sentence of five years and a maximum of 20 years (Israel, 2005:5). Not surprisingly, most of the victims listed in the legislation were attacked by strangers. Although the victimizations of these children and adults were particularly vicious and unconscionable, they do not represent the usual occurrence of sexual victimization in the United States.

While flaming the public's emotions, the get-tough politics further detract critical attention from what Blumstein calls the "crime/punishment conundrum" (1998). Two explanations that are discussed focus on the impact of drug offenses and the diminishing effectiveness of increased incapacitation. In the context of a 14-year, tenfold increase in the number of prisoners accounted for by drug offenses, Blumstein observes that incarceration may have minimal impact on drug activities because replacements for drug marketeers are easily recruited. Therefore, incarcerating drug offenders does not necessarily disrupt the drug markets and drug-related crimes. In contrast, incapacitating violent predators removes these offenders from continued activity.

A second issue considered by Blumstein is the diminishing returns of incarcerating more offenders. "One important component of deterrence is the stigma associated with the sanction, and the potential threat of a stigma is diminished considerably when one's reference group already widely carries that stigma" (p. 134). In this context, promoting and expanding incarceration policies are counterproductive strategies. Instead of reactive legislation, focusing on primary prevention, early intervention, and effective reforms and restorative justice strategies would be more productive and cost-effective. Greenwood suggests that this set of strategies could be "two or three times more cost-effective than three strikes" (1998:139).

Rational Thinking about Correctional Policy

Greenwood offers some optimism in observing that "slowly the tide is beginning to turn" (1998:137). Based on his review of recent polls and state legislation, he concluded that (1998:137):

> Many state officials are beginning to recognize that wise invest-
> ments in early prevention are not only effective ways of reduc-
> ing crime, but reduce the need for future prison cells as well.

In addition, Greenwood cites evidence that "a large block of voters" understands that building more prisons is not the best policy for deal-ing with crime.

Recently, the National Center on Addiction and Substance Abuse at Columbia University estimated that alcohol and illegal drugs con-tributed to the incarceration of 80 percent of the 2 million inmates in American prisons and jails. Concurring with that estimate, Bob Lam-pert, the Director of the Department of Corrections in Wyoming, contends that 80 percent of that state's inmates have substance abuse problems (St. Gerard, 2004:2). Although drug use or abuse is associ-ated with the offender's incarceration, the Center reports that most of these offenders are "not treated for addiction before they are released from the institution" (Wren, 1998:A8).

There is some evidence that drug treatment as opposed to incar-ceration is gaining prominence. In 2000, Californians approved Propo-sition 36, which mandates drug treatment rather than incarceration for first- and second-time drug possession offenders (Ehlers, Schiraldi & Ziedenberg, 2004:27). This legislation is also applicable to three-strike defendants if they have been released from prison for a minimum of five years prior to being arrested for drug possession (Ehlers, Schi-raldi & Ziedenberg, 2004:28). Similarly, in Pennsylvania, Senate Bill 217 was enacted. This legislation requires the Department of Correc-tions to evaluate offenders to determine if they are eligible for alter-native sentencing and drug treatment (Collis, 2004:1). In Kansas, Senate Bill 123 became effective in November of 2003. Felony drug offenders who are nonviolent are sentenced to treatment programs rather than prison. In addition to affording drug offenders another chance, the State of Kansas is also saving money. It is estimated that it costs $6,500 for drug treatment rather than $19,000 for incarcera-tion (Ranney, 2005).

Although the 1994 Violent Crime Control and Law Enforcement Act allocated some money for drug treatment for inmates and parolees, there is no compelling evidence that states have uniformly adopted such strategies. The legislation also authorized federal money for drug courts in local jurisdictions, which are designed to move offenders into treatment programs versus prisons (Wren, 1998:A8). Not all states have enthusiastically developed and expanded drug court programs, but their numbers are certainly increasing.

These policies are impressive, but they are not sufficient. Funding for drug treatment and prevention programs is woefully lacking. King and Mauer (2005) note the disparate relationship between funding for enforcement versus treatment and prevention efforts. Even though the federal government spends $19 billion dollars a year for the war on drugs, the funding has been distributed in a 2:1 ratio, with enforcement getting the larger share (King & Mauer, 2005:31).

Early release mechanisms for elderly inmates also merit consideration. It is possible that older inmates could be cared for far more economically and humanely in community-based settings. This kind of a program does not appear to be controversial, and it would allow limited prison operating budgets to focus more attention on younger inmates who will return to the community at the conclusion of their sentences (see Auerhahn, 2002).

As Cullen (2005) notes, there is still strong support among Americans that rehabilitation is a worthy goal (p.13). There also appears to be a softening in public attitudes among both liberals and conservatives regarding offenders. With a growing emphasis on offenders returning to the community, there is an impetus for prison administrators to improve the programs that will make successful reentry a reality (Slevin, 2005). These programs include drug treatment, job training, and education in parenting and life skills.

Americans' penchant for three-strikes laws may also be fading. Schiraldi, Colburn, and Lotke (2004) found that ". . . the percentage of Americans favoring mandatory sentences such as three strikes laws declined as the 1990s waned, from 55 percent in 1995 to only 38 percent by 2001" (p. 2). Schiraldi and colleagues (2004) contend that more than one-half of the states have revised their sentencing laws, eliminated mandatory sentences, or reformed parole policies to alleviate crowding and reduce their rate of incarceration (2004:11). Three prisons in New York are supposed to be closed due to the fact that the prison population has decreased by 9 percent in the last four years (DiMascio, 2004:3). These public opinion and legislative changes signal a different direction in correctional policy.

There are also some initiatives regarding public and private institutions that can be explored. Austin and Coventry (2001) proposed a collaborative effort between the public and private sector to test changes in correctional policy in various areas such as counseling and vocational training in prison and after the inmate is released (p. 60). The flexibility of the private sector might also be suited to test the effects of reducing long prison sentences. Rather than simply trying to find a system that is cheaper but just as unsuccessful as public-sector prisons, these kinds of innovations could enlighten policymakers about current practices (Austin & Coventry, 2001:60).

There are plenty of lessons to be learned from inmates. In 2005, in conjunction with the World Congress on Criminology in Philadelphia, inmates at the State Correctional Institution at Graterford met with scholars from 24 countries to discuss their theory on the process of transformation. The goal is to reach inmates who will be returning to the communities to refrain from further criminal activity and to ". . . model a new, non-criminal culture for youngsters in their neighbourhoods" (DiMascio, 2005a:3). With more than 41,000 inmates in state facilities, Pennsylvania lifers have the opportunity to work on eradicating crime and improving the lives of community residents (DiMascio, 2005a:2-3). These kinds of programs can be duplicated in other states.

If policymakers and citizens are genuinely interested in reducing crime, they can do more. At the outset, policies can prioritize and invest in children. Policymakers could commit necessary resources to ascertain that low-income pregnant girls and women receive proper prenatal care, that children receive necessary immunizations, and that nurses be dispatched to inner-city neighborhoods to offer help to parents in taking care of their children. Once again, there is public support for early intervention in the lives of children (Cullen, 2005:22). Greenwood's findings indicate that early intervention strategies such as parent training and graduation incentives are more cost-effective than reactive sentencing law (1998:139).

It is also important that child abuse be investigated and reported more vigorously, and that the criminal justice system intervene early in the process to make certain that abusive parents or relatives are not permitted to victimize children repeatedly. Recent research by Harlow indicated that one in 10 male state prison inmates reported being physically abused before age 18 and one in four female inmates reported being victimized by physical abuse before age 18 (1999:1). Harlow also found that state inmates who had been previously victimized were more likely to be serving a sentence for violent crime than those inmates who reported that they had not been victimized (1999:3).

Similarly, Pollock (2004) found that 57 percent of female inmates in state prisons reported being abused, and 38 percent of them said that the abuse occurred prior to their eighteenth birthday (p. 86). While fewer male inmates (14%) than female inmates reported that they had been abused before their eighteenth birthday (Pollock, 2004:86), all of these victimizations are troubling. Social welfare agencies have to devote additional resources to hire and train child care workers, and they will also need to create and fund enhanced community services and select personnel specifically focused on the problems of child abuse. From foster care and permanent termination of parental rights to counseling for victims and support for them, the government will have to take a more active role.

The public must also prevail upon legislators and policymakers to revise existing correctional policies. Unfortunately, crime control policies have generally been dichotomized into either incarcerating offenders in prisons or allowing them to go free (Merlo, 1995). These are not the only available options. Intermediate sanctions such as electronic monitoring, intensive supervision probation, halfway houses, shorter prison terms, and drug treatment programs need to be expanded and made available to more offenders. These kinds of strategies are important, but they must also be used judiciously. In some instances, there is the threat of net-widening when it comes to intermediate sanctions.

Recent research on parole can inform the debate on appropriate policies. Solomon, Kachnowski, and Bhati (2005) studied mandatory and discretionary parolees as well as offenders who were released unconditionally, having served their full sentences. The largest group of parolees was comprised of the mandatory releases—offenders who have served their sentence less any good time credits and are released to finish their sentence in the community. Their findings indicate that there is very little difference overall in the rates of recidivism between the mandatory and discretionary releases—offenders who were granted parole by a parole board or other authority. However, their findings illustrate that certain offenders, particularly women, public order offenders, male property offenders, and those offenders who engage in technical violations, benefited from discretionary release and were less likely to be rearrested if supervised after leaving prison (Solomon, Kachnowski & Bhati, 2005:2).

These findings, coupled with the research conducted on parolees returning home in Chicago, can help shape the future direction of parole. In the Chicago study, the support of the family was an important resource for offenders. In addition, offenders who returned to disadvantaged neighborhoods (even different neighborhoods than they lived in previously) were more likely to return to criminal activity and less likely to find employment (Urban Institute, 2004:3). Perhaps attention has to be focused on the environments where offenders reside, strategies to strengthen family support, and job opportunities.

Congress also considered passage of the Second Chance Act, which will provide funding for offenders who are being released in the community. From housing to drug treatment, there are plenty of supports that could be in place for unconditional release and parole offenders. Funding and the research to assess what is working are essential. Volunteers can also play a bigger role in the prisoner reentry process. In Wisconsin, volunteers are used in corrections to help monitor jail conditions and to assist with inmates and offenders on probation and parole (Terry, 2000:9). Whether it is mentoring services, educational and vocational programs, or self-help, there are many qualified residents who can participate. The mentoring would be particularly helpful as inmates make the adjustment from prison to community.

Criminologists and criminal justice administrators also have a role to play in communicating with the public, practitioners, and policymakers (Merlo, 2000). Testifying before the legislature and the Congress and speaking to citizen groups in the community would inform the public and the agencies that these kinds of policies will force economic constraints without guaranteeing public safety (see Cullen, 2005:28). There is no empirical evidence to support the position that severe punishments alone deter criminal behavior. Not only must we assess the cost of and the likelihood of success for these policies, but also recognize that their continuation will come at the expense of other programs intended to help children and young people.

In discussing the importance of public opinion, retired Oklahoma state corrections professional Jack Crowley observed that (1998:39):

> Public policies on crime and justice, so often enacted as a reaction to public opinion, have led to longer and tougher sentences for offenders, even as those who work in the criminal justice system acknowledge that locking people up does little to rehabilitate them.

Crowley questions why corrections administrators spend so much time reacting to public opinion and policy rather than working to modify and shape opinions and policies. In the absence of informed, rational policy decisions, the politicization of crime control has resulted in distorted images of crime and punishment as well as reactive sentencing and incarceration policies that are not only costly but counterproductive. As previously discussed, the public indicates a preference for rehabilitation and early intervention strategies. Given the decrease in crime, the costs of incarceration, and the information about failed policies, this might be the right time to change course in correctional policy.

DISCUSSION QUESTIONS

1. How would you describe correctional policy and the current situation in the United States prison system to a visitor from another nation? Are there certain characteristics that are unique to the United States?

2. Explain some of the consequences of a correctional strategy that emphasizes long-term incarceration (such as three-strikes legislation).

3. Review the penalties for crack cocaine versus powder cocaine. Prepare an argument suggesting a rationale for why the penalties should be the same.

4. Explain the changes that have occurred in the use of parole. What do you foresee for the future of parole? Why?

5. What are some of the strategies that states and the federal government have utilized to deal with the increased prison population? Make an argument for an alternative strategy.

6. Discuss the opportunity costs associated with an increased reliance on long-term incarceration. What should states do?

7. Discuss the post-modern penology. What are its human costs? Defend the "no-frills prison" concept. Do you think that these kinds of prisons are more likely to deter crime? Why?

8. Elaborate on the politicization of crime as it affects correctional policy.

9. What will be the role of the private sector in corrections? What do you foresee for the future? Are there lessons we should have learned? What changes do you recommend?

10. Illustrate the media's effect on correctional policy. How can the media and politicians become better informed about the realities of crime? What role should you play?

11. Provide a rationale for moving away from our heavy reliance on incarceration. Create a correctional policy that will incorporate community-based correctional alternatives along with incarceration. How will it improve the status quo?

REFERENCES

Adams, Kenneth (1996). "The Bull Market in Corrections." *The Prison Journal* 76(4):461-467.

Allen, Mike (2005). "House Passes Bill to Make Gang Crimes Federal Offenses." *Washington Post* (May 12). *http://www.washingtonpost.com/*

Auerhahn, Kathleen (2002). "Selective Incapacitation, Three Strikes, and the Problem of Aging Prison Populations: Using Simulation Modeling to See the Future." *Criminology & Public Policy* 1(3):353-387

Austin, James (1995). "Correctional Options: An Overview." *Corrections Today* 57(1):48.

Austin, James, and Garry Coventry (2001). *Emerging Issues on Privatized Prisons.* Washington, DC: U.S. Department of Justice, Office of Justice Programs, Bureau of Justice Assistance.

Bales, William D., Laura E. Bedard, and Susan T. Quinn (2005). "Recidivism of Public and Private State Prison Inmates in Florida." *Criminology & Public Policy* 4(1):57-82.

Baum, Noah, and Brooke Bedrick (1994). "Trading Books for Bars: The Lopsided Funding Battle between Prisons and Universities." San Francisco: Center on Juvenile and Criminal Justice.

Beck, Allen J. (2005). "Sexual Violence Reported by Correctional Authorities, 2004." *Bureau of Justice Statistics Special Report.* Washington, DC: U.S. Department of Justice, Office of Justice Programs.

Benekos, Peter J., and Alida V. Merlo (1995). "Three Strikes and You're Out! The Political Sentencing Game." *Federal Probation* 59 (March):3-9.

Blumstein, Alfred (1998). "U.S. Criminal Justice Conundrum: Rising Prison Populations and Stable Crime Rates." *Crime & Delinquency* 44(1):127-135.

Bonczar, Thomas P. (2003). "Prevalence of Imprisonment in the U.S. Population, 1974-2001." *Bureau of Justice Statistics Special Report.* Washington, DC: U.S. Department of Justice, Office of Justice Programs.

Bureau of Justice Statistics (2004). "Data Collections for the Prison Rape Elimination Act of 2003." *Bureau of Justice Statistics Status Report.* Washington, DC: U.S. Department of Justice, Office of Justice Programs.

Burright, David K. (1990). "Privatization of Prisons: Fad or Future?" *FBI Law Enforcement Bulletin* (February):1-4.

Butterfield, Fox (1997a). "Homicides Plunge 11 Percent in U.S., F.B.I. Report Says." *New York Times* (June 2):A1, A12.

Butterfield, Fox (1997b). "Punitive Damages: Crime Keeps on Falling, but Prisons Keep on Filling." *New York Times* (September 28):Section 4, 1,4.

Butterfield, Fox (1998). "Prison Population Growing Although Crime Rate Drops. *New York Times* (August 9):A14.

Camp, Camille Graham, and George M. Camp (1998). *The Corrections Yearbook 1998.* Middletown, CT: Criminal Justice Institute.

Chiricos, Ted, Kelly Welch, and Marc Gertz (2004). "Racial Typification of Crime and Support for Punitive Measures." *Criminology* 42(2):359-389.

Clark, Charles S. (1994). "Prison Overcrowding." *The Congressional Quarterly Researcher* 4(5):97-120.

Clark, John, James Austin, and D. Alan Henry (1997). "Three-Strikes and You're Out: A Review of State Legislation." *Research in Brief.* Washington, DC: National Institute of Justice.

Clear, Todd, and George Cole (1997). *American Corrections*, 4th ed. Belmont, CA: Wadsworth.

Collis, Ann (2005). "Felon Voting Rights." *Correctional Forum* (September):14.

Collis, Ann (2004). "Sentencing Alternatives to Incarceration: Senate Bill 217 Passes." *Correctional Forum* (December):1, 13.

Congressional Digest (1994). "The Federal Role in Crime Control." (June-July). Washington, DC.

Corrections Digest (1994). "Senate Crime Bill Will More Than Double American Prison Population by Year 2005." (March 9):1-4.

Correctionscorp (1998). "1997 Summary Statistics Table." June 2. *http://www.correctionscorp.com/*

Crawford, Charles (2000). "Gender, Race, and Habitual Offender Sentencing in Florida." *Criminology* 38(1):262-280.

Criminal Justice Newsletter (1994). "State Chief Justices Oppose Senate Crime Bill Provisions." (February 15):1-3.

Criminal Justice Newsletter (1997a). "Three-Strikes Law Said to Have Little Effect on Prison Crowding." (October 15):3-4.

Criminal Justice Newsletter (1997b). "Gun Crime Mandatory Sentences Take Effect in California." (December 15):1-2.

Criminal Justice Newsletter (1997c). "Alcohol and Drugs Implicated in 80 Percent of Incarcerations." (December 15):4-5.

Criminal Justice Newsletter (1997d). "Drop in Crime Said to be Less in States with Three-Strikes Laws." (March 18):1-2.

Crowley, Jack (1998). "Changing Public Opinion: Correctional Administrators Have an Obligation to Attempt to Influence Public Opinion." *Corrections Today* (February):38-40.

Cullen, Francis T. (2005). "The Twelve People Who Saved Rehabilitation: How the Science of Criminology Made a Difference." *Criminology* 43(1):1-42.

Cullen, Francis T., and Karen E. Gilbert (1982). *Reaffirming Rehabilitation.* Cincinnati: Anderson.

Davis, Sareta M., Alida V. Merlo, and Joycelyn M. Pollock (2006). "Female Criminality: Ten Years Later." In Alida V. Merlo and Joycelyn M. Pollock (eds.), *Women, Law & Social Control*, 2nd ed., pp. 191-210. Boston: Allyn & Bacon.

Dickey, Walter (1996). "The Impact of 'Three Strikes and You're Out' Laws: What Have We Learned? *Overcrowded Times* 7(5):3-2.

DiMascio, William (2004). "In Other States." *Correctional Forum* (March):3.

DiMascio, William (2005a). "Grave Injustice." *Correctional Forum* (September):2-3.

DiMascio, William (2005b). "In Other States." *Correctional Forum* (September):3.

Dreier, Peter (2005). "How the Media Compound Urban Problems." *Journal of Urban Affairs* 28(2):193-201.

Durham, Alexis M. (1994). *Crisis and Reform: Current Issues in American Punishment.* Boston: Little, Brown.

Durose, Matthew, and Patrick A. Langan (2003). "Felony Sentences in State Courts, 2000." *Bureau of Justice Statistics Bulletin.* Washington, DC: U.S. Department of Justice, Office of Justice Programs.

Ehlers, Scott, Vincent Schiraldi, and Jason Ziedenberg (2004). "Still Striking Out: Ten Years of California's Three Strikes Law." Washington, DC: Justice Policy Institute.

Fabelo, Tony (1996). "Whatever Is Next After the Prison-Building Boom Will Be Next In Texas." *The Prison Journal* 76(4):475-483.

Feeley, Malcolm M., and Jonathan Simon (1992). The New Penology: Notes on the Emerging Strategy of Corrections and Its Implications." *Criminology* 30(4):449-474.

Gaes, Gerald G. (2005). "Prison Privatization in Florida: Promise, Premise, and Performance." *Criminology & Public Policy* 4(1):83-86.

Gilliard, Darrell K., and Allen J. Beck (1998). "Prisoners in 1997." *Bureau of Justice Statistics Bulletin*. Washington, DC: U.S. Department of Justice, Office of Justice Programs.

Glaze, Lauren E., and Seri Palla (2004). "Probation and Parole in the United States, 2003." *Bureau of Justice Statistics Bulletin*. Washington, DC: U.S. Department of Justice, Office of Justice Programs.

Gordon, Diana (1990). *The Justice Juggernaut: Fighting Street Crime, Controlling Citizens*. New Brunswick, NJ: Rutgers University Press.

GovTrack (2005). "H.R. 3132: Children's Safety Act of 2005. *http://www.govtrack. us/congress/bill.xpd?bill=h109-3132*

Greenwood, Peter W. (1998). "Investing in Prisons or Prevention: The State Policy Makers' Dilemma." *Crime & Delinquency* 44(1):136-142.

Harland, Alan T. (1996). "Editorial Introduction." *The Prison Journal* 76(4):381-384.

Harlow, Caroline Wolf (1999). "Prior Abuse Reported by Inmates and Probationers." *Bureau of Justice Statistics Selected Findings*. Washington, DC: U.S. Department of Justice, Office of Justice Programs.

Harrison, Paige M., and Allen J. Beck (2005). "Prison and Jail Inmates at Midyear 2004." *Bureau of Justice Statistics Bulletin*. Washington, DC: U.S. Department of Justice, Office of Justice Programs.

Innes, Stephanie (1998). "Construction Not Answer, Critics Say." *Tucson Citizen* (August 3):A1, 4.

Institute of Governmental Studies (2004). "Proposition 66: Limitation on 'Three Strikes' Laws." Berkeley, CA: Institute of Governmental Studies, University of California. *http://igs.Berkeley.edu/library/htThreeStrikesProp66.htm*

Irwin, John (1996). "The March of Folly." *The Prison Journal* 76(4):489-494.

Israel, Michael (2005). *Criminal Justice Washington Newsletter*, 109th Congress, 1st Session, #13. (September 26).

Jamison, Ross (2003). *Is Maryland's System of Higher Education Suffering Because of Prison Expenditures?* Washington, DC: Justice Policy Institute

Johnson, W. Wesley, Katherine Bennett, and Timothy J. Flanagan (1997). "Getting Tough on Prisoners: Results from the National Corrections Executive Survey, 1995." *Crime & Delinquency* 43(1):24-41.

Justice Policy Institute (2005). *Press Release: Race and Imprisonment in Texas*. Washington, DC: Justice Policy Institute. *http://www.justicepolicy.org/article. php?id=487*

Kappeler, Victor E., and Gary W. Potter (2005). *The Mythology of Crime and Criminal Justice*, 4th ed. Long Grove, IL: Waveland.

Kappeler, Victor E., Mark Blumberg, and Gary W. Potter (1996). *The Mythology of Crime and Criminal Justice*, 2nd ed. Prospect Heights, IL: Waveland.

King, Ryan S., and Marc Mauer (2005). *The War on Marijuana: The Transformation of the War on Drugs in the 1990s.* Washington, DC: The Sentencing Project.

Kovandzic, Tomislav V., John J. Sloan, III., and Lynne M. Vieraitis, L.M. (2004). " 'Striking Out' as Crime Reduction Policy: The Impact of 'Three Strikes' Laws on Crime Rates in U.S. Cities." *Justice Quarterly* 21(2):207-239.

Lane, Michael (1986). "A Case for Early Release." *Crime & Delinquency* 32(4):399-403.

Lanza-Kaduce, Lonn, and Karen F. Parker (1998). *A Comparative Recidivism Analysis of Releasees From Private and Public Prisons in Florida.* Private Corrections Project (January). Gainesville, FL: University of Florida, Center for Studies in Criminology and Law. *http://web.crim.ufl.edu/*

Logan, Charles H. (1990). *Private Prisons: Cons and Pros.* New York: Oxford University Press.

Maruschak, Laura M., and Allen J. Beck (2001). "Medical Problems of Inmates, 1997." *Bureau of Justice Statistics Special Report.* Washington, DC: U.S. Department of Justice, Office of Justice Programs.

Matson, Scott, and Roxanne Lieb (1997). *Sexual Predator Commitment Laws.* Olympia, WA: Washington State Institute for Public Policy.

Mauer, Marc (1994). "Americans Behind Bars: The International Use of Incarceration, 1992-1993." *Report*, 1-27. Washington, DC: The Sentencing Project.

Mauer, Marc (1996a). "Punishing More Wisely." *Legal Times* (2 September).

Mauer, Marc (1996b). "Three Strikes Policy is Just a Quick-Fix Solution." *Corrections Today* (July):23.

Mauer, Marc (1997). "Racial Disparities in Prison Getting Worse in the 1990s." *Overcrowded Times* 8(1):1, 8-12.

Mauer, Marc, Ryan S. King, and Malcolm C. Young (2004). *The Meaning of "Life": Long Prison Sentences in Context.* Washington, DC: The Sentencing Project.

Mays, G. Larry (1996). "What Does the Future Hold and What Can We Do About It?" In G. Larry Mays and Tara Gray (eds.), *Privatization and the Provision of Correctional Services: Context and Consequences*, pp. 155-158. Cincinnati: Anderson.

Merlo, Alida V. (1995). "Prison Crowding: Contracting for Life Imprisonment and Preparing for More Problems." Paper presented at the annual meeting of the American Society of Criminology, Boston, MA, November 15, 1995.

Merlo, Alida V. (1997a). "The Costs and Consequences of the Increased Utilization of Long-Term Incarceration in America." Paper presented at the annual conference of the Australian and New Zealand Society of Criminology, Brisbane, Queensland, Australia, July 9, 1997.

Merlo, Alida V. (1997b). "The Crisis and Consequences of Prison Overcrowding." In Joycelyn M. Pollock (ed.), *Prisons Today and Tomorrow*, pp. 52-83. Gaithersburg, MD: Aspen.

Merlo, Alida V. (2000). "Juvenile Justice at the Crossroads: Presidential Address." *Justice Quarterly* 17(4):639-661

Merlo, Alida V., and Peter J. Benekos (1998). "Charting Correction Policy for the 21st Century: The Role of the Media, Politics and Ideology." Paper presented at the annual meeting of the Academy of Criminal Justice Sciences, Albuquerque, NM, March 13, 1998.

Merlo, Alida V., and Peter J. Benekos (1999). "Politics, Media & Corrections." *American Jails* XXIII(2):590-565.

Merlo, Alida V., and Joycelyn M. Pollock (eds.) (1995). *Women, Law and Social Control.* Needham Heights, MA: Allyn & Bacon.

Mortenson, Tom (1996). "Black Men in College or Behind Bars." *Overcrowded Times* 7(2):4, 15, 20.

National Center for Policy Analysis (1996). "Privatizing the Prison System." *http://public-policy.org/~ncpa/studies/s181/s181n.html*

National Legal Aid and Defenders Association (1997). *Cocaine Sentencing: Making Things Worse.* Washington, DC: National Legal Aid and Defenders Association.

New York Times (1993). "Hunt for Kidnapped Girl 12, Is Narrowed to Small Woods." (December 3):A22.

New York Times (1997). "Governor Pataki's Message to Judges." (December 16):A20.

New York Times (1998a). "Lawyer for Rapist Who Killed Argues Against Death Penalty." (February 17):A16.

New York Times (1998b). "Jury Recommends Death for Killer of Prostitute." (February 26):A18.

Ogle, Robbin S. (1999). "Prison Privatization: An Environmental Catch-22." *Justice Quarterly* 16(3):579-600.

Petersilia, Joan, and Elizabeth Piper Deschenes (1994). "Perceptions of Punishment: Inmates and Staff Rank the Severity of Prison Versus Intermediate Sanctions." *Prison Journal* (74):306-328.

Pollock, Joycelyn M. (2004). *Prisons and Prison Life: Costs and Consequences.* Los Angeles: Roxbury.

Ranney, Dave (2005). "Drug Treatment Appears to be Sound Alternative to Prison Time, So Far." *Lawrence Journal-World* (January 30). *http://www.justicepolicy. org/article.php?id=475*

Ritzer, George (2004). *The McDonaldization of Society*, rev. ed. Thousand Oaks, CA: Pine Forge Press.

Sandoval, Joseph (1996). "Three Strikes is Good Criminal Justice Policy." *Corrections Today* (July):22.

Schiraldi, Vincent, James Colburn, and Eric Lotke (2004). *Three Strikes and You're Out: An Examination of the Impact of 3-Strike Laws 10 Years After Their Enactment.* Washington, DC: Justice Policy Institute.

The Sentencing Project (1999). *Facts on Prisons and Prisoners.* Washington, DC: The Sentencing Project.

The Sentencing Project (2005). *Comments and Recommendations Submitted to the United States Sentencing Commission for the 2005-2006 Amendment Cycle.* Washington, DC: The Sentencing Project.

Shichor, David (1997). "Three Strikes as a Public Policy: The Convergence of the New Penology and the McDonaldization of Punishment." *Crime & Delinquency* 43(4):470-492.

Skolnick, Jerome H. (1995). "What Not to Do About Crime—The American Society of Criminology 1994 Presidential Address." *Criminology* 33(1):1-13.

Slevin, Peter (2005). "Prison Experts See Opportunity for Improvement." *Washington Post* (July 26):A03. *http://www.washingtonpost.com*

Smith, Phil (1993). "Private Prisons: Profits of Crime." *Covert Action Quarterly* (Fall). *http://mediafilter.org/MFF/Prison.html*

Solomon, Amy L., Vea Kachnowski, and Avinash Bhati (2005). *Does Parole Work? Analyzing the Impact of Postprison Supervision on Rearrest Outcomes.* Washington, DC: The Urban Institute.

Sprott, Jane B. (1996). "Understanding Public Views of Youth Crime and the Youth Justice System." *Canadian Journal of Criminology* 38(3):271-291

Stephan, James J. (2004). "State Prison Expenditures, 2001." *Bureau of Justice Statistics, Special Report.* Washington, DC: U.S. Department of Justice.

Stephan, James J., and Jennifer C. Karberg (2003). *Census of State and Federal Correctional Facilities, 2000.* Washington, DC: U.S. Department of Justice, Office of Justice Programs.

St. Gerard, Vanessa (2004). "Local Forum: Wyoming." *On the Line* 26(4):2.

Tatge, Mark (1998). "Employees Criticize Privately Run Prison." *The Plain Dealer* (August 30):A1, 18.

Terry, W. Clinton, III (2000). "Opening the Courts to the Community: Volunteers in Wisconsin's Courts." *Bureau of Justice Assistance Bulletin.* Washington, DC: U.S. Department of Justice, Office of Justice Programs.

Thomas, Charles W. (2005). "Recidivism of Public and Private State Prison Inmates in Florida: Issues and Unanswered Questions." *Criminology & Public Policy* 4(1):89-100.

Toch, Hans (1996). "Prison Reform in a Federalist Democracy." *The Prison Journal* 76(4):495-501.

Tonry, Michael, and Kate Hamilton (1995). *Intermediate Sanctions in Overcrowded Times.* Boston: Northeastern University Press.

Tonry, Dylan T. (1996). "Probation and Parole Population Up 3.2 Percent in 1995." *Overcrowded Times* 7(4):5-6.

Turner, Michael G., Jody L. Sundt, Brandon K. Applegate, and Francis T. Cullen (1995). "Three Strikes and You're Out Legislation: A National Assessment." *Federal Probation* 59(3):16-35.

Uniform Crime Reports (2004). *Crime in the United States 2004.* Washington, DC: U.S. Government Printing Office. *http://www.fbi.gov/ucr/2004/04prelim.pdf*

Urban Institute (2004). "Chicago Prisoners 'Experiences Returning Home." Washington, DC: The Urban Institute.

U.S. General Accounting Office (1998). *Truth In Sentencing: Availability of Federal Grants Influenced Laws in Some States*. February 4. Washington, DC: U.S. General Accounting Office.

U.S. General Accounting Office (1996). *Private and Public Prisons: Studies Comparing Operational Costs and/or Quality of Service*. August. Washington, DC: U.S. General Accounting Office.

USA Today (2004). "Elderly Inmates Swell Prisons, Driving Up Health Care Costs." (February 28). *http://www.usatoday.com/news/nation/2004-02-28-elderly-inmates_x.htm*

Vaughn, Michael S. (1993). "Listening to the Experts: A National Study of Correctional Administrators' Responses to Prison Overcrowding." *Criminal Justice Review* 18 (Spring):12-25.

Verhovek, Sam Howe (1996). "Texas Caters to a Demand Around U.S. for Jail Cells." *New York Times* (February 9):A1, A10.

vonZielbauer, Paul. (2005). "Company's Troubled Answer to Fragile Alabama Inmates." *New York Times* (August 1):A1, A11.

Warr, Mark. (1995). "The Polls-Poll Trends: Public Opinion on Crime and Punishment." *Public Opinion Quarterly* 56(2):296-310.

Welsh-Huggins, Andrew (2005). "Prisons Raise Patrols for Inmate Suicides." Associated Press (August 2). *http://www.sfgate.com/cgi-bin/article.cgi?f=/n/a/2005/08/01/national/a230932DSS.DTL*

White, Ahmed A. (2001). "Rule of Law and the Limits of Sovereignty: The Private Prison in Jurisprudential Perspective." *The American Criminal Law Review* 38(1):111-146.

Wren, Christopher S. (1998). "Clinton to Require State Efforts to Cut Drug Use in Prisons." *New York Times* (January 12):A1, A8.

Ziedenberg, Jason, and Vincent Schiraldi (2002). *Cellblocks or Classrooms?* Washington, DC: Justice Policy Institute.

Zimbardo, Philip G. (1994). "Transforming California's Prisons into Expensive Old Age Homes for Felons: Enormous Hidden Costs and Consequences for California's Taxpayers." *Report*, November:1-16. San Francisco: Center on Juvenile and Criminal Justice.

CASES

United States v. Booker, 125 S. Ct. 738 (2005).

5

Juvenile Justice:
Deconstructing Adolescence and Dismantling the Juvenile Court

Reflections on crime reveal that youths and young criminals have been the focus of fear and the target of punitive public policies. Since the sensational youth gang violence in the 1980s and the "horrific series of shooting sprees by public school students" in the late 1990s (Gest, 2001:83), lawmakers have been guided by punitive ideology in designing reactive legislation. Even as data indicate encouraging downward trends in juvenile crime, and especially violent crime (Snyder, 2005; Uniform Crime Reports, 2004), negative images of youths continue to captivate the media's attention and perpetuate the theme of a society under siege by violent youths. As Macallair and Males observed, "the pervasive assumption that today's youths are more violent than past generations is leading to the gradual abandonment of a separate juvenile justice system" (2000:1).

YOUTH CRIME: MEDIA IMAGES VERSUS DATA

In August 2005, Snyder reported that based on FBI data, "juvenile arrests for violence in 2003 were the lowest since 1987" (2005:4). From 1994 to 2003, the data reflected a 32 percent decrease in the number of juvenile arrests for violent crimes (i.e., murder, forcible rape, robbery, aggravated assault) (p. 4). These data, however, are often overshadowed by headlines that capture more of the public's attention:

"Senseless Youth Violence in Seattle." (CBS News, September 2000).

"Youth Violence: Still An Epidemic." (CBS News, January 2001).

"Youth Violence is Sharply on Rise." (*Boston Globe*, August 2004).

"Psychiatrist: Zoloft Caused Mania in Youth." (ABC News, February 2005).

"Teen Who Killed 9 Claimed Nazi Leanings." (MSNBC, March 2005).

"Boston Targets Cape Verdean Youth Violence." (*Boston Globe*, July 2005).

In October 1997, as the FBI was announcing a 9 percent decrease in the rate of violent crime committed by youths—from 511.9 arrests per 100,000 in 1995 to 464.7 per 100,000 in 1997 (Uniform Crime Reports, 1997)—one newspaper juxtaposed three stories on the front page about youths who had committed murders (*Erie Times News*, 1997):

"15-Year-Old Charged in Murder of Boy Selling Candy for School Fund-Raiser" (New Jersey)

"Teen Stabs Mother to Death, Then Kills Two Others During Shooting Rampage at School" (Mississippi)

"17-Year-Old Convicted of Killing Best Friend's Mother" (Massachusetts)

These headlines and the accompanying stories do more to influence the public's perceptions and predispositions toward youths than findings that violent youthful offenders represented "about one-third of 1 percent of all juveniles ages 10-17 living in the U.S." (Snyder, 2005:4). Arrest data for youths under age 18 indicate that juveniles accounted for 16 percent of all arrests in 2003 (see Figure 5.1). Data in Figures 5.2 and 5.3 show that rates of juvenile arrests for violent and property crimes have been declining since 1994. In the last 25 years, as a percent of all arrests, juvenile arrests for murder have accounted for less than one of every 10 arrests, except in 1995 (Butts, 2000). See Table 5.1 for a broad picture of juveniles as offenders.

Figure 5.1
Percent of Arrests Involving Juveniles, 2003

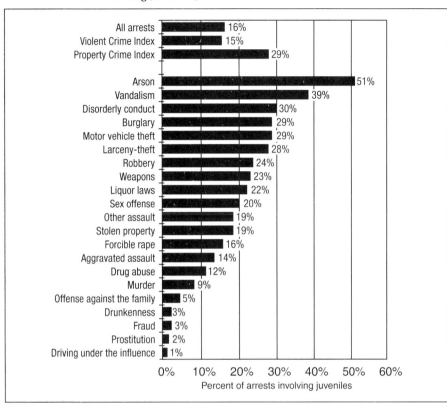

Source: Howard N. Snyder (2005). *Juvenile Arrests 2003*. Washington, DC: Office of Juvenile Justice and Delinquency Prevention.

Figure 5.2
Arrests per 100,000 Juveniles Ages 10-17, Violent Crime Index

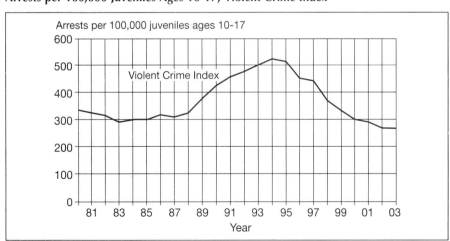

Source: Howard N. Snyder (2005). *Juvenile Arrests 2003*. Washington, DC: Office of Juvenile Justice and Delinquency Prevention.

Figure 5.3
Arrests per 100,000 Juveniles Ages 10-17, Property Crime Index

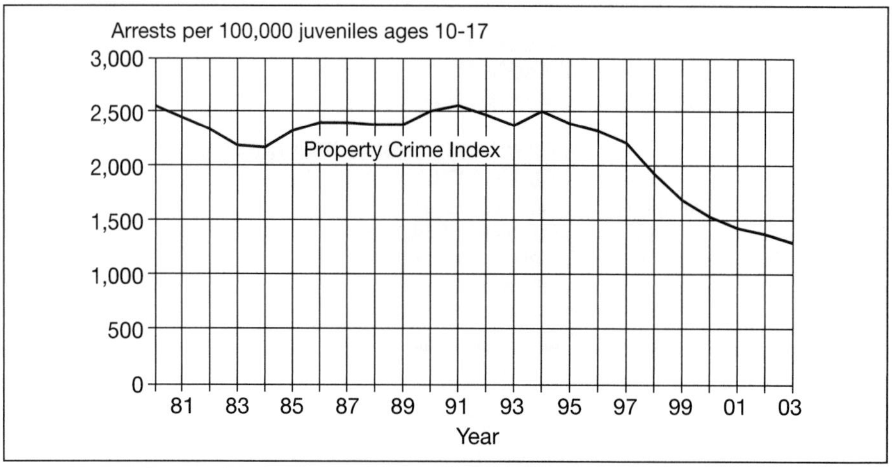

Source: Howard N. Snyder (2005). *Juvenile Arrests 2003*. Washington, DC: Office of Juvenile Justice and Delinquency Prevention.

Despite this good news about decreases in youth violence, it is tragedies—such as the deaths of 15 people at Columbine High School in 1999 (Lawrence, 2004) and the case of the King brothers (ages 12 and 13) in Florida in 2002, who were charged as adults for killing their father (Canedy, 2002)—that capture the public's emotions and sustain images of youth violence. The concerns about reducing school violence and providing students with a safe environment in which to learn are salient issues in the United States (Lawrence, 1998). The killing and wounding that occurred at Columbine not only serve to reinforce these concerns but also to convey inaccurately that school violence is on the increase. While some data indicate that schools have in fact become safer (DeVoe et al., 2004; Lewin, 1997), it is the perception that these kinds of tragedies are random and can happen to anyone that underlies public responses and legislative remedies.

Such news coverage distorts the true picture of crime and sustains the public preoccupation with crime and fear of victimization. For example, in contrast to noteworthy reductions in violent crime, "murder coverage on America's television network newscasts increased by more than 700 percent between 1993 and 1996—a period during which the actual murder rate declined by 20 percent" (Morin, 1997:34). Butts and Snyder explain how the public's understanding can be distorted (1997:11):

> Today, the public hears about every incident, whether it happened in a different town or on a different continent. Moreover, the details of every incident are repeated several times—at arrest, trial, sentencing, etc. The growing publicity

about these cases may suggest to the public that they are occurring more frequently, even if juvenile crime trends indicate otherwise.

The consequence of these perceptions is the designation of the adolescent as "Public Enemy # 1" (Magill, 1998) and the creation of public policy that is based on exaggerated premises. According to Lewin, legislative proposals recognize that while crime figures are falling, "young people are committing worse crimes and need to be dealt with more harshly" (1998:A13). Based on their analysis, Macallair and Males concluded that there is "a need for policy makers and the media to re-examine popular assumptions about youth crime and ...a need to reconsider current trends in youth crime policies" (2000:7). Before examining some of this legislation, a review of juvenile justice history provides a context within which to understand the politics of juvenile justice reform.

Table 5.1
Juveniles as Percent of All Arrests for Murder

1980	9%
1995	15%
1999	9%
2003	9%

Source: Federal Bureau of Investigation. *Crime in the United States*, Annual. Washington, DC: U.S. Department of Justice.

JUSTICE FOR JUVENILES

One hundred years ago, the image of "wayward" children who were engulfed by the forces of the Industrial Revolution and the dynamics of an expanding and increasingly diverse urban population captured the attention of concerned citizens. The "child savers" (as they were called) believed that miscreant youths were subjected to additional harms as a result of being handled by the criminal court. In that "Progressive Era," which adopted positivist assumptions of behavior, reformers emphasized the need to act in the best interests of the children and to protect them from the immoral influences and negative social conditions that propelled them into delinquency (Bortner, 1988). This view of the need for a separate system to handle troubled youths reflected faith in individualized treatment and confidence in the "virtues of traditional institutions" to intervene on behalf of the children (Bortner, 1988:46).

f the first formal juvenile court in Chicago in 1899
te would exercise authority to remove children from
ined, and uncaring environments and would act *in*
best interests of each child (Albanese, 1993). Unlike
proceedings that established guilt and assigned punishment,
the intent of the juvenile model was to determine the child's needs and
to provide appropriate treatment. This presumed an informal process
guided by principles of substantive rationality, which established a distinct legal status for youths (Bortner, 1988). In essence, the significant
characteristics of this system included:

- emphasis on treatment (rehabilitation model);

- reliance on informal proceedings;

- concern with the best interests of the child rather than
  behaviors;

- acceptance of the positivist assumptions of behavior;
  and

- faith in the good intentions of the court to be guided by
  parens patriae.

The "orthodox" view of juvenile court history recognizes the good
intentions and humanitarian motivations of the "child savers." However, Platt has developed a cogent "revisionist" argument that this
movement was more likely motivated by alarm about lower-class
immigrants and ensuing value conflicts and that it resulted in a system
designed to exercise control and authority to resocialize poor juveniles
(1977). Platt suggests that the increased power of the state to regulate
youths (i.e., social control) more accurately characterizes this era of
reform. In citing the "growing concern with youth crime and urban violence," Platt recognized that social conditions and not the plight of individual youths prompted the "new penology" of juvenile justice
(1977:178).

Both the orthodox and revisionist views of juvenile justice reform
recognize the expanded authority of the state to intervene in the lives
of youths and to do so without the procedural constraints required for
handling adults. In effect, adolescence became a distinct legal status that
by 1966 was recognized by the Supreme Court as providing the worst
of both worlds for children (*Kent v. United States*, 383 U.S. 541,
[1966]). In other words, with informal hearings, youths were denied
procedural safeguards; with inadequate performance and treatment outcomes, youths were denied due process and rehabilitation. According
to Albanese (1993), the Court's response to this state of the juvenile
justice system in the 1960s and 1970s was to "reform" the juvenile
court by requiring greater due process. This was essentially a recon-

ceptualization of the juvenile court from an informal, rehabilitative system to one with more due process and adversarial concerns. This also facilitated and accelerated a "convergence" between the juvenile and criminal courts. Feld (1993) has argued that with the emphasis on crime control and due process, the juvenile court has been "transformed" (1) from informal to formal practices, (2) from a "best interests" to a "just deserts" philosophy, and (3) from the developmental model of adolescence to the deterrence model of punishment. Based on the performance of the contemporary juvenile court, the original intentions have long been discarded. Feld questions the justification of maintaining a separate "punitive" system for young adults.

TRANSFORMING JUVENILE JUSTICE

Feld's observations identify important issues regarding the future of juvenile justice. The ideology of getting tough on crime and the use of bumper-sticker slogans to determine public policy (e.g., "old enough to do the crime, old enough to do the time"; "adult crime, adult time") underscore a conservative, neoclassical approach to juvenile justice that recognizes: (1) a rational choice model to explain criminality, (2) criminal court jurisdiction, and (3) legislation that reconstructs the image of youths.

Rational Choice

A basic rationale of the juvenile court has been the principle that youths are engaged in developmental processes and tasks of transitioning from childhood immaturity and dependence to adult responsibility and independence (Adams & Gullotta, 1983; Henggeler, 1989; Rice, 1987). As a result, "youthfulness was considered an excusing factor from full criminal responsibility" (Bortner, 1988:51). However, as crime became identified as a national crisis in the 1970s and 1980s, the focus of public policy shifted from rehabilitation to just deserts and punishment. By the late 1980s and early 1990s, the media—and, consequently, the public and politicians—found another public enemy: juvenile offenders, especially violent youths, became the new Willie Horton (Vogel, 1994).

In the context of classical ideological assumptions prevalent in criminal court, rational choice was also used as an explanation for youthful offending. As the focus shifted from the best interests of the child to public safety, and from *parens patriae* to punishment, the focus on accountability and deterrence further diminished the treatment ideals and clouded the developmental perspective. The image of violent youths, gangs, drugs, and guns justified efforts to increase penalties for youthful offenders. A system that had converged toward more due process and formal rationality now embraced rational decisionmaking and moved away from individualized treatment to categorical punishments. In this model, deterministic, positivist explanations of juvenile delinquency were replaced with classical assumptions of deliberate and willful youth criminality.

Jurisdictional Reform

With the greater emphasis on formal rationality, and the accompanying challenges to the assumptions justifying separate systems for juveniles, "a fundamental change in the jurisprudence of sentencing occurred as the offense rather than the offender began to dominate the decision" (Feld, 1993:405). As a result, concern with violent crime, drugs, and gangs increased pressure to get tough with youthful offenders. This was facilitated by removing selected youths from juvenile court and transferring them to the domain of criminal court.

Essentially, judicial waiver provides the juvenile court with a mechanism for identifying youths who are not amenable to care and treatment and for transferring jurisdiction to criminal court. As Feld (1993) noted, almost all states have this discretionary practice of handling designated juveniles as adults. Data indicate that states increased their use of this jurisdictional transfer: the number of cases waived to criminal court from 1985 to 1994 increased 71 percent—from 7,200 to 12,300 (Sickmund, Snyder & Poe-Yamagata, 1997:31). This prominent increase in the number of waived cases was also documented in Pennsylvania, where the number of juvenile cases sent to criminal court from 1985 to 1995 increased 134 percent (227 to 533) while the total number of juvenile court dispositions increased only 27 percent (29,137 to 36,997) (Merlo, Benekos & Cook, 1997:7). Even though these waivers represent less than 2 percent of all formally handled delinquency cases (i.e., 1.4%), data indicate that in the 1990s there was a greater likelihood of transferring youths, especially for crimes against persons: in 1994, 44 percent of waived cases were for person offenses, compared to 33 percent in 1985 (Sickmund, Snyder & Poe-Yamagata, 1997:31).

Because of declining crime and the use of legislative exclusion, the number of youths judicially waived in 2000 decreased to less than 6,000 (of these, 40 percent were for person offenses compared to 44 percent in 1994) (Puzzanchera et al., 2004:34). As explained by Lemmon and colleagues, "Under statutory exclusion, cases that meet certain age, offender, or other criteria are processed directly by the criminal courts, bypassing the juvenile system completely" (2005:215).

Legislative Reform

The data on waivers show that juvenile courts have been responsive to the get-tough, "adult crime–adult time" momentum. However, politicians have also been adding to the transformation by imposing statutory exclusions that automatically disqualify an increasing number of youths from juvenile court. In addition to the 41 states that revised jurisdictional authority, laws regarding juveniles have also changed sentencing options, confidentiality, victims' rights, and correctional programming (Sickmund, Snyder & Poe-Yamagata, 1997:28). As Boxes 5.1 and 5.2 indicate, legislatures have enacted increasingly tough measures against juveniles. These reforms further narrow the distinctions between juvenile court and criminal court, and reinforce perceptions that juveniles are only younger criminals who need to be held accountable and receive just punishments for their criminal offending.

Box 5.1

Juvenile court proceedings and records are more open as provisions reduce confidentiality

Between 1985 and 1995 legislatures made significant changes in how information about juvenile offenders is treated by the justice system—often in tandem with changes in jurisdictional authority. At year-end 1995—

- 22 States have open hearings for certain cases (10 are new or modified laws).

- 39 States permit release of certain juveniles' names and/or photos (11 are new or modified laws).

- 18 States prohibit sealing or expunging certain juvenile court records (8 are new or modified laws).

- 45 States allow release of juvenile court records to certain types of people—prosecution, law enforcement, social agencies, schools, the victim, or the public (21 are new or modified laws).

- 47 States allow police to fingerprint and 44 States allow them to photograph certain juveniles; 44 States provide for an offense history repository for juvenile arrest/disposition information (26 are new or modified laws).

Source: Melissa Sickmund, Howard N. Snyder, and Eileen Poe-Yamagata (1997). *Juvenile Offenders and Victims: 1997 Update on Violence*, pp. 28-29. Washington, DC: Office of Juvenile Justice and Delinquency Prevention.

The transformations of the juvenile court that promote the rational choice model of crime and the increased use of both judicial and legislative exclusions may appeal to the public and win support for politicians, but there is no convincing evidence that they make communities safer. Schwartz concluded that "treating juveniles as adults when they are 16 or 17 years old may seem appealing as a 'get tough' measure. However, there is no credible evidence that such policies are effective crime control measures" (1989:71). Research by Bishop and colleagues, for example, indicates that youths transferred to the adult court jurisdiction of Florida had higher rates of recidivism compared to similar youths retained in juvenile court (1996:183). Moran (1996) also reported an increased likelihood of reoffending for juveniles transferred to adult court.

Box 5.2

From 1992 through 1995, legislatures in 47 States and the District of Columbia enacted laws that toughened their juvenile justice system

State	Changes in law or court rule*			State	Changes in law or court rule*		
Alabama	J			Montana		S	C
Alaska	J			Nebraska			
Arizona		S	C	Nevada	J		C
Arkansas	J	S	C	New Hampshire	J	S	C
California	J		C	New Jersey		S	C
Colorado	J	S	C	New Mexico	J	S	
Delaware	J	S	C	New York			
D. of Columbia	J	S		North Carolina	J		C
Florida	J	S	C	North Dakota	J		C
Georgia	J	S	C	Ohio	J	S	C
Hawaii			C	Oklahoma	J		C
Idaho	J	S	C	Oregon	J		C
Illinois	J	S	C	Pennsylvania	J		C
Indiana	J	S	C	Rhode Island	J	S	
Iowa	J		C	South Carolina	J		C
Kansas	J		C	South Dakota	J		
Kentucky	J			Tennessee	J		C
Louisiana	J	S	C	Texas	J	S	C
Maine			C	Utah	J		C
Maryland	J		C	Vermont			
Massachusetts		S		Virginia	J	S	C
Michigan		S	C	Washington	J		C
Minnesota	J	S	C	West Virginia	J		
Mississippi	J		C	Wisconsin	J	S	C
Missouri	J	S	C	Wyoming	J		C

* J = Jurisdiction, S = Sentencing, C = Confidentiality

■ These laws involve increased eligibility for criminal court processing and adult correctional sanctioning and decreased confidentiality for a subset of juvenile offenders.

Source: Authors' adaptation of P. Torbet's *State Responses to Serious and Violent Juvenile Crime.*

Source: Melissa Sickmund, Howard N. Snyder, and Eileen Poe-Yamagata (1997). *Juvenile Offenders and Victims: 1997 Update on Violence*, pp. 28-29. Washington, DC: Office of Juvenile Justice and Delinquency Prevention.

Myers (2003) studied the outcomes of juvenile waivers in Pennsylvania and found that recidivism was higher for youths who were sent to adult criminal court. In addition, he found that "youths transferred to adult court were rearrested more quickly following final disposition than were their counterparts who remained in juvenile court" (p. 92). If the rationale "of treating juvenile offenders as adults" is to send a message that violent youths "will no longer be tolerated," the findings by Myers and others fails to support a deterrent effect (Myers, 2003:94).

Another element of this deterrence rationale is that youthful offenders will be more likely to receive punishment in the adult court than if they were handled in juvenile court. Lemmon and his colleagues, however, "found no significant difference in the certainty of punishment between juvenile and adult courts" (2005:227). In raising questions about the "efficacy of deterrence policies," Lemmon and colleagues acknowledge that exclusionary policies such as the ones mentioned above are "often a political solution to a complex social problem" (2005:219).

While this evidence raises doubts about the effectiveness and intended outcomes of punitive treatment of youths, a study by the Justice Policy Institute concludes that the commingling of adults and juveniles in correctional institutions is a disastrous experience for youths (Ziedenberg & Schiraldi, 1997). The survey identified that juveniles incarcerated with adults are eight times more likely to commit suicide, five times more likely to report being raped and sexually assaulted, twice as likely to report being beaten by prison staff, and 50 percent more likely to be attacked with a weapon. The Children's Defense Fund identified three especially egregious occurrences taking place when youths were confined in adult facilities: a 17-year-old male who robbed a pizza store in Ohio was stabbed to death by six adults; a 16-year-old male who burned a fence in Texas hanged himself after being raped and beaten; and a 15-year-old female who ran away from home was raped by a deputy jailer (Edelman, 1998).

> Close to a century ago, the juvenile justice system was developed because children were subjected to unspeakable atrocities in adult jails, and were returned to society as hardened criminals. As the system developed, it became clear that housing young offenders and adult prisoners together was self-destructive and self-defeating (Ziedenberg & Schiraldi, 1997:1).

In the early 1970s, the government's response to these types of incidents (e.g., youths housed with adults) was to seek additional legislation to protect juveniles. In 1974, the Juvenile Justice and Delinquency Prevention Act mandated: (1) the deinstitutionalization of status offenders, (2) the separation of juveniles and adults, and (3) the removal of adolescents from jails (Albanese, 1993). However, by the late 1990s, politics and ideology shifted, and Congress was considering Senate Bill 10, which (among other get-tough initiatives with youths) would have reversed the Juvenile Justice and Delinquency Prevention mandate and would have permitted youths to be incarcerated with adults (Senate Bill 10, 1997). The Violent and Repeat Juvenile Offender Act, which clearly reflects the classical views of deterrence through increased severity of sanctions, may be more a political reaction to fears and frustrations regarding crime than a rational public policy. This is the "new" politics of juvenile crime, and it is consistent with the punitive and retributive ideology that characterizes the criminal justice system.

The assumptions and intentions of Senate Bill 10 demonstrate the transformation of the juvenile court and suggest the impact that media stories, classical ideology, and politics have had on dismantling juvenile justice. When violent crimes involving youthful offenders occur, the dynamics are set for emotional reactions, fear, demonization of youths, and calls for punishment—all of which further distort perceptions of juvenile delinquency and exacerbate what is wrong with the criminal justice system.

YOUTH VIOLENCE AND MORAL PANIC

The incidents of public school violence in the late 1990s and early 2000s also illustrate Fishman's (1978) concept of a "crime wave." He analyzed how the media identify and report stories that fit an established theme, thus creating the impression that a particular crime is becoming epidemic. This pattern was evident in the tragedies in 1997 and 1998 involving kids, guns, and homicides at five schools. These incidents captured national attention and prompted alarm regarding school safety and the pathology of youth violence. They presaged the Columbine tragedy and firmly established the theme of school violence.

In October 1997, in Pearl, Mississippi, two students were killed and seven wounded. In December of the same year, three youths were killed in West Paducah, Kentucky. In March 1998, four students and a teacher were killed in Jonesboro, Arkansas. In April of that year, a teacher chaperoning a middle-school dance was killed in Edinboro, Pennsylvania, and in May, 24 students were wounded and two were killed in Springfield, Oregon, when a 15-year-old opened fire in the cafeteria. In two of these incidents, the youth also allegedly killed one or both of his parents: in Pearl, 16-year-old Luke Woodham killed his mother, and in Springfield, 15-year-old Kip Kinkel shot and killed his parents the night before his shooting spree in Springfield (King & Murr, 1998). These five incidents occurred within seven months and left 48 people wounded and 11 students, two teachers, and three parents dead. In each case, the homicides involved guns and at least one adolescent was charged with the killings. The aftermath precipitated Congressional hearings on youth violence and included interviews with citizens and experts on violence and school crime (Meckler, 1998:A4).

On April 1, 1998, during the debate on Senate Bill 10, the Violent and Repeat Juvenile Offender Act, Senator Patrick Leahy (D-Vt.) responded to the March 24, 1998, shooting at Westside Middle School in Arkansas by urging colleagues "not to politicize the important issue of juvenile crime" (Violent and Repeat Juvenile Offender Act of 1997):

> Mr. President, the recent shootings outside a school in Jonesboro, Arkansas, that left four young students and a teacher dead and scores of others wounded in both body and mind are shocking. Just over the last few months, we have seen deadly shootings carried out by juveniles in rural communities in Kentucky, in Mississippi and now in Arkansas. Clearly, juvenile crime is not just an urban problem. These shootings leave scars on the loved ones of those killed and injured and on the communities involved that take a long time to heal.

> We may never fully comprehend how such crimes against children could be executed by other children. But one thing should be clear: The issue of juvenile crime should not be used for cheap grandstanding or short-sighted political gain. We need to find constructive approaches to this problem that build upon past successes and respect the proper roles of State, local and Federal authorities.

The following academic year, on April 20, 1999, it was the incident at Columbine High School in Littleton, Colorado, that shocked the nation as "the worst school shooting incident in the history of the United States" (Lawrence, 2004:89). The nature of the shooting and extensive media coverage reinforced fears and parent anxiety about school safety. The images of Eric Harris, 18, and Dylan Klebold, 17, captured the headlines. Stories about their arsenal of weapons, the 13 students and one teacher they killed, and the suicides that ended the shooting spree were retold for weeks, as law enforcement personnel, school officials, surviving students, and parents told their stories to the media (Lawrence, 2004:89). The school shootings (and media attention) have continued (see Table 5.2), which reinforces fears and justifies policies that make schools more secure and less tolerant.

These stories and the images of school violence were revived in August 2005, when Mitchell Johnson was released from prison. On March 24, 1998, Johnson (then 13), along with Andrew Golden (then 11), killed four students and a teacher, and wounded 10 others at Westside Middle School in Jonesboro, Arkansas. Johnson was released after serving seven years, and "many still question the fairness of releasing Johnson on his 21st birthday because of a now-closed loophole in the law" (Nelson, 2005:par. 2). In her article about Johnson's release, Melissa Nelson not only reviewed the facts of the Jonesboro incident but also chronicled other "schoolyard assaults in which teenagers attacked their classmates" (par. 9). The effect was to portray a pattern of violence by youths and to question their sentences. Interviews with survivors and victims' families reflected emotional reactions, including anger over the length of the sentences and questions about "whether justice has been served" (Nelson, 2005:par. 12). This attention prompted the sheriff to offer protection to Johnson's mother. (Golden is scheduled to be released in 2007.)

Table 5.2
Recent School Shootings

Nov. 19, 1999 Deming, N.M.	Victor Cordova Jr., 12, shot and killed Araceli Tena, 13, in the lobby of Deming Middle School.
March 10, 2000 Savannah, Ga.	Two students killed by Darrell Ingram, 19, while leaving a dance sponsored by Beach High School
May 26, 2000 Lake Worth, Fla.	One teacher, Barry Grunow, shot and killed at Lake Worth Middle School by Nate Brazill, 13, with .25-caliber semiautomatic pistol on the last day of classes
March 5, 2001 Santee, Calif.	Two killed and 13 wounded by Charles Andrew Williams, 15, firing from a bathroom at Santana High School
March 7, 2001 Williamsport, Pa.	Elizabeth Catherine Bush, 14, wounded student Kimberly Marchese in the cafeteria of Bishop Neumann High School; she was depressed and frequently teased.
March 30, 2001 Gary, Ind.	One student killed by Donald R. Burt, Jr., a 17-year-old student who had been expelled from Lew Wallace High School.
Sept. 24, 2003 Cold Spring, Minn.	Two students are killed at Rocori High School by John Jason McLaughlin, 15.
March 21, 2005 Red Lake, Minn.	Jeff Weise, 16, killed grandfather and companion, then arrived at school where he killed a teacher, a security guard, 5 students, and finally himself, leaving a total of 10 dead.

Source: Adapted from Infoplease.com (2005). "A Time Line of Recent Worldwide School Shootings." Pearson Education. *http://www.infoplease.com/ipa/A0777958.htm*

Zero Tolerance

The 1998 killing of eighth-grade teacher John Gillette in Edinboro, Pennsylvania, while he was chaperoning a middle-school dance, demonstrated the emotional response and panic that can spread through a community after such a devastating crime. Less than one week after Gillette was killed by 14-year-old Andrew Wurst, three boys, ages 11, 12, and 14, were arrested for making terroristic threats in a middle school located outside of Edinboro. The youths, who allegedly threatened to shoot someone at the next middle school dance (Guerriero & Palattella, 1998:C1), were expelled from school and charged with misdemeanors.

The next day, police were called to two other area schools: one in response to a "weapon" and the other to a teen who promised to make the day "memorable" (Hahn & Eckert, 1998:A1). Both the local and state police were called to investigate the incident at the second school, where police determined that a "big misunderstanding" had occurred and "no serious threats" had been made (Hahn & Eckert, 1998:A1).

In partial response to the Edinboro shooting and the general concerns about school violence, the Catholic diocese of a nearby city (Erie, Pennsylvania) banned all middle-school dances associated with parochial schools (*Erie Times News*, 1998b:B4). In the days following the Edinboro killing, the local media replayed and referred to the incident—which one police officer acknowledged as causing "understandable hysteria" (Hahn & Eckert, 1998:C1)—as they continued to report various other stories on school violence. In addition, there was disagreement regarding what responses should be taken by school officials to allegations and threats of violence by students in the local schools. Some citizens and officials claimed that schools were overreacting while others supported the policy that students' remarks about violence should be taken seriously, even if spoken in jest (Guerriero, 1998:C1).

In Toledo, Ohio, in response to school misbehaviors, school officials rely on police and the juvenile justice system to handle unruly students (Rimer, 2004). Students can be handcuffed by police and taken into custody for dress code violations and for being disruptive (Rimer, 2004).

In St. Petersburg, Florida, in March 2005, a five-year-old girl was handcuffed by police for being an "unruly kindergartner" (Tobin, 2005). The girl had climbed on a table, torn papers off the bulletin board, and hit the assistant principal. When police arrived, the girl had stopped her "tantrum," but she was handcuffed and placed in the police car. The girl was later released, and no charges were filed. The case received wide attention because the incident—"two seconds of the tantrum and eight seconds of handcuffing"—was captured on videotape and released to the media (Tobin, 2005:par. 36). A police department investigation determined that policy had not been violated in handcuffing the girl, and the officers were not disciplined. The department, however, did change its policy, which now requires a supervising officer to be present when handcuffing children younger than eight years old (*New York Times*, 2005b). In Cincinnati, Ohio, police were reprimanded for violating policy after handcuffing a five-year-old boy for fighting on a school bus (*Sun Sentinel*, 2005). In January 2005, two officers responded to a fight on a bus and restrained the youth. The boy, Izell Finch, was not arrested, and the city settled a lawsuit with the mother.

The tragic homicide in Edinboro mentioned above occurred in a rural, middle-class community that fit the theme of school-related shootings that was receiving national attention in the 1997–1998 school year. From Pearl, Mississippi, to Littleton, Colorado, young, white, adolescent males in rural and suburban middle America were using guns to inflict terror on fellow students and teachers. Some had experienced rejection from peers, ex-girlfriends, or parents, and there may have been indications and warnings that these youths were seeking retaliation (King & Murr, 1998). The killings had "shock value" because they "took place in the heart of middle America" and not in the inner-city areas where minority youths had been killing each other with increasing frequency since the mid-1980s (King & Murr, 1998:33). Moreover, the "hysteria" about student statements that intimated school violence resulted in less tolerance and sensationalism to student threats (Join Together Online, 1998):

> In Forestville, Kentucky, an 18-year-old male was arrested and handcuffed after he threatened to kill his baseball coach for not putting him in the starting lineup. The youth claimed he was "just joking."

> In Ebensburg, Pennsylvania, "two 12-year-old boys were suspended after saying they wanted to kill seven classmates."

> A Tennessee student in kindergarten was charged with bringing a handgun to school and threatening "to kill his teacher for putting him in time-out."

In related cases, two sixth-grade girls from a rural middle school near Edinboro, Pennsylvania, were charged with making terroristic threats for passing a note in which they wished another girl was dead after gaining the affections of a desired boyfriend (*Erie Times News*, 1998a:B4). Even though school officials disciplined the girls, the mother of the "targeted" girl contacted police and filed charges against the note passers. On the other side of the country, in Half Moon Bay, California (near San Francisco), a 14-year-old eighth grader was suspended for writing two compositions for English class in which he described violence used against the principal (*New York Times*, 1998a). This was the first student to be suspended under a 1998 California law for threatening violence against students, teachers, or administrators. One of his papers, titled "The Riot," described a student rebellion in which the library was burned, the science labs were blown up, and the principal was severely beaten. His parents filed a lawsuit protesting his suspension.

This small sampling of stories about the aftermath of school-related shootings fits the public view ("frame") that crimes committed by juveniles (especially violent crimes) are escalating, thus supporting the corollary that youths are out of control. The school shooting "crime wave" might be traced to February 19, 1997, in Bethel, Alaska, when a 16-year-old youth killed the school principal and another student (King & Murr, 1998:33). The subsequent incidents came to be viewed as evidence that the United States was experiencing an "epidemic" of school shootings. Each new case of

Fellow students hug at a memorial service for the victims of the Columbine High School shooting rampage in Littleton, Colorado. Media coverage of school shootings inundates the public with emotional images such as this, feeding the public view that juvenile crime is escalating, even as juvenile crime rates decline. *(AP Photo/Eric Gay)*

reported school violence easily fit the constructed crime frame (Sasson, 1995) and reinforced the media theme of youth violence. In his study of how citizens make sense of crime stories, Sasson observed that "whatever the cause of popular fear and concern over crime, the issue's significance for politics and public policy depends on how it is constructed or framed" (1995:3). The incidents and tragedies were real, and the coverage provided by the media accentuated: (1) the victims' grief, (2) the details and images of the crimes, and (3) the replay of the earlier stories. This type of media coverage "shapes perceptions and directs much public discourse on the crime issue" (Potter & Kappeler, 1998:7).

Essentially, school shootings became the "condensation symbol" used by the media (as well as the public and politicians) to further demonize youths and displace images of "juvenile delinquents" with stories of violent, dangerous "young criminals." Media reports "constructed" the crime wave (Fishman, 1978) and created the climate for a moral panic. Potter and Kappeler describe how incidents such as school shootings become moral panics and are "perceived as a threat to the stability and well-being of society" (1998:7):

> The media provide copious details and information (not necessarily accurate); this is followed by attention from law enforcement officials, politicians, and editorial writers who begin to comment on the panic. "Experts" then join the fray and try to explain the panic and offer policy options for dealing with it.

This type of media attention and official discourse distorts images of crime and generally results in reactive public policies that fail to address the underlying problems. For example, in 1997, while the headlines focused on the Pearl, Mississippi, and West Paducah, Kentucky, school shootings, a less-covered story was the release of a report on the general decline in school crimes (Lewin, 1997). The findings, from a study by the National School Safety Center, concluded that greater attention to school safety (e.g., metal detectors, locker searches, uniformed guards) was contributing to fewer incidents of crimes committed in schools. The decrease in reported school violence paralleled the national decline of all homicides committed by juveniles and especially those committed with firearms (Sickmund, Snyder & Poe-Yamagata, 1997:13).

Data from the FBI indicate that homicides by youths peaked in 1994 and have been declining ever since (Uniform Crime Reports, 2004). A 1998 report by the Justice Policy Institute also documented a 30 percent decrease in juvenile homicide arrests between 1994 and 1996 (Lewin, 1998). In fact, Males (1998) reported that while 20 to 30 youths a year are killed in schools by guns, 2,000 to 3,000 children and youth are murdered each year by parents or caretakers. However, the media stories of kids, guns, and schools create a different perception and contribute to the moral panic.

While the school shootings noted above were receiving media attention, school crime rates continued to decline into the early 2000s (DeVoe et al., 2004). From 1992 to 2002

> school crime dropped from 48 violent victimizations per 1,000 students to 24 per 1,000. Between 1995 and 2003, the percentage of students who reported being a victim of crime of violence or theft at school also declined—from 10 percent to 5 percent. In 2002, as in previous years, students from one to 18 years of age were more likely to be victims of nonfatal serious violent crime away from school than at school (U.S. Department of Justice, 2004:par. 1).

In their report, "Indicators of School Crime and Safety: 2004," DeVoe and colleagues found that in 2003, only 1 percent of students ages 12 to 18 "reported being victims of violent incidents" (2004:ix). In the

1999-2000 academic year, of 2,140 homicides of youths ages five to 19, only 16 occurred at school (p. 7). The peak number of school homicides (34) was recorded in the 1997-1998 academic year and, in 2000-2001, the number had dropped to 10 (DeVoe et al., 2004:7).

The significance of these figures in the larger context is that school shootings by youths are a relatively small problem in comparison to homicidal child abuse. The school shootings, however, "galvanized" public alarm and prompted experts and politicians to offer simple explanations and quick responses (Lewin, 1998). This crime-wave mentality focused on youths as killers, and the resulting panic further eroded support for the rationale of a separate juvenile court. The greater harm to children as victims was overshadowed by the few sensationalized crimes of children as offenders. It is not surprising, therefore, that in the context of the deterrence-punishment politics of public policy, the response to juveniles was to get even tougher.

Get Tougher

In his discussion of crime as a social problem, Sasson (1995) identified the "faulty system" as one of the frames of reference used to analyze and explain crime and to prescribe corresponding actions to curtail it. This is a "law and order" frame that perceives that "people do crimes because they know they can get away with them" and "the only way to enhance public safety is to increase the swiftness, certainty and severity of the punishment" (Sasson, 1995:14). This is the classical ideology of deterrence and punishment that is evident in the public discourse and political response to the "epidemic" of school shootings.

In the aftermath of the shooting in Edinboro, a Pennsylvania state representative introduced legislation "that would mandate trial as an adult for anyone 13 or older accused of violent acts on school property" (Neri, 1998:A1). The legislator, Victor Lescovitz, justified his proposal because of "concern that a juvenile convicted in juvenile court won't be behind bars long enough either for rehabilitation or for him or her to pay their debt to society" (Neri, 1998:A4). The language not only reflects the incapacitative, get-tough response to crime, but also dismisses the juvenile court as a viable system for achieving the retributive or rehabilitative social goals. The transformation of the juvenile court and its convergence with the criminal court are facilitated by the moral panic and legislative response to school violence.

As discussed earlier, Feld (1993) reviewed these phenomena and suggested that the concepts of childhood and adolescence are being questioned as the rationale for separate courts dissipates. Applebome's essay on the changing image of children in contemporary society recognizes that distinctions between childhood and adulthood are blurring (1998). Because "childhood is as much a cultural construction as a biological one," the innocence attributed to children 100 years ago at the founding of the juvenile court is being reexamined and rejected as states respond to school shootings by "dismantling juvenile justice systems at a furious clip" (Applebome, 1998:WK1). This reaction is: (1) encouraged by celebrated cases, (2) guided by classical ideology, and (3) promoted by politicians who would deconstruct adolescence by lowering the age and expanding the scope of criminal jurisdiction for youths. By proposing that 11-year-olds should be eligible for the death penalty, one Texas legislator epitomized the quick-fix, get-tough mentality that has "endangered (the) notion of childhood" (Applebome, 1998:WK4). This selection of age 11 appears to be a knee-jerk reaction to the fact that an 11-year-old was involved in the school shootings in Jonesboro, Arkansas, in March 1998.

In a similar and broader response to the few "violent and repeat juvenile offenders," the Senate proposed to reform juvenile law in order to enable federal courts to sentence juveniles as adults (Senate Bill 10, 1997). Concluding that "violent crime by juveniles constitutes a growing threat to the national welfare that requires an immediate and comprehensive governmental response," the Violent and Repeat Juvenile Offender Act of 1997 would have lowered to 14 the age at which juveniles could be tried as adults and be subject to the "same procedures and penalties as adults," including "being sentenced to death" (Senate Bill 10, 1997:Sec. 5032). The legislation would have permitted incarcerating youths with adults and would essentially have been "an abandonment of the basic premise of the county's juvenile justice system" (American Civil Liberties Union, 1998:1).

In the 106th Congress, both the Senate and the House of Representatives introduced juvenile offender legislation. Senate Bill 254, the Violent and Repeat Juvenile Offender Accountability and Rehabilitation Act of 1999, resembles its predecessor, Senate Bill 10. The 1999 version would also allow juveniles 14 or older to be handled by the adult criminal court and sentenced as adults, but it prohibits the execution of youths under the age of 18 (Senate Bill 254, 1999).

We feel that eliminating the juvenile court is not a realistic solution to juvenile crime. As noted earlier, almost all states have had mechanisms to transfer dangerous and violent adolescents to criminal court (Merlo, Benekos & Cook, 1997). This recent rush to mandate lower ages, draft tougher sentences, and demonize youths appears to be a reaction to (1) media coverage of celebrated cases, (2) punitive and retributive ideologies and goals of justice, and (3) the politicization of juvenile justice. As Wilson acknowledges, "Politically, Washington must pretend it can do a lot about crime. Practically, it can do very little" (1997:1).

WHAT CAN BE DONE?

As noted, the 1997–1999 school shootings were extreme tragedies that captured media, public, and political attention, but these incidents do not represent or reflect the crimes committed by the majority of juveniles. Legislating jurisdictional changes for juveniles would not likely prevent young, rural, white adolescent males from copying sensational school violence committed by other adolescents (Lewin, 1998). There are many variables that contribute to these crimes, but tougher punishments for younger kids will not curtail accessibility to guns, diminish learned aggression, promote social and emotional development, improve communication skills, enhance parenting abilities, or deter the stresses of adolescent development. In testimony submitted to the Maine legislature, Sally Sutton, Executive Director of the Maine Civil Liberties Union, said: "Unfortunately, it seems that the politicization of the juvenile crime issue has become the greatest impediment to finding a comprehensive solution to the problem itself. Tragically, our public policy is being driven by rhetoric, not rationality" (1997:1). From another ideological perspective, even Bill Powers of the National Rifle Association recognizes that "the problem of troubled youth and violence is a problem that's not addressed by the quick, easy legislative answer" (*Erie Daily Times*, 1998:A7). According to one former director of a Children and Youth Services Agency, a starting point is to recognize that "the vast majority of our children are overwhelmingly sensitive, intelligent, hardworking individuals and that needs to be front and center all the time. High emotion in the absence of careful analysis cannot be the basis for sound social policy" (Gardner, 1998:A8).

From media headlines, it appears that the politics of punishment and the popularity of incapacitation preclude "intelligent debate" on what to do about juvenile crime (Mattingly, 1998a:5). There are, however, several encouraging initiatives and interventions occurring throughout the United States that offer more than get-tough legislation for confronting delinquents and youthful criminals. The next section reviews some strategies, programs, and system reforms that contradict the pessimism that is reflected in punitive legislation such as the Violent and Repeat Juvenile Offender Act of 1997, which would have in part lowered the age for juveniles to be treated like adults (Mattingly, 1998b:7).

Strategies

Risk Factors. While the classic knee-jerk answer to the question of crime is to increase punishment as a deterrent, the positivist approach begins with an effort to examine and understand what contributes to criminality. Generally referred to as the "causes" of crime or, as Wilson prefers to call them, the "precursors" (1998:7), factors have been identified that put youths at risk for criminal behavior. For example, insightful research directed by Loeber and Farrington (1998) focused on serious and violent juvenile (SVJ) offenders. It documented both risk and protective factors in the careers of these offenders. The findings of a "distinguished panel of researchers" have been acclaimed as "hopeful and compelling" in recognizing how SVJ offenders differ from non-SVJ offenders (Bilchik, 1998a). While SVJ offenders represent a small group, they commit a disproportionate amount of crime and have contributed to the moral panic over juvenile delinquency.

The SVJ model indicates that there are three developmental pathways to serious and violent juvenile offending: (1) the authority conflict pathway that progresses to disobedience and antiauthority behaviors; (2) the overt pathway that begins with minor aggressions and escalates to serious and dangerous violence; and (3) the covert pathway that culminates in moderate and less serious criminality. The findings also reveal predictor variables for SVJ offending (Bilchik, 1998a:3):

1. Persistent precocious behavior problems during the elementary school-age years (e.g., sexual behavior and experimentation with illegal substances).

2. For children between the ages of 6 and 11, nonserious delinquent acts, aggression, substance use, low family socioeconomic status, and antisocial parents.

3. For youth between the ages of 12 and 14, weak social ties, antisocial peers, nonserious delinquent behavior, poor school attitude and performance, and psychological conditions such as impulsivity.

4. For adolescents, joining delinquent gangs. Rates of SVJ offending increase after joining a gang and decrease after leaving a gang. Drug dealing.

The Loeber–Farrington model summarized by Bilchik is a research-based, epidemiological initiative to identify factors that place youths at risk for—or protect them from—delinquent careers. This strategy recognizes (1) early childhood experiences, (2) gang involvement, and (3) drug dealing as salient predictors of serious offending. In his discussion of what drives serious juvenile crime, Shepherd (1997) also included the availability of handguns as an important factor. In the context of these efforts to examine the antecedents of serious offending, Kennedy (1997) described how "guns and gangs" escalated youth violence in Boston. Similarly, Arnette and Walsleben (1998) focused on "school environments" and how they contributed to truancy and delinquency.

These findings and reports are supported by the Office of Juvenile Justice and Delinquency Prevention and the Office of Justice Programs. They are part of the general strategy to understand the risk factors of delinquency, especially serious juvenile offending. A second strategy is to focus on minimizing their effects and preventing delinquent careers.

Prevention. One of Loeber and Farrington's (1998) conclusions was that risk for serious offending is not monocausal and, therefore, primary prevention requires multiple efforts. In response, Bilchik concluded that "priority should be given to preventive actions that reduce risk factors in multiple domains" (1998a:3). This is illustrated in Box 5.3 and indicates that both microsocial and macrosocial goals are necessary for approaching this integrative preventive strategy.

Box 5.3
Effective Early Intervention Programs to Mediate Risk Factors Known to Predict Serious and Violent Juvenile Offending

Involving parents:
- Parent management training
- Functional family therapy
- Family preservation

Involving children:
- Home visitation of pregnant teenagers
- Social competence training
- Peer mediation and conflict resolution
- Medication for neurological disorders and mental illness

Involving schools:
- Early intellectual enrichment (preschools)
- School organization interventions

Involving the community:
- Comprehensive community mobilization
- Situational crime prevention
- Intensive police patrolling, especially crime "hot spots"
- Legal and policy changes restricting availability and use of guns, drugs, and alcohol
- Mandatory laws for crimes involving firearms

Source: Shay Bilchik (May 1998). "Serious and Violent Juvenile Offenders." *Juvenile Justice Bulletin.* Washington, DC: Office of Juvenile Justice and Delinquency Prevention, p. 5.

Drugs. Prevention strategies are designed to target specific risk factors. For example, the drug–crime problem generates its own agenda to control availability of illicit drugs (supply) and to reduce drug use (demand). Recognizing the consequences of drugs on youths and delinquency, the Office of National Drug Control Policy (ONDCP) identified prevention of youth drug use as the primary goal of its 10-year drug control strategy (McCaffrey, 1998a). This Comprehensive Youth-Oriented Prevention Strategy included an anti-drug media campaign and school drug prevention programs with emphasis on: preventing tobacco use among youths, working with the child welfare system, expanding partnerships with health care professionals, and expanding community anti-drug coalitions. Of the five drug-control goals designated by the ONDCP, Goal 1, the youth prevention strategy, represented the largest budget percentage increase requested in fiscal year 1999: a 15 percent increase from $1.76 million in fiscal year 1998 to $2.02 million in fiscal year 1999 (McCaffrey, 1998b).

In 2005, the ONDCP continued to stress prevention by focusing on programs that involved parents and media campaigns (National Drug Control Strategy, 2005a). The three national priorities were: stopping drug use, healing drug users, and disrupting the drug markets. The ONDCP reported that prevention messages were being received by the target population (youths ages 12-17) and that "those who had been exposed to such messages are significantly less likely to abuse drugs" ("New Report Shows That Teens Who Receive Anti-Drug Messages Are Less Likely to Use Drugs," 2005:par. 1). John Walters, Director of the ONDCP, also reported a 17 percent decrease in drug use by youths since 2001 ("New Ads Help Parents Address Teen Drug Use," 2005).

In fiscal year 2006, however, the drug control budget for the National Youth Anti-Drug Media Campaign was reduced to $120 million (National Drug Control Strategy, 2005b). [This line item was reduced from $180 million in 2003, to $170 million in 2004, to $145 million in 2005 (National Drug Control Strategy, 2004, 2005b)]. Nonetheless, the 2006 Report noted that other "demand reduction programs," such as those supported by the Departments of Education and Health and Human Services, would receive "funding to support important prevention efforts" (National Drug Control Strategy, 2005a:par. 1).

In addition to funding prevention strategies, in 1998, former Drug Czar Barry McCaffrey also questioned the drug war metaphor and the use of language that distorts the understanding of the drug problem and exacerbates the politicization of drug policy. This contrasts significantly with the call for more use of military technology, reconnaissance, and the use of the National Guard to combat drugs, as was proposed by former Senator Bob Dole, the Republican presidential candidate in 1996 (Seelye, 1996). Dole used a familiar "war cry" when he urged that more military power was needed to win the war on drugs.

As a strategic plan, however, the ONDCP drug prevention policy is only a statement that formulates goals and objectives and reflects understanding of the drug–crime patterns. It orients policy and, in this case, recognizes the importance of committing resources for prevention—not for combat.

Guns. Guns, like drugs, are also criminogenic elements. Efforts to prevent and reduce gun violence by youths, therefore, also incorporate supply and demand reduction strategies. A Boston project supported by the National Institute of Justice adopted such an approach to disrupt the illegal gun market and target high-incident neighborhoods in which gang turf activity and violence prevailed (Kennedy, 1997). The strategy involved the cooperation of the police, probation officers, and street workers to reduce serious youth violence. In Los Angeles, Operation Ceasefire also relied on a collaborative strategy in targeting gun violence (Tita, Riley, Ridgeway & Greenwood, 2005).

Some states have responded to juvenile gun violence by enacting and strengthening legislation that restricts youths' access to firearms (National Criminal Justice Association, 1997). In 1995, 13 states had legislation holding parents accountable for family firearms, and a number of states had established "gun-free schools" and "safety zones" (National Criminal Justice Association, 1997:34). A significant element of these strategies is to prevent juvenile gun violence by controlling availability and access to firearms. The school-related shootings in 1997–1999 focused new attention on these strategies.

Schools. Another prevention strategy is keeping kids in school. School dropout rates are related to delinquency as well as to teen pregnancy, gang involvement, unemployment and underemployment, and low income (Cantelon & LeBoeuf, 1997). As a delinquency prevention strategy, keeping young people in school requires: (1) making schools safe and (2) designing programs that target at-risk youths and their families. As Cantelon and LeBoeuf (1997) reported, this necessitates:

> bringing together in one place a support system of caring adults who ensure that the student has access to the resources that can help him or her build self-worth and the skills needed to embark on a more productive and constructive life (p. 27).

This approach is known as Communities in Schools (CIS), and it represents a holistic model and a collaboration-driven partnership that uses the school environment to assess and meet specific needs (educational, health, recreational, employment, legal) of the at-risk youths. The process is designed to facilitate service delivery in order to prevent and reduce dropout.

Another salient school safety concern is bullying. While this type of victimization "has not been recognized as a serious problem in the United States until fairly recently" (Lawrence, 2004:97), it is now viewed as widespread, underreported, and harmful to students, teachers, and the school learning environment (Sampson, 2002:1). Several effective (and some noneffective) strategies to counter bullying have been identified. Based on the "whole-school" approach developed by Olweus in Scandinavia, Sampson has identified specific responses that reduce bullying (2002:20-23). (See Box 5.4.)

Box 5.4
Strategies for Reducing Bullying.

- Increasing student reporting of bullying.
- Developing activities in less-supervised areas.
- Reducing the amount of time students can spend less supervised.
- Staggering recess, lunch, and/or class-release times.
- Monitoring areas where bullying can be expected (e.g., bathrooms).
- Assigning bullies to a particular location or to particular chores during release times.
- Posting classroom signs prohibiting bullying and listing the consequences for it.
- Providing teachers with effective classroom management training.
- Having high-level school administrators inform late-enrolling students about the school's bullying policy.

Source: Rana Sampson (March 2002). *Bullying in Schools.* Washington, DC: U.S. Department of Justice, Office of Community Oriented Policing Services, pp. 20-23.

Sampson points out that "zero tolerance" policies do not solve bullying problems and may discourage reporting and exacerbate the problem of bullying (2002:24). Based on his research, Lawrence also underscores the importance of increasing the awareness of bullying among students, teachers, and parents, and recognizing its effects for both victims and bullies (2004:98).

Because schools provide opportunities to reach youths with delinquency prevention initiatives, an important partnership among the Office of Juvenile Justice and Delinquency Prevention and the U.S. Departments of Education, and Health and Human Services has resulted in the Safe Schools/Healthy Students Initiative (Caliber Associates, 2000). These agencies work to link schools and communities in providing community-wide prevention and child development services that emphasize social skills, prosocial behaviors, and drug prevention.

Intervention. A third strategy for reducing youth crime is secondary prevention, that is, programs directed toward youths who have already become involved in delinquent behaviors. Even in the case of serious and violent juvenile offenders, some interventions have proved to be effective (see Table 5.3). The risk of recidivism is a salient concern, but appropriate programs that incorporate multimodal interventions and aftercare can increase positive outcomes (Bilchik, 1998a:6).

Table 5.3
Effectiveness of Interventions for Serious and Violent Juvenile Offenders

Treatment Type: Noninstitutionalized Offenders	Treatment Type: Institutionalized Offenders
Positive effects, consistent evidence	
Individual counseling Interpersonal skills Behavioral contracting	Interpersonal skills Teaching family home
Positive effects, less consistent evidence	
Multiple services Restitution, probation/parole	Cognitive-behavioral treatment Community residential programs Multiple services
Mixed but generally positive effects, inconsistent evidence	
Employment-related programs Academic programs Advocacy/casework Family counseling Group counseling	Individual counseling Guided group Group counseling
Weak or no effects, inconsistent evidence	
Reduced caseload, probation/parole	Employment-related programs Drug abstinence Wilderness/challenge
Weak or no effects, consistent evidence	
Wilderness/challenge Early release, probation/parole Deterrence programs Vocational programs	Milieu therapy

Note: Interventions were conducted primarily as single-component rather than multimodal programs. Results from multiple-services programs suggest that some of the interventions that showed less than consistent positive effects individually may have more significant effects when combined.

Source: Shay Bilchik (May 1998). "Serious and Violent Juvenile Offenders." *Juvenile Justice Bulletin*. Washington, DC: Office of Juvenile Justice and Delinquency Prevention.

Similarly, the National Institute of Justice sponsored a report titled "Preventing Crime: What Works, What Doesn't, What's Promising" (Sherman et al., 1997), which examined the outcomes of various initiatives, including prevention and intervention programs. The report noted that in spite of cynicism about rehabilitation, which has contributed to increased transfers of juveniles to adult court, there is evidence that some programs are effective with some offenders. Based on a meta-analysis, the authors concluded that while there are no panaceas or silver bullets, there are programs successful in reducing recidivism (pp. 9-16):

> First, treatment must directly address characteristics that can be changed (dynamic) and that are directly associated with an individual's criminal behavior (criminogenic factors). . . . The final principle of effective treatment is the need to deliver treatment in a style and mode that addresses the learning styles and abilities of offenders.

As a result of the encouraging findings, the report endorses intervention strategies as worthy of continued support, funding, and continuous evaluation.

The National Criminal Justice Association also identified promising juvenile justice initiatives and concluded that some programs "not only have a positive impact on troubled youth, but are a good investment when compared with the costs associated with the behavior of serious, violent, and chronic juvenile offenders" (1997:10-11).

Balance and Collaboration. A final approach to delinquency recognizes the importance of developing integrated initiatives. For example, the National Criminal Justice Association identified two important themes in recent state reforms and program developments: (1) the promotion of "community-based, public/private sector responses" and (2) the utilization of "school-based programs and activities" (1997:12). The findings reported by Loeber and Farrington (1998) also stress the importance of involving schools and the community, and of developing "partnerships" among juvenile justice, public-health, welfare, law enforcement, and children's services to enhance the accountability and effectiveness of programs. The Communities in Schools (CIS) model reflects this strategy and is an example of how local communities work with schools to "build a self-sustaining structure to provide . . . basics for their youth" (Cantelon & LeBoeuf, 1997:3).

The "SafeFutures" strategy also demonstrates these elements and relies on collaboration to design and develop delinquency reduction interventions (SafeFutures, 1998):

- Reducing risk factors and increasing protective factors for delinquency.

- Providing a continuum of services for juveniles at risk for delinquency with appropriate immediate interventions.

- Developing a full range of graduated sanctions designed to hold delinquent youths accountable to the victim and the community, to ensure community safety, and to provide appropriate treatment and rehabilitation services.

The strategy emphasizes a "continuum of care in the communities" (SafeFutures, 1998) and incorporates the components of the Balanced and Restorative Justice Model of juvenile justice (BARJ). BARJ (Bazemore & Umbreit, 1994) focuses on three objectives for responding to delinquent youths: (1) holding them accountable for their behavior, (2) ensuring community safety, and (3) providing opportunities for effective program interventions (see Box 5.5). The restorative justice dimension is emphasized by holding youths accountable with victim mediation, community service, and restitution. This model requires that juvenile courts have a "meaningful range of graduated sanctions . . . that hold (youth) immediately and appropriately accountable . . . without needlessly drawing them too deeply into the juvenile justice system" (Shepherd, 1997:12).

BARJ's balanced approach is not only concerned with the best interests of youths but also the protection and interests of the community. As a strategy, this model provides the juvenile court with a broader mission that requires more community involvement and agency partnerships. It also offers a viable alternative to abandoning the juvenile court. As an example, a 1998 statement of recommendations and a newly articulated mission for the juvenile justice system in Pennsylvania were developed by the Juvenile Advisory Committee of the Pennsylvania Commission on Crime and Delinquency. They incorporated three elements of balance and collaboration (Sharp, 1998): (1) community protection, (2) victim restoration, and (3) youth redemption.

The four main strategies—(1) research to demonstrate risk and protective factors, (2) research-based prevention initiatives, (3) intervention programs based on what works, and (4) collaborations and partnerships that require the community to work with various child care and juvenile justice systems to develop a continuum of accountability—reflect objectives and trends for the twenty-first century. These strategies focus on attacking the problem of juvenile crime rather than reacting to youthful offenders. Doing something proactive is a refreshing challenge to the "nothing works" mantra of the 1970s and 1980s. The research literature provides evidence of the effectiveness of these strategies and reports on initiatives that incorporate elements of these strategies in the design of meaningful programs that work. A few of these programs are presented in the next section.

Box 5.5

The Participants in a Balanced and Restorative Juvenile Justice System

Crime Victims	Offenders	Citizens, Families, and Community Groups
◆ Receive support, assistance, compensation, information, and services.	◆ Complete restitution to their victims.	◆ Are involved to the greatest extent possible in rehabilitation, community safety initiatives, and holding offenders accountable.
◆ Receive restitution or other reparation from the offender.	◆ Provide meaningful service to repay the debt to their communities.	
◆ Are involved and are encouraged to give input at all points in the system as to how the offender will repair the harm done.	◆ Face the personal harm caused by their crimes by participating in victim offender mediation or other victim awareness programs.	◆ Work with offenders on local community service projects.
		◆ Provide support to victims.
◆ Have the opportunity to face the offenders and tell their story.	◆ Complete work experience and active and productive tasks that increase skills and improve the community.	◆ Provide support to offenders as mentors, employers, and advocates.
◆ Feel satisfied with the justice process.		◆ Provide work for offenders to pay restitution to victims and service opportunities that allow offenders to make meaningful contributions to the quality of community life.
◆ Provide guidance and consultation to juvenile justice professionals on planning and advisory groups.	◆ Are monitored by community adults as well as juvenile justice providers and supervised to the greatest extent possible in the community.	
	◆ Improve decisionmaking skills and have opportunities to help others.	◆ Assist families to support the offender in obligation to repair the harm and increase competencies.
		◆ Advise courts and corrections and play an active role in disposition.

Source: Gordon Bazemore and Susan E. Day (1996). "Restoring the Balance: Juvenile and Community Justice." *Juvenile Justice* 3(1):9.

Programs

In 1998, the Annual Training Conference for the Pennsylvania Juvenile Court Judges' Commission (JCJC) responded to the demand for information and training on "effective violence and delinquency prevention programs" by presenting "Programs That Work" (Pennsylvania Juvenile Court Judges' Commission, 1998:1). The training featured 10 "blueprint" programs that have been recognized as research-based and effective in "reducing the onset, prevalence, or offending rates of violent behavior," and have demonstrated at least a one-year post-treatment deterrent effect (Pennsylvania Juvenile Court Judges' Commission, 1998:1). At the Judges' Commission Annual Training in 2005, the Conference featured presentations by David Olds and Clay Yeager on the nurse–family partnership and its success in preventing violence (Pennsylvania Juvenile Court Judges' Commission, 2005).

The programs encompass approaches from pregnancy prevention to violence reduction and are focused on factors such as cognitive restructuring, behavioral-interpersonal skill development, school adjustment, substance abuse, and serious and chronic offending. Several of them are school-based, involving community collaborations and incorporating multimodal interventions based on reducing risk factors and promoting protective factors (Center for the Study and Prevention of Violence, 2002-2004).

The "nothing works" perspective on intervention strategies and programs that characterized the 1970s and 1980s has been replaced by an evidence-based approach (Walker, 2006). In addition to the Blueprints for Violence Prevention noted above (see http://www.colorado.edu/cspv), the Office of Juvenile Justice and Delinquency Prevention maintains the Model Programs Guide (MPG) (see http://www.ojjdp.ncjrs.org). This is a searchable database that profiles more than 250 evidence-based programs organized into five categories: (1) prevention, (2) immediate sanction, (3) intermediate sanction, (4) residential care, and (5) reentry.

Based on evaluation criteria, programs are rated exemplary, effective, or promising, and "users identify programs that match their community's target population characteristics and priority risk and protective factors" (OJJDP News @ a Glance, 2005:par. 11). The Guide permits easy access to identifying programs that are specific to offenders, problems, and communities; program profiles include contact information, references, and evaluation information about the programs (OJJDP News @ a Glance, 2005). (The MPG can be accessed at http://www.dsgonline.com/mpg2.5/mpg_index.htm)

Schools. In the aftermath of the school-related shootings of the late 1990s (and with exaggerated media attention on school violence), school-based interventions to promote safety have received renewed interest. Although one legislator proposed that teachers should begin carrying guns (Rosenberg, 1998), several more rational and less political responses have focused on reducing fear and restoring safety (Arnette & Walsleben, 1998). Programs that promote positive social skills and peer-mediated activities are directed at five behaviors or factors that contribute to school-related crime and violence (Arnette & Walsleben, 1998): (1) bullying, (2) gangs, (3) weapons, (4) substance abuse, and (4) community violence.

One study, for example, found that 64 percent of school-associated violent deaths in 1992–1994 were related to either "interpersonal dispute" or "gang-related activities," while just 11 percent were attributed to "disputes over romantic relationship" and 6 percent to "drug-related activities" (Kachur et al., 1996). Based on these data, programs that target conflict resolution and gang resistance could have significant impact on school violence. In this effort, students in Boston who

to school are required to attend a conflict resolution and
~~g program offered by the Counseling and Intervention
...erg, 1998). The Center reports a 9 percent recidivism
rate for an intervention program that offers an alternative to sus-
pending students and sending them home. Similarly, the Safe Alternative
and Violence Education (SAVE) Program in San Jose, California, provides a skills course taught by police for students who are caught
carrying weapons (Rosenberg, 1998).

In addition, the U.S. Department of Justice is continuing to fund
School Resource Officers (SROs) for law enforcement agencies to
assign officers to work in schools ("COPS Office Announces $5.4
Million in Grants to Hire New Law Enforcement Officers in America's
Schools," 2005). With the 2005 grant of $5.4 million, the Office of
Community Oriented Policing Services In Schools Program "has pro-
vided more than $753 million to fund and train over 6,600 SROs"
(COPS, 2005:par. 5).

Gangs. Efforts to combat gang-related violence include (National
Criminal Justice Association, 1997:23):

- Preventing youths from joining gangs.
- Transforming existing gangs into neighborhood clubs.
- Mediating and intervening in conflicts between gangs.

While various programs have been developed to meet all three objectives, the prevention approach generates better results (Howell, 1995). As
an example, the popular Gang Resistance Education and Training (GREAT)
program uses school-based curricula and after-school activities to reduce
youth violence and dissuade gang membership (Arnette & Walsleben,
1998). Law enforcement officers are trained and certified to deliver the
GREAT program in more than 1,300 communities. Preliminary results of
short-term effects are encouraging and indicate that program participants demonstrate more prosocial attitudes and behaviors, including less
impulsivity and less delinquency (Arnette & Walsleben, 1998:6).

As an outcome of teaching resistance and conflict resolution skills
to students, those who complete GREAT have exhibited reduced gang
affiliation and more negative attitudes about gangs. In addition, they
develop higher self-esteem and have more friends who are involved in
prosocial activities. These findings indicate that GREAT is achieving its
goals (*Juvenile Justice Update*, 1998:11). Another popular program
that targets drugs, however, does not appear to be successful in meeting
its goals. Results indicate that the popular DARE (Drug Abuse Resistance
Education) program does not reduce drug use (*Juvenile Justice Update*,
1998). The findings are not conclusive, but they raise doubts about the
effectiveness of the program and require additional evaluation.

A more collaborative community-based program sponsored by the Boys and Girls Clubs of America is also demonstrating a positive initial impact. Gang Prevention Through Targeted Outreach connects local clubs with courts, police departments, schools, and social service agencies to enhance interpersonal skills, school performance, and community involvement (Arnette & Walsleben, 1998:7). The outreach program involves the participants in prosocial activities with positive adult and peer role models in an effort to bond the students with these models and to provide them with alternatives to gangs.

Arnold Schwarzenegger, as chair of the Inner-City Games Foundation, talks with middle-school students during an appearance to promote the Greater Houston Inner-City Games. The Foundation provides opportunities for inner-city youths to participate in sports and educational, cultural, and community enrichment programs and encourages them to stay off drugs and out of gangs. *(AP Photo/Planet Hollywood, Brett Coomer)*

Guns. Programs for reducing gang-related crime and violence also require efforts to reduce availability and use of guns. The Boston Gun Project delivered a zero-tolerance message and joined the forces of police, probation, and parole officers as well as street workers in an effort to stop the gun violence (Braga, Kennedy, Piehl & Waring, 2001; Kennedy, 1997). This collaborative project targeted gangs and "hot spots." It demonstrated its serious intentions by arresting one gang member for possession of a single bullet. Coupled with the offender's 15-year history of felonies, his arrest resulted in a lengthy prison sentence of nearly 20 years (Kennedy, 1997:2). The Boston program was so effective that between July 10, 1995, and December 11, 1997 (a period of 29 months), not one youth was killed with a gun (*Criminal Justice Newsletter*, 1997:5). In addition to zero-tolerance and "fast-track" sanctions, the partnership among police, school officials, churches, probation officers, courts, and community groups worked to offer at-risk youths various programs to reduce school dropout levels, provide after-school job counseling, and encourage nonviolent dispute resolution (*Criminal Justice Newsletter*, 1997). The success of this project encouraged other cities to model such cooperative efforts to reduce youth violence (*Law Enforcement News*, 1997).

One element of success has been the installation of police-probation officer patrols that have a "preventive effect on gang and youth violence" (*Law Enforcement News*, 1997:6). These patrols appear to enhance the authority and consequences of probation and to provide incentive for youths on probation to participate in the services and programs available to them. Presenting the "clenched fist" as well as the "outstretched hand," the program reflects a balanced approach to working with youths while emphasizing prevention (Harden, 1997). This collaborative, problem-oriented response to the problem of kids and guns can be contrasted with the legislation, signed in August 1998 by New York governor George E. Pataki, that mandates that students as young as 14 who carry loaded guns to school can be prosecuted as adults (*New York Times*, 1998b). This response increases the penalty from 18 months of juvenile incarceration to a maximum of four years of prison for carrying a loaded gun and up to seven years if there was "intent" to use the firearm on school grounds. This is another example of legislation that fails to consider why kids carry guns, what will happen to youths while they are incarcerated, how much it will cost for confinement, or what the future prospects are for youths when they are released from prison.

Community Mobilization. One of the characteristics of successful programs is the existence of partnerships and community-based collaborations that are forged to implement comprehensive interventions. For example, the experience in Allegheny County, Pennsylvania, "exemplifies a large-scale, comprehensive, and proactive effort to mobilize the community to achieve a collaborative and coordinated antiviolence approach" (Hsia, 1997:1). In this community, concerns with juvenile crime (especially violent crime) motivated leaders from law enforcement, public and private agencies, and citizens' groups to coordinate their efforts on youth crime prevention. The community leaders convened a retreat to assess the fragmented response to youth crime and to develop a plan for unifying and coordinating initiatives.

As a result, the Youth Crime Prevention Council was established in 1994. The Council included significant memberships from Law Enforcement Agency Directors (LEADs) who recognized that youth violence was "not just a law enforcement issue but a societal one which required communitywide prevention efforts" (Hsia, 1997:2). The council assessed the community needs, developed priorities, implemented plans, and maintained leadership and coordination of the community efforts. Several activities were initiated or increased, including: (1) after-school safe places, (2) family support centers, (3) mentoring, (4) health/wellness, and (5) community-oriented policing. In addition, massive community education was conducted to "present a realistic picture of youth crime in the county" and to mobilize and involve the community in the various crime prevention collaborations (Hsia, 1997:4).

In the first year of its efforts (1994-1995), Al
rienced a "13 percent decline in the overall
arrested and a 30 percent decline in the numbe
for violent crime" (Hsia, 1997:10). These dec
state-wide arrests declined only 2 percent and !
This preliminary information provides "enc(
cess" that demonstrate the positive outcomes that can bc .cu..
with this type of comprehensive, collaborative project (Hsia, 1997:10).
The experience reflects effective public policy and underscores the following five principles:

- Perseverance in bringing together a large number of community leaders.

- Sensitivity to the turfs, tensions, and conflicts among
  policymakers, agencies, and citizen groups.

- Access to information and technical assistance from
  experts and academic/research institutions.

- Funding support from federal, state, local, and private
  sources.

- Commitment to sustaining and building on successes.

Data from 1995 to 1996 reveal a continued decrease in the number of
juveniles arrested for murder and manslaughter: 27 percent in Allegheny
County compared to 10 percent state-wide. However, during the second year, Allegheny County reported a 10 percent increase in the
total number of juveniles arrested for violent crime, while the state experienced less than a 1 percent increase (Pennsylvania State Police,
1997). For Allegheny County, this increase was due primarily to a 35
percent increase in the number of juveniles arrested for rape in
Allegheny County (1995 to 1996). Researchers are continuing to
monitor arrests and to evaluate the impact of the collaboration on delinquency and youth crime in Allegheny County.

Alternatives to Placement

GROW. Successful collaboration has also been demonstrated with
programs that focus on secondary prevention (that is, treatment) of
juvenile offenders. As an effort to reduce the costs of placement by
implementing an effective community-based alternative, Santa Cruz
County, California, developed the Graduated Return to Opportunities
Within Families and Community (GROW) to keep "seriously at-risk
juveniles" at home or, if placed, to return them home more quickly than
in the past (Rubin, 1998:12). GROW is a co-directed, partnered pro-

m between probation and mental health agencies that offers intense and integrated services to conduct-disordered juveniles. GROW emphasizes human services contacts with numerous interactions and interventions, including drug treatment, behavioral-cognitive counseling, community service projects, competency building, vocational internships, and family involvement and parental training (Rubin, 1998). Probation officers enforce the conditions of community placement, while mental health staff members provide a variety of treatments.

Focusing on institutional alternatives and shortened institutional stays, GROW appears to be successful due to the "integration of interagency services" (Rubin, 1998:13). This "system of care" model redirects efforts and resources toward developing individualized treatment plans that "strengthen protective factors and seek to avoid risk factors" (p. 12). Between 1989 and 1997, not only was the average number of out-of-home placements reduced from 104 to 67 per year, but Santa Cruz County saved nearly $11 million in eight years (Rubin, 1998:2).

CICTP. A similar program in Erie County, Pennsylvania, has also experienced some success in reducing the number of youths in placement as well as the related costs of treatment programming (Garase, 1998). The Collaborative Intensive Community Treatment Program (CICTP) provides an integration of interventions from social service agencies, probation, and schools, and includes individual and group counseling, a family training component, cultural sensitivity and victim awareness, anger management, prosocial skill development, moral reasoning, psychological-education groups (regarding alcohol and other drugs), and recreational therapy. This community-based initiative accepts adjudicated, placement-bound youths and coordinates a continuum of services that both control the youths and provide multimodal programs.

After one year of operation (1996–1997), 71 youths were programmed into CICTP; 48 (68%) successfully completed all phases of treatment, and 23 (32 percent) were terminated prior to completion. A comparison of 35 CICTP graduates with 39 out-of-home-placement juveniles determined that for approximately one-half the cost, the CICTP youths had comparable readjudication rates and also demonstrated improvements in some of the targeted skills. While not "decidedly" better than placement, this program achieved comparable outcomes with less expense and developed a continuum of care that included a family component and integrated service delivery (Garase, 1998:105):

> Therefore, CICTP attained its stated goals of reducing the fiscal and administrative burden of residential placement and reducing the clinical and behavioral need for residential placement. With careful implementation, intensive supervision programs may become an expanded component of the dispositional continuum in juvenile justice.

Boot Camps. While the programs reviewed above are not widely known by the public or promoted by the media, they have achieved encouraging results. Boot camps, however, which have received public endorsement and media attention, have not been as impressive in accomplishing their stated goals (Bourque et al., 1996; MacKenzie, Gover, Armstrong & Mitchell, 2001).

The juvenile boot camp, which offers an alternative to traditional placement, is modeled after adult shock incarceration/boot camp programs. The appeal of photos of youths in uniforms performing drills and exercises has helped to popularize these programs, but the evaluations are less optimistic. While the programs do tend to promote positive attitudes and self-esteem in youths, attrition and recidivism suggest that the programs are not achieving their intended outcomes. One area of particular weakness is aftercare, the long-term reality of adjusting to the community, as opposed to the short-term, highly structured intervention of the boot camp.

Evaluating the boot camp program underscores the fact that being popular with the public and politicians does not necessarily make a program an effective intervention. Much like juvenile awareness programs or "Scared Straight" programs, these quick-fix interventions are not realistic responses to the factors that place (and keep) youths at risk for delinquent behavior (Finkenauer & Gavin, 1998). As Whitehead and Lab concluded, these types of programs "are appealing because they are cheap and based on traditional values" (1996:177). While they may have some relevant program components (for example, boot camps include substance abuse education, vocational training, and academic instruction), an emphasis on severity of punishment and reliance on the deterrence doctrine tend to misdirect good intentions.

Summary of Programs. This small sampling of secondary prevention and community treatment programs suggests the success that can be achieved when comprehensive, cooperative efforts are implemented. Many of the programs build on the effective strategies mentioned earlier. They focus on reducing risk factors and enhancing protective factors. The findings reported by Loeber and Farrington (1998) suggest that the integration of existing services and programs and the implementation of multimodal, comprehensive interventions are promising approaches. Although there is "no simple answer to the treatment and control of delinquents in the community" (Whitehead & Lab, 1996:338), some encouraging findings of "what works" are summarized in a National Criminal Justice Association report on core intervention initiatives (1997:79):

- Strengthening and preserving families.
- Taking steps to facilitate agency collaboration.

- Encouraging local responses and community-based solutions.

- Ensuring accountability and tough sanctions for those juveniles who do commit crimes of violence.

System Reform

Even as the various strategies and programs noted above are endorsed and implemented, it is evident that the larger questions concern the future of the juvenile justice system. The traditionalist or preservationists seek to maintain the juvenile court as a "non-criminal, quasi-civil court with exclusive jurisdiction over young offenders" (Butts & Harrell, 1998:2). However, in their discussion of juvenile justice policy options, Butts and Harrell conclude that the original mission of the juvenile court has been eroded and the politicization of crime has resulted in an emphasis on punishment and increased formality in juvenile court procedures (1998:13):

> Three decades of reform have largely dissolved the traditional juvenile court, and the system that remains is rapidly losing political viability. Policy makers may soon need to devise an entirely new process for handling young offenders.

Feld (1993), arguing that the convergence of the juvenile and criminal courts has all but dismantled the juvenile court, has proposed the abolition of the juvenile court. Other "abolitionists" have also recommended eliminating the concept of delinquency and sending all offenders to the same criminal courts (Butts & Harrell, 1998). State statutes, of course, do provide for the transfer of designated juveniles (i.e., serious, violent, repeat) to criminal court, and these laws are being used at an increasing pace, from nearly 7,000 in 1985 to 9,700 in 1995, a 33 percent increase (Stahl, 1998:2). However, Shepherd has argued that this "adultification" is misguided and represents another "attempt at a 'quick fix'" (1997:12):

> [I]t addresses the juvenile justice system's perceived inadequacies by ignoring the real problem and dealing with youth in another setting that is even more bankrupt.

Policy Options. Reflecting on the future of juvenile justice policy, Ohlin (1998) examined how severe criticisms of rehabilitation programs and a lack of confidence in the juvenile court have undermined juvenile justice. He also recognized the role of the media in accentuating violence and reinforcing exaggerated fears of victimization. In response, he proposed six broad policy issues, including the need for a more general youth policy that promotes the following strategies (1998:148-153): (1) to reduce the alienation of youths, (2) to enhance community resources for youth programs, (3) to encourage more state and local responsibility in coordinating these efforts, and (4) to develop school curricula that are relevant to youths and meet career-oriented needs.

In effect, Ohlin has suggested a youth-friendly perspective as opposed to the "demonization of youth" policies that reflect conservative-punitive ideologies as solutions to the problems of adolescence. He states that while most youths engage in some delinquent acts, most eventually desist, and only a very few are involved in chronic and/or serious crime. He believes that it is important not to develop policy for all delinquents based on the few who are used as examples to create moral panic and fuel the politicization of juvenile justice policy.

Shay Bilchik, former Administrator of the Office of Juvenile Justice and Delinquency Prevention (OJJDP), voiced support for the balanced approach as a model for juvenile justice in the twenty-first century (1998b:97):

> The only effective long-term response to the problem of juvenile delinquency and violence lies in improving the juvenile justice system and preventing delinquency before it occurs.

In 1998, the Discretionary Grant Program for OJJDP underscored this approach and encouraged system-level changes that included "collaborative involvement of public and private sectors" to deliver a wide continuum of services (Office of Juvenile Justice and Delinquency Prevention, 1998:55).

While these system reforms are difficult to achieve and even more difficult to sustain, they present encouraging initiatives that involve communities in confronting youth crime and in building partnerships. Such policies reinforce the juvenile justice system and maintain a commitment to positivist, developmental views of youth and delinquency. In the policy debate, however, Butts and Harrell observe that "those in favor of abolishing the concept of delinquency appear increasingly likely to prevail" (1998:9). As an alternative, they propose building "new courts" for youths.

Specialty Courts. As a compromise to both the preservationist and abolitionist perspectives on the juvenile court, the present system does offer some alternatives for determining what to do with juvenile offenders. As Figure 5.4 illustrates, youths who commit less serious crimes can still be handled in the juvenile court, where appropriate programs can be used for secondary prevention. For the few serious, violent youthful offenders, transfer to criminal court is the increasingly popular practice. While this may present an acceptable compromise, Butts and Harrell note that simply shifting youths into the adult system will not

Figure 5.4
Specialty Courts

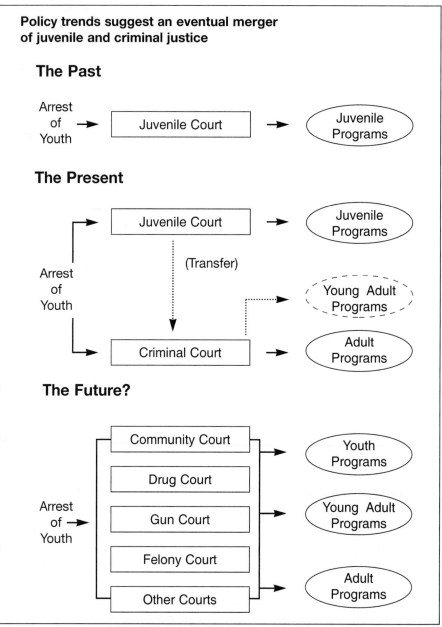

Source: Jeffrey A. Butts and Adele V. Harrell (1998). *Delinquents or Criminals: Policy Options for Young Offenders.* Washington, DC: The Urban Institute, p. 9. Reprinted with permission of The Urban Institute.

correct the problems of overcrowded court dockets, large supervision caseloads, and poorly monitored programs (1998:8). They propose that the system expand on its development of innovative court models that offer speciality services that can diversify the juvenile justice system (p. 9):

> In recent years, while the juvenile court has been adopting the
> criminal court's emphasis on punishment and due process, the
> rest of the justice system has been experimenting with new,
> alternative court models . . . These new courts offer a good
> starting point for developing a new system of courts for
> youthful offenders.

For example, drug courts use the legal authority of the court to
intervene with nonviolent drug-related offenders. Court programs
require drug treatment and maintain strict offender monitoring. The
model also requires expedited case management and interagency cooperation (e.g., district attorney, probation department, drug treatment
specialists). In their review of the drug court phenomenon, Inciardi,
McBride, and Rivers conclude that these courts offer great promise, not
only as a viable response to the drug offender but also as an incentive
to make system improvements that are necessary in order to develop
and implement effective drug court programs (1996:88). In the mid-
1990s, about 25 of 250 drug courts in the United States were dedicated
to juveniles (Butts & Harrell, 1998:10). By 2003, there were approximately 300 juvenile drug courts in operation in 46 states and the District of Columbia, and another 100 of these youth specialty courts were
being planned (Butts & Roman, 2004).

The adoption of specialty courts in the juvenile justice system
incorporates some of the initiatives and collaborative strategies
described earlier and demonstrates a commitment to developing comprehensive prevention and treatment-based programs. In addition,
the "future" model outlined by Butts and Harrell also permits some
political and ideological balance: accountability and strict sanctions
imposed by the court as well as community-based, intensive drug
treatment. These types of alternative courts are not a panacea to juvenile delinquency and youth violence, but they expand the continuum
of options and resist abandoning the concept of adolescence. This is
important because "even if states abolish the practice of sending
young offenders to separate court, children and adolescents will continue to be cognitively, emotionally and socially different from adults"
(Butts & Harrell, 1998:i).

DISCUSSION: CHANGING THE FOCUS

It is evident that media coverage of sensational youth crimes has
helped to politicize juvenile justice and to accelerate the convergence
of the juvenile and criminal courts. As Yanich found in his content
analysis of local television news stories about crime, "murder is the

offense that dominates KidsCrime coverage wildly out of proportion to its occurrence in reality . . . However, our understanding of the juvenile circumstances regarding crime are overtaken by those sensational images" (2005:130). This chapter has proposed that by focusing on prevention of delinquency (primary and secondary), the policy debate can move beyond "coddling verses getting tough," beyond "treatment versus punishment," and can continue to emphasize and develop strategies and programs that work in stopping and reducing the incidence of crime among youths. This facilitates more rational and moderate thinking and less ideological extremism. As a model for dealing with juvenile delinquents, this orientation promotes a balanced approach of accountability, public safety, and competency development. Politicians can endorse the comprehensive, integrated process and still stress the sanctions and accountability while noting the cost-effectiveness of early intervention and community-based strategies. In this regard, Shepherd is mindful that legislators and policymakers have to be held accountable to sound policy rather than sound bites (1997:13). The political and media preoccupation with violent offenders, which has resulted in a redirection of resources toward incarceration policies, must be countered with policy that recognizes the effectiveness of early intervention (Ohlin, 1998). Consensus on the importance of prevention and risk reduction can help bridge ideological differences and the availability of scientifically tested programs provides strategies to focus these efforts.

Efforts to resist the further erosion of the juvenile court and the juvenile justice system—and the deconstruction of childhood and adolescence—become even more difficult when headlines reinforce the moral panic over youth crime. At a time when school violence, crime, and delinquency have declined, news that Jason McLaughlin was sentenced to life in prison for the 2003 deaths of two students at Rocori High School in Cold Spring, Minnesota, rekindles the super-predator image of youthful offenders (*New York Times*, 2005a). This contributes to the fear of being a victim of violent crime, which is a "key factor" in producing and sustaining "punitive attitudes toward juveniles" (Yanich, 2005:110).

Even though trends in youth crime have exhibited a sustained decline since the nexus of guns, gangs, and drugs in the 1980s and 1990s resulted in a spike of violence, youths are still at risk to become both victims and offenders. In addition to adolescent tumult, Siegel and Welsh identify five "pressing problems" that affect certain segments of the youth population and keep them at risk (2005:3-4): (1) poverty, (2) health, (3) family, (4) substandard living conditions, and (5) inadequate education.

Recognizing the effectiveness of preventive and early intervention programs, a commitment to reaffirming the mission of the juvenile justice system is warranted.

DISCUSSION QUESTIONS

1. Does the public's perception of youth crime match the official data? Why? Explain the role of the media and politics in shaping juvenile justice policy.

2. Trace the evolution of the juvenile justice system. What has changed in the last 100 years? Why?

3. Describe the legislative reforms that have occurred regarding the waiver or transfer of jurisdiction from juvenile court to adult criminal court. What has been the result of these legislative initiatives? Is recidivism reduced? Are the juveniles or society better served? Why?

4. How did the school shootings become the "condensation symbol" for altering our image of youths? How did these incidents create a "moral panic"? What are the lessons of the school shootings? What effect will they have on juvenile justice in the next century?

5. Elaborate on some strategies that can be utilized to reduce school violence. Can you provide a rationale for selecting these programs versus simply relying on increased penalties? How do you "sell" these programs to the public?

6. What elements are needed to create successful programs? What role can politicians play in this process? Can the media also become involved? How?

7. What do you envision for the juvenile court in the twenty-first century? Do you see a role for specialty courts? Explain.

8. Why has juvenile justice become such a "hot button" issue? What effect has its predominance had on our policy initiatives? How do you foresee its position in the future? Why?

9. If increasingly more juveniles are transferred into the adult court, there will ultimately be more juveniles in adult prisons. Will these demographic changes have an effect on prisons? Explain.

10. Recently, some elected officials have advocated harsher sanctions for violent offenders and the transfer of juveniles to the adult criminal court at age 13 or 14. Prepare a list of your recommendations for dealing with violent juvenile offenders.

REFERENCES

Adams, Gerald R., and Thomas Gullotta (1983). *Adolescent Life Experiences*. Belmont, CA: Wadsworth.

Adler, Jerry, and Peter Annin (1998). "Murder at an Early Age." *Newsweek* (August 24):28.

Albanese, Jay (1993). *Dealing with Delinquency: The Future of Juvenile Justice*, 2nd ed. Chicago: Nelson-Hall.

American Civil Liberties Union (1998). "Congress Considers Jailing Children With Adults." *http://aclu.org/* (May 26, 1998).

Applebome, Peter (1998). "No Room For Kids in a World of Little Adults." *New York Times* (May 10):WK4.

Arnette, June L., and Marjorie C. Walsleben (1998). *Combating Fear and Restoring Safety in Schools*. Washington, DC: Office of Juvenile Justice and Delinquency Prevention.

Bazemore, Gordon, and Susan E. Day (1996). "Restoring the Balance: Juvenile and Community Justice." *Juvenile Justice* 3(1):3-14.

Bazemore, Gordon, and Mark S. Umbreit (1994). *Balanced and Restorative Justice: Program Summary* (October). Washington, DC: Office of Juvenile Justice and Delinquency Prevention.

Beck, Allen J., and Timothy A. Hughes (2005). "Sexual Violence Reported by Correctional Authorities, 2004." *Bureau of Justice Statistics Special Report*. Washington, DC: U.S. Department of Justice, Office of Justice Programs.

Belluck, Pam (1998a). "Chicago Boys, 7 and 8, Charged With Murdering 11-Year-Old Girl." *New York Times* (August 11). *http://www.nytimes.com*

Belluck, Pam (1998b). "Murder Charges Dropped Against 2 Boys in Chicago." *New York Times* (September 5):A1, 10.

Bilchik, Shay (1998a). *Serious and Violent Juvenile Offenders*. Washington, DC: Office of Juvenile Justice and Delinquency Prevention.

Bilchik, Shay (1998b). "A Juvenile Justice System for the 21st Century." *Crime & Delinquency* 44(1):89-101.

Bishop, Donna M., Charles E. Frazier, Lonn Lanza-Kaduce, and Lawrence Winner (1996). "The Transfer of Juveniles to Criminal Court: Does It Make A Difference?" *Crime & Delinquency* 42(2):171-191.

Bluth, Andrew (1998). "Judge Rules Boys Held in Girl's Death May Go Home to Await Trial." *New York Times* (August 14). *http://www.nytimes.com*

Bortner, M.A. (1988). *Delinquency and Justice: An Age of Crisis*. New York: McGraw-Hill.

Bourque, Blair B., Roberta C. Cronin, Daniel B. Felker, Frank R. Pearson, Mei Han, and Sarah M. Hill (1996). *Boot Camps for Juvenile Offenders: An Implementation Evaluation of Three Demonstration Programs*. Washington, DC: National Institute of Justice.

Braga, Anthony A., David M. Kennedy, Anne Morrison Piehl, and Elin J. Waring (2001). *Reducing Gun Violence: The Boston Gun Project's Operation Ceasefire.* Washington, DC: U.S. Department of Justice, Office of Justice Programs, National Institute of Justice.

Butterfield, Fox (1997). "Drop in Homicide Rate Linked to Crack's Decline." *New York Times* (October 27):A10.

Butts, Jeffrey A. (2000). *Youth Crime Drop.* Washington, DC: The Urban Institute. *http://www.urban.org/UploadedPDF/youth-crime-drop.pdf*

Butts, Jeffrey A., and Adele V. Harrell (1998). *Crime Policy Report: Delinquency or Criminals: Policy Options for Young Offenders.* Washington, DC: The Urban Institute.

Butts, Jeffery A., and John Roman (eds.) (2004). *Juvenile Drug Courts and Teen Substance Abuse.* Washington, DC: Urban Institute Press.

Butts, Jeffrey, and Howard Snyder (1997). *The Youngest Delinquents: Offenders Under Age 15.* Washington, DC: Office of Juvenile Justice and Delinquency Prevention.

Caliber Associates (2005). *2000 Report to Congress: Title V Community Prevention Grants Program.* Washington, DC: Office of Juvenile Justice and Delinquency Prevention.

Canedy, David (2002). "Florida Boys Admit Killing Father and Get Shorter Sentences in Deal." *New York Times* (November 15):A1, 20.

Cantelon, Sharon, and Donni LeBoeuf (1997). *Keeping Young People in School: Community Programs That Work.* Washington, DC: Office of Juvenile Justice and Delinquency Prevention.

Center for the Study and Prevention of Violence (2002-2004). *Blueprints for Violence Prevention.* *http://www.colorado.edu/cspv*

"COPS Office Announces $5.4 Million in Grants to Have New Law Enforcement Officers in America's Schools" (July 2005). Washington, DC: U.S. Department of Justice. *http://www.cops.usdoj.gov/print.asp?Item=1546*

Criminal Justice Newsletter (1997). "Murder of a Youth in Boston Ends Noted 29-Month Respite." 28(23):5-6.

DeVoe, Jill F., Katharin Peter, Phillip Kaufman, Amanda Miller, Margaret Noonan, Thomas D. Snyder, and Katrina Baum (2004). *Indicators of School Crime and Safety: 2004.* Washington, DC: U.S. Department of Justice, Bureau of Justice Statistics and U.S. Department of Education, National Center for Education Statistics.

Edelman, Marion Wright (1998). "Adult Jails and Prisons Are No Place for Children." Children's Defense Fund Reports (March). *http://www.childrensdefense.org/*

Erie Daily Times (1998). "NRA Under the Gun in Wake of School Violence." (June 5):A7.

Erie Times News (1997). "15-Year-Old Charged in Murder of Boy Selling Candy for School Fund Raiser"; "Teen Shoots Mother to Death, Then Kills Two Others During Shooting Rampage at School"; "17-Year-Old Convicted of Killing Best Friend's Mother." (October 2):A1.

Erie Times News (1998a). "Two Students Charged With Threatening Peer." (May 17):B4.

Erie Times News (1998b). "Erie Diocese Bans Middle School Dances." (May 31):B4.

Feld, Barry (1993). "Juvenile (In)Justice and the Criminal Court Alternative." *Crime & Delinquency* 39:403-424.

Finkenauer, James O., and Patricia W. Gavin (1998). *Scared Straight: The Panacea Phenomenon Revisited*. Prospect Heights, IL: Waveland.

Fishman, Mark (1978). "Crime Waves as Ideology." *Social Problems* 25(5):531-543.

Garase, Maria Lynn (1998). *An Evaluation of the Erie County, Pennsylvania, Collaborative Intensive Community Treatment Program*. Unpublished Manuscript. Erie, PA: Mercyhurst College Institute for Child and Family Policy.

Gardner, Jule (1998). "Forever Changed: In the Wake of Violence, Climate at School Functions is Under Scrutiny." *Erie Times News* (June 7):A1, 8.

Gest, Ted (2001). *Crime & Politics: Big Government's Erratic Campaign for Law and Order*. New York: Oxford University Press.

Guerriero, John (1998). "Professor: District's Response Was Correct." *Erie Daily Times* (May 1):C1, 4.

Guerriero, John, and Ed Palattella (1998). "Lawyer Claims School Officials Overreacting." *Erie Daily Times* (May 1):C1, 4.

Hahn, Tim, and Pam Eckert (1998). "Threats Reported at Millcreek, Fairview Schools." *Erie Times News* (May 2):A1,2.

Harden, Blaine (1997). "Boston's Approach to Juvenile Crime Encircles Youths, Reduces Slayings." *Washington Post* (October 23):A3.

Henggeler, Scott W. (1989). *Delinquency in Adolescence*. Newbury Park, CA: Sage.

Howell, James C. (ed.) (1995). *Guide For Implementing the Comprehensive Strategy for Serious, Violent, and Chronic Juvenile Offenders*. Washington, DC: Office of Juvenile Justice and Delinquency Prevention.

Hsia, Heidi M. (1997). *Allegheny County, PA: Mobilizing to Reduce Juvenile Crime*. Washington, DC: Office of Juvenile Justice and Delinquency Prevention.

Inciardi, James A., Duane C. McBride, and James E. Rivers (1996). *Drug Control and the Courts*. Thousand Oaks, CA: Sage.

Join Together Online (1998). "Schools Taking Student Threats Seriously." *http://www.jointogether.org/gv/* (May 13, 1998).

Juvenile Justice Update (1998). "Early Evaluative Results of GREAT Program Are Encouraging." (June/July):11.

Kachur, S. Patrick, Gail M. Stennies, Kenneth E. Powell, William Modzeleski, Ronald Stephens, Rosemary Murphy, Marci-jo Kresnow, David Sleet, and Richard Lowry (1996). "School-Associated Violent Deaths in the United States, 1992 to 1994." *Journal of the American Medical Association* 275(22):1729-1733.

Kennedy, David M. (1997). *Juvenile Gun Violence and Gun Markets in Boston*. Washington, DC: National Institute of Justice.

King, Patricia, and Andrew Murr (1998). "A Son Who Spun Out of Control." *Newsweek* (June 1):32-22.

Law Enforcement News (1997). "Anti-violence Effort, a Hit in Boston, Now Making its Mark in Other Cities." (October 31):1, 6.

Lawrence, Richard (1998). *School Crime and Juvenile Justice*. New York: Oxford University Press.

Lawrence, Richard (2004). "Violence and Education: Controlling the School Yard." In Alida V. Merlo and Peter J. Benekos (eds.), *Controversies in Juvenile Justice and Delinquency*, pp. 89-110. Newark, NJ: LexisNexis/Anderson.

Lemmon, John H., Thomas L. Austin, P. J. Verrecchia, and Matthew Fetzer (2005). "The Effect of Legal and Extralegal Factors on Statutory Exclusion of Juvenile Offenders." *Youth Violence and Juvenile Justice* 3(3):214-234.

Lewin, Tamar (1997). "Despite Recent Carnage, School Violence is Not on Rise." *New York Times* (December 3):A14.

Lewin, Tamar (1998). "Experts Wrestle With Why Kids Turn Into Killers." *New York Times* (March 26). *http://www.nytimes.org*

Lewis, Anthony (1997). "Crime and Politics." *New York Times* (May 19):A13.

Loeber, Rolf, and David Farrington (eds.) (1998). *Serious and Violent Juvenile Offenders*. Thousand Oaks, CA: Sage.

Macallair, Daniel, and Michael Males (2000). *Dispelling the Myth: An Analysis of Youth and Adult Crime Patterns in California Over the Past 20 Years*. San Francisco: Center on Juvenile and Criminal Justice. *http://www.cjcj.org*

MacKenzie, Doris Layton, Angela R. Gover, Gaylene Styve Armstrong, and Ojmarrh Mitchell (2001). *A National Study Comparing the Environments of Boot Camps with Traditional Facilities for Juvenile Offenders*. Washington, DC: U.S. Department of Justice, National Institute of Justice.

Magill, Sherry (1998). "Adolescents: Public Enemy #1." *Crime & Delinquency* 44(1):121-126.

Males, Michael (1998). "Kids Most At Risk From Violent Adults, Not From Other Kids." *Erie Morning News* (June 2):A7.

Mattingly, Marion (1998a). "Interview: Bobby Scott on Avoiding Sound-Bite Policy and Taking Effective Action Against Juvenile Crime. *Juvenile Justice Update* (December/January):5-6, 15.

Mattingly, Marion (1998b). "Shay Bilchik Speaks Out on S.10." *Juvenile Justice Update* (June/July):7-8.

McCaffrey, Barry R. (1998a). *The National Drug Control Strategy, 1998: A Ten-Year Plan*. Washington, DC: Office of National Drug Control Policy.

McCaffrey, Barry R. (1998b). *FY 1999 Budget Highlights: Federal Drug Control Programs*. Washington, DC: Office of National Drug Control Policy.

Meckler, Laura (1998). "U.S. House Subcommittee Tries To Understand Youth Violence." *Erie Daily Times* (April 29):A4.

Merlo, Alida V., Peter J. Benekos, and William J. Cook (1997). "'Getting Tough' With Youth: Legislative Waiver as Crime Control." *Juvenile and Family Court Journal* 48(3):1-15.

Moran, Richard (1996). "Proposals to Cut Juvenile Crime—Politics or Reality?" *Juvenile Justice Update* 2(5):5.

Morin, Richard (1997). "An Airwave of Crime." *The Washington Post National Weekly Edition* (August 18):34.

Myers, David L. (2003). "The Recidivism of Violent Youths in Juvenile and Adult Court: A Consideration of Selection Bias." *Youth Violence and Juvenile Justice* 1(1):79-101.

National Criminal Justice Association (1997). *Juvenile Justice Reform Initiatives in the States: 1994-1996.* Washington, DC: Office of Juvenile Justice and Delinquency Prevention.

National Drug Control Strategy (2004). *Fiscal Year 2005 Budget Summary* (March 2004). Washington, DC: The White House. Annual Reports. *http://www.white housedrugpolicy.gov/publications/policy/05budget*

National Drug Control Strategy (2005a). *Stopping Use Before It Starts: Education and Community Action.* Washington, DC: Office of National Drug Control Policy. *http://www.whitehousedrugpolicy.gov/publications*

National Drug Control Strategy (2005b). *Fiscal Year 2006 Budget Summary* (February 2005). Washington, DC: The White House. Annual Reports. *http://www.white housedrugpolicy.gov/publications/policy/06budget*

Nelson, Melissa (2005). "Ark. Readies for Release of School Shooter." *Seattle Post-Intelligencer* (August 10). *http://seattlepi.nwsource.com/*

Neri, Albert J. (1998). "Bill Would Require Adult Trials in Cases of School Violence." *Erie Morning News* (June 2):A1, 4.

"New Ads Help Parents Address Teen Drug Use" (June 2005). Washington, DC: Office of National Dug Control Policy, National Youth Anti-Drug Media Campaign. *http://www.mediacampaign.org/newsroom/press05*

"New Report Shows That Teens Who Receive Anti-Drug Messages Are Less Likely to Use Drugs" (July 2005). Washington, DC: Office of National Drug Control Policy. *http://www.whitehousedrugpolicy.gov/news/press05*

New York Times (1998a). "Violence-Ridden Composition Brings Eighth-Grader Suspension." (May 8). *http://www.nytimes.com*

New York Times (1998b). "Law Permits Trial of Youths as Adults for Guns at School." (August 19). *http://www.nytimes.com*

New York Times (2005a). "Teen in Minn. Shootings Gets Life Sentence." *http://www.nytimes.com*

New York Times (2005b). "Chief: Handcuffing Girl Not a Violation." (August 4). *http://www.nytimes.com*

Office of Juvenile Justice and Delinquency Prevention (1998). *Discretionary Grant Programs: Parts C and D.* Washington, DC: Office of Juvenile Justice and Delinquency Prevention.

OJJDP News @ a Glance (2005). "OJJDP Offers Enhanced Model Program Guide." (July/August). *http://www.ncjrs.org/html/ojjdp/news_at_glance/210414/top story.html*

Ohlin, Lloyd E. (1998). "The Future of Juvenile Justice Policy and Research." *Crime & Delinquency* 44(1):143-153.

Olweus, Dan (1994). "Bullying: Too Little Love, Too Much Freedom." *School Safety Update* (May):1-4.

Pennsylvania Juvenile Court Judges' Commission (2005). 2005 Annual Training Conference. *http://www.jcjc.state.pa.us*

Pennsylvania Juvenile Court Judges' Commission (1998). "Annual Training to Feature Programs That Work." *Pennsylvania Juvenile Justice* (June):6.

Pennsylvania State Police (1997). *Pennsylvania State Data Center.* Harrisburg, PA: Pennsylvania State Police.

Platt, Anthony M. (1977). *The Child Savers: The Invention of Delinquency*, 2nd ed. Chicago: University of Chicago Press.

Potter, Gary W., and Victor E. Kappeler (1998). *Constructing Crime: Perspectives on Making News and Social Problems*. Prospect Heights, IL: Waveland.

Puzzanchera, Charles, Anne L. Stahl, Terrance A. Finnegan, Nancy Tierney, and Howard N. Snyder (2004). *Juvenile Court Statistics 2000*. Pittsburgh: National Center for Juvenile Justice.

Rice, F. Philip (1987). *The Adolescent: Development, Relationships, and Culture*, 5th ed. Boston: Allyn & Bacon.

Rimer, Sara (2004). "Unruly Students Facing Arrest, Not Detention." *New York Times* (January 4):A1, 15.

Rosenberg, Debra (1998). "Lessons From the Front." *Newsweek* (June 8):34.

Rubin, H. Ted (1998). "How Santa Cruz County's GROW Program Uses Interdisciplinary Teams to Curb Out-of-Home Placements." *Juvenile Justice Update* (June/July):1-2, 12-14.

Sachs, Susan (1998). "A Chilling Crime and a Question: What's in a Child's Mind?" *New York Times* (August 16):WK1.

SafeFutures (1998). *http://www.ncjrs.org/ojjdp/safefutures/index.html*

Sampson, Rana (2002). *Bullying in Schools*. Washington, DC: U.S. Department of Justice, Office of Community Oriented Policing Services.

Sasson, Theodore (1995). *Crime Talk: How Citizens Construct a Social Problem*. New York: Aldine de Gruyter.

Schwartz, Ira (1989). *(In)Justice for Juveniles: Rethinking the Best Interests of the Child*. Lexington, MA: Lexington Books.

Seelye, Katherine Q. (1996). "Dole Says Clinton Has Failed in War on Drugs." *New York Times* (August 20). *http://www.nytimes.org*

Senate Bill 10 (1997). "The Violent and Repeat Juvenile Offender Act of 1997." *http://rs9.loc.gov/cgi-bin/bdquery/z?d105:SN00010:@@@L#summary*

Senate Bill 254 (1999). "Violent and Repeat Juvenile Offender Accountability and Rehabilitation Act." See *http://rs9.loc.gov/*

Sharp, Ronald E. (1998). "New Mission for Juvenile Justice System." *Pennsylvania Commission on Crime and Delinquency Quarterly* 12(11):1-2.

Shepherd, Robert Jr. (1997). "Doing Justice to Juvenile Justice—What Changes Does the System Really Need?" *Juvenile Justice Update* (August/September):1-2, 11-13.

Sherman, Lawrence W., Denise Gottfredson, Doris MacKenzie, John Eck, Peter Reuter, and Shawn Bushway (1997). *Preventing Crime: What Works, What Doesn't, What's Promising*. Washington, DC: National Institute of Justice.

Sickmund, Melissa, Howard Snyder, and Eileen Poe-Yamagata (1997). *Juvenile Offenders and Victims: 1997 Update on Violence*. Washington, DC: Office of Juvenile Justice and Delinquency Prevention.

Siegel, Larry J., and Brandon C. Welsh (2005). *Juvenile Delinquency: The Core*, 2nd ed. Belmont, CA: Thompson Wadsworth.

Snyder, Howard N. (1997). *Juvenile Arrests 1995*. Washington, DC: Office of Juvenile Justice and Delinquency Prevention.

Snyder, Howard N. (2005). *Juvenile Arrests 2003*. Washington, DC: Office of Juvenile Justice and Delinquency Prevention.

Stahl, Anne L. (1998). *Delinquency Cases in Juvenile Courts, 1995*. Washington, DC: Office of Juvenile Justice and Delinquency Prevention.

Sun Sentinel (2005). "Mom of Handcuffed Boy Settles Lawsuit." (August 16). *http:// www.sun-sentinel.com*

Sutton, Sally (1997). In the States. (February 25). New York: American Civil Liberties Union.

Tita, George, K. Jack Riley, Greg Ridgeway, and Peter Greenwood (2005). *Reducing Gun Violence: Operation Ceasefire in Los Angeles*. Washington, DC: U.S. Department of Justice, National Institute of Justice.

Tobin, Thomas C. (2005). "Mom Moving Girl In Video Out of Florida." *St. Petersburg Times ONLINE*. (April 26). *http://www.sptimes.com*

Uniform Crime Reports (1997). *Crime in the United States 1996*. Washington, DC: U.S. Government Printing Office.

Uniform Crime Reports (1998). *Crime in the United States 1997*. Washington, DC: U.S. Government Printing Office.

U.S. Department of Justice (2004). "Nation's School Crime Rate Continues to Decline." (November 29). Press Release. *http://www.ojp.usdoj.gov*

Violent and Repeat Offender Act of 1997 (Senate-April 1, 1998) *Congressional Record ONLINE*. Thomas. Available: *http://thomas.loc.gov/cgi-bin/query/ D?r105:3:./temp/~r105UlUqXr::*

Vogel, Jennifer (1994). "Throw Away the Key: Juvenile Offenders Are the Willie Hortons of the '90s." *UTNE Reader* (July/August):56-60.

Walker, Samuel (2006). *Sense and Nonsense About Crime and Drugs: A Policy Guide*, 6th ed. Belmont, CA: Thompson Wadsworth.

Westcott, Scott (1998). "It Will Never Be The Same." *Erie Daily Times* (April 29):A1,3.

Whitehead, John T., and Steven P. Lab (1996). *Juvenile Justice: An Introduction*, 2nd ed. Cincinnati: Anderson.

Wilson, James Q. (1998). "Forward: Never Too Early." In Rolf Loeber and David Farrington (eds.), *Serious and Violent Juvenile Offenders*, ix-xi. Thousand Oaks, CA: Sage.

Wilson, James Q. (1997). "What, If Anything, Can the Federal Government Do About Crime?" *Perspectives on Crime and Justice: 1996-1997 Lecture Series*, Volume 1 (November):1-22. Washington, DC: National Institute of Justice.

Yanich, Danilo (2005). "Kids, Crime, and Local Television News." *Crime & Delinquency* 51(1):103-132.

Ziedenberg, Jason, and Vincent Schiraldi (1997). *The Risks Juveniles Face When They Are Incarcerated With Adults*. Washington, DC: Justice Policy Institute.

CASES

Kent v. United States, 383 U.S. 541 (1966).

6

Criminal Justice Policy:
The Legacy of Get-Tough Legislation*

In 2005, the U.S. Supreme Court in *U.S. v. Booker* (125 S. Ct. 738 [2005]) determined that federal judges were no longer constrained by the federal sentencing guidelines. This was a significant departure from the practice that had been in place since 1987. In a 5–4 decision, the justices ruled that the federal sentencing provisions violated the defendant's rights as guaranteed under the Sixth Amendment. Furthermore, the justices indicated that the sentencing guidelines were advisory rather than mandatory. Previously, federal court judges had been required to follow the range of sentences stipulated in the guidelines. Enhancement penalties enabled judges to augment the defendant's sentence after he or she had been convicted, and these factors could be based upon a preponderance of the evidence rather than proof beyond a reasonable doubt. As a result, offenders such as Freddie Booker were subjected to longer sentences based upon mitigating factors that had not been proven beyond a reasonable doubt to the jury. In Booker's case, the result was a sentence of 30 years in a federal prison (rather than 21 years and 10 months), which the judge imposed based upon evidence that Booker had more cocaine (possession) than the amount for which he was found guilty (*U.S. v. Booker*, 125 S. Ct. 738 [2005]).

---

*An earlier version of this chapter was presented at the Annual Meeting of the Academy of Criminal Justice Sciences, March 17, 2005, Chicago, Illinois.

Almost immediately after the decision was announced, the influence of ideology, politics, and the media on criminal justice policy became readily apparent. Officials in Congress began to lament the deleterious effects of the Court's decision and to assert that a new federal sentencing code would be quickly enacted to replace the existing one. Their proclamations suggested that the revised sentencing legislation would be even tougher on offenders. In fact, the Court's decision in *Booker* appears to be related to the tough stance Congress took in the proposed gang legislation. Although not intended to replace the federal sentencing provisions, Congress enacted H.R. 1279, the Gang Deterrence and Community Protection Act, in May of 2005. The legislation is before the Senate, and is expected to reach the President's desk (GovTrack, 2005). Ostensibly, this legislation focuses on gangs and gang members. However, it targets any group of three or more individuals who are engaged in two or more gang crimes (one of them has to be a crime of violence) that are separate episodes. If convicted under this legislation, offenders serve a mandatory 10-year minimum sentence. The legislation also establishes additional harsher mandatory sanctions (including the death penalty) for other offenses (The Sentencing Project, 2005b).

This swift response from elected officials demonstrates: (1) the dominance and continued popularity of an ideology that is punitive and harsh toward offenders, (2) elected officials' eagerness to maintain their stance on crime control and their certainty regarding how best to address crime, and (3) the media portrayal of sensationalized crime and criminals, and the concomitant perceived public demand for tougher sanctions designed to incapacitate offenders for long periods of time.

Simultaneously, several developments and initiatives in the last five years, including legislative policies and judicial decisions, indicate that crime control policy is changing. In the 1980s and 1990s, the politics of the war on drugs and the ideologies of deterrence, incapacitation, and punishment contributed to rapid growth of prison populations, increased spending for prison construction, and demonization of criminals. However, with decreasing crime rates and concerns about other issues, such as terrorism as well as budget constraints, crime has faded as a political and public policy priority (Turpin, 2000). While attention has shifted to other issues, the consequences of the get-tough era of crime control persist.

One of the most evident consequences of the era is its effect on the nation's prison population. There are more than 2.1 million offenders incarcerated in state and federal prisons and jails and, while the rate of growth has slowed, populations continue to increase. By the middle of 2004, more than 25,000 offenders were added to the prison population (Harrison & Beck, 2005:1). At the end of 2003, state prisons were either at capacity or up to 16 percent above capacity, and federal prisons were

39 percent above capacity (Harrison & Beck, 2005:1). Arguably, prison populations are affected by sentencing policies and parole revocation practices rather than crime rates (Petersilia, 2003; Seiter, 2002). For example, mandatory sentences and sentencing guidelines have not only resulted in more offenders being sentenced to prison but also in longer sentences for those who are imprisoned (Tonry, 2004:134).

Although the impact on prison populations of *United States v. Booker* (125 S. Ct. 738 [2005]) is as yet unknown, judges will have more sentencing discretion, which could result in shorter prison sentences (Greenhouse, 2005). This Court decision creates the opportunity (if not need) for a new debate about sentencing policy that has already underscored ideological differences regarding penal policy and renewed "the struggle between Congress and the judiciary for control over setting criminal punishment" (Hulse & Liptak, 2005:A27).

Another indication of both the consequences of get-tough legislation and evidence of changing views on correctional ideology is in California, where the huge adult prison population [more than 166,000 prisoners, reflecting an incarceration rate of 506 per 100,000 compared to the average state incarceration rate of 433 (Harrison & Beck, 2005:3)] and the state's "massive" budget problems [$8 billion in debt (DiMascio, 2005)] have prompted a reassessment of the California Department of Corrections and Rehabilitation (Warren, 2005). With fiscal as well as ideological motivations, Governor Schwarzenegger has called for an emphasis on "rehabilitation" and a corrections system that "corrects" (Warren, 2005). In his view, rehabilitation and preparing offenders for reentry will reduce recidivism, which will reduce the prison population, which ultimately will reduce the state's corrections costs.

These policy formulations indicate that the pendulum is swinging "toward preventing crime, rehabilitating inmates, and keeping ex-convicts from returning to prison reflecting Schwarzenegger's view that 'Corrections should correct'" (Sacramento County Deputy Sheriffs' Association, 2005:par. 8).

In the context of re-examining these issues and developments—sentencing policy, prison crowding, and correctional ideology—this chapter reviews four consequences of the get-tough era of crime control that have precipitated emergent (and re-emergent) initiatives: (1) sentencing, (2) prisons, (3) reentry, and (4) collaboration.

SENTENCING ISSUES

Three recent developments illustrate the complexities of the sentencing dilemma. First, in the Summer of 2004, the U.S. Supreme Court indicated that it would not support sentencing guidelines that allowed for enhancements or extra time for offenders without formally charging them and convicting them of additional offenses. In the case of *Blakely v. Washington* (124 S. Ct. 2531), the justices, by a 5–4 decision, determined that Washington state's sentencing guidelines were unconstitutional and that judges could no longer increase offenders' sentences for aggravating factors (e.g., if an offender played a leadership role in the crime). The justices determined that the Washington statute was invalid because it allowed judges instead of juries to augment a defendant's sentence on the basis of these factors (*Blakely v. Washington*, 124 S. Ct. 2531 [2004]; McGough, 2004:A-6).

Given the similarities between the Washington statute and the federal sentencing guidelines, there was widespread speculation after *Blakely* that the U.S. Supreme Court would apply its decision to the federal system (McGough, 2004:A-6). Prior to hearing oral arguments in the federal cases that challenged the same issue, Justice Sandra Day O'Connor, who did not support the majority decision, reportedly told a group of judges that the [*Blakely*] decision "looks like a No. 10 earthquake to me" (Denniston, 2004:A12). Justice O'Connor's comment illustrates the complexity and the controversy surrounding the issue of sentencing in the courts.

Second, during the first week of the Fall 2004 term, the U.S. Supreme Court heard oral arguments in the consolidated cases of *U.S. v. Booker* and *U.S. v. Fanfan* (125 S. Ct. 738 [2005]). Both federal defendants had been convicted of drug offenses. After being convicted of possessing and distributing crack cocaine, Freddie J. Booker was sentenced to 30 years in prison, despite the fact that a jury had determined that he had distributed a smaller amount of cocaine, which typically would have meant a lighter sentence than the judge imposed. The second defendant, Ducan Fanfan, lived in Massachusetts and was convicted by a federal court in Maine of conspiring to distribute crack cocaine. Rather than sentence Fanfan to the 15 to 19 years stipulated in the federal sentencing guidelines, the judge departed from those guidelines, based on the Court's decision in *Blakely*, and sentenced Fanfan to six years (Denniston, 2004:A12). The cases were consolidated, and the Court's decision was released in January 2005. In their decision, the justices determined that the defendant's Sixth Amendment right to a jury trial was violated when the judge used the federal sentencing guidelines to increase the length of an offender's sentence when the offender had not been convicted of those additional offenses beyond a reasonable doubt. Second, the justices determined that the federal sentencing guidelines are advisory rather than mandatory. In short, judges can consult the guidelines, but they can use their own discretion in sentencing (Greenhouse, 2005:A1; *U.S. v. Booker*, 125 S. Ct. 738 [2005]).

The effect of the Court's decision is not yet fully known. The federal sentencing guidelines had been used to sentence approximately 60,000 offenders each year (Cohen, 2004:A1). Clearly, *Booker* reinstates judicial discretion, at least in the short term. However, there is no evidence to suggest that *Booker* has caused the turmoil in the system that was predicted. Preliminary analysis suggests that many federal court judges continue to apply the guidelines exactly as they are written, but in an advisory manner. It is expected that some defendants will appeal their sentences, and these appeals will have to be determined on a case-by-case basis (The Sentencing Project, 2005a). However, judges, defense attorneys, and prosecutors realize that the newly restored discretion may disappear quickly. In the wake of the Court's ruling, officials from the Justice Department as well as members of Congress were meeting to try to draft legislation that would renew the spirit of the 1984 Sentencing Reform Act, which attempted to reduce disparity in sentencing and laid the groundwork for the mandatory federal sentencing guidelines now determined to be unconstitutional. Simultaneously, some lawmakers also advocated a slower approach and an admonition to avoid the "quick fix" (Cohen & Fields, 2005:1).

Finally, in November 2004, voters in California defeated Proposition 66, a referendum to the three-strikes law requiring that the first and/or second strike be a violent crime as opposed to any felony offense (Institute of Governmental Studies, 2004). As a result, the original three-strikes law remains unchanged in California. According to Ehlers, Schiraldi, and Ziedenberg (2004), the three-strikes legislation that Californians initially supported in 1994, and again in 2004, will not only require nonviolent offenders to serve an extra 164,314 years in prison, but also will cost an extra $10.5 billion in prison and jail expenditures (p. 23).

This legislation and the political pronouncements that a new federal criminal code will be even tougher on criminals test the public's steadfast determination to continue with sanctions that mandate long terms of incarceration for felony offenders, even if they have not been convicted of any violent crimes. These developments also highlight the importance of establishing programs to ensure the successful reintegration of offenders. By focusing on the requisite skills, treatment, education, and values necessary to return to the community, correctional administrators and staff help to ensure that the long-term effects of incarceration can translate into a lower recidivism rate and a safer community.

PRISON CROWDING

Remnants of the conservative ideology that dominated correctional policy in the 1980s and 1990s persist today. They are particularly apparent in the use of incarceration in federal and state prison systems to sanction offenders. In June of 2004, the prison population in the United States had grown by approximately 2 percent over the previous year; there were a total of 1,494,216 inmates in the federal and state prison systems (Harrison & Beck, 2005:1). The state with the largest prison population was Texas, and California was a close second. Together, these two states incarcerate approximately 335,163 inmates or 22 percent of the total inmates incarcerated at midyear in 2004 (Harrison & Beck, 2005:1).

In order to comprehend fully the extent to which incarceration is utilized, it is helpful to examine how many residents of the United States have served or are serving sentences in state or federal prisons. In 2001, according to Bonczar, about one in 37 adult residents had served time in state or federal prison (2003:3). For African Americans, the problem is especially troublesome. In 2001, approximately 16.6 percent of adult African-American men were current or former inmates in the federal or state prison systems. The rate of incarceration for African-American men is six times that of white males, and twice that of Hispanic males (Bonczar, 2003:5). By June of 2004, one out of every 138 residents in the United States was either in prison or jail (Harrison & Beck, 2005:2). By 2010, if these current incarceration rates continue, it is anticipated that ". . . 1 in 29 persons age 18 or older" will have served a sentence in prison (Bonczar, 2003:7). For younger Americans, the predictions are especially dire. Bonczar contends that if the United States continues to use imprisonment to the extent that it currently does, one in 15 persons born in 2001 will serve a sentence in the state or federal system during his or her lifetime (2003:7).

The transition from a prison population of approximately 200,000 in 1974 to approximately 1.5 million in 2004 has occurred steadily over a 30-year period. The increase in the use of incarceration encompasses periods of time that have been characterized by both rising and falling violent crime rates. It has been driven by the realities of crime as well as a conservative ideology, politics, and the media, and it has been costly. For fiscal year 2001, the total for prison expenditures for all 50 states was $29.5 billion. The most expensive costs were incurred by the State of California, which spent $4.2 billion on its prisons (Stephan, 2004:2).

In mid-year 2004, the incarceration rate was 486 inmates per 100,000 residents, but there are regional and state variations. For example, in Louisiana it was 814 inmates per 100,000, and in Maine it was 149 inmates per 100,000. Clearly, correctional policies are not uniform throughout the United States. Perhaps the most startling revelation was the number of women incarcerated in June of 2004. For the second year in a row, there were more than 100,000 women (6.9% of all inmates) incarcerated in federal and state prisons, and this represented an approximate 3 percent increase from the previous year. Although men comprise the overwhelming majority of inmates, the number of women incarcerated has increased dramatically since 1995 (Harrison & Beck, 2005:4-5).

As previously mentioned, the large number of inmates incarcerated has also resulted in prison overcrowding. By the middle of 2004, both federal and state prison systems report operating over capacity, and there does not seem to be much evidence of these conditions abating anytime soon. The problem is particularly acute in the federal prisons, which were 39 percent above capacity, compared to state prisons, which were estimated "to be operating between 100 percent of their highest capacity and 16 percent of their lowest capacity" (Harrison & Beck, 2004:7). In the last decade, the population of federal inmates has almost doubled, with a 93 percent increase (The Sentencing Project 2004:1). Although not all states have experienced overcrowding problems, these data suggest that the federal government and the states are finding it difficult to provide beds, staff, programs, and services to satisfy the demand they are experiencing.

Overcrowded prisons are worrisome for correctional administrators and inmates. The spread of contagious diseases such as tuberculosis (which can be fatal) is increased when inmates are housed in open dormitory areas or in close proximity to one another. Institutions that have space limitations and rely on double-bunking or dormitory housing may increase the likelihood of transmitting tuberculosis from inmate to inmate or from inmate to staff (Pollock, 2004:121). Even without contagious diseases, prison incarceration is a stressful experience. In their research, Lawrence and Andrews (2004) found that crowding in prison is associated with an increase in stress and arousal among inmates, and it diminishes their psychological well-being. According to Pollock, "overcrowding stresses even the most even-tempered and mentally healthy inmate" (2004:125).

The effects of overcrowding can be quite serious. One inmate died in 2005 after an altercation with correctional officers in a state-administered jail in Baltimore, Maryland. Taking place in what was characterized in media accounts as an overcrowded and violent institution, the inmate's death was classified as a homicide. As a result, eight officers were terminated from their positions, and a new warden, Mitchell Franks, assumed leadership of the institution (*New York Times,* 2005:A18).

Prison overcrowding can primarily be attributed to: the increased use of incarceration for drug offenders, the use of sentencing statutes

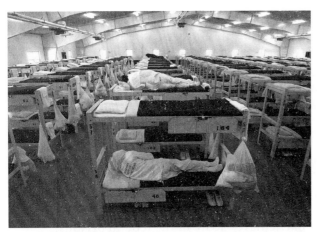

Hundreds of beds fill one of the prison dormitories at the Elmore Correctional Facility in Elmore, Alabama. In 2004, Alabama Prison Commissioner Donal Campbell announced that long-term sentencing reform was needed to get a handle on the growing inmate population. *(AP Photo/Dave Martin)*

like the three-strikes law in California, chronic offender laws, and sentence enhancement provisions. In addition, states' greater reliance on incarceration today than in the past, the accompanying decrease in the use of parole and early release mechanisms for offenders, and the increase in returnees (i.e., offenders who have been paroled and are returned to prison for violations of the conditions of parole) influence population growth.

The get-tough philosophy that affected criminal justice policy beginning in the late 1970s has reinforced the use of incarceration for felons. Both the number of new admissions to prison and the number of returnees continue to increase. In 2002, 69 percent of all the defendants who were convicted of a felony in the state courts were sentenced to a term of incarceration. These felons were either sentenced to prison (41%) or to local jails (28%) (Durose & Langan, 2004:3). For those defendants who were convicted of a drug offense, 66 percent were sentenced to incarceration in either the local jail or the state prison (Durose & Langan, 2004:3). Clearly, drug offenders have been targeted by correctional policies and shibboleths like the war on drugs. As for the returnees, the numbers have continued to increase, but not to the same extent as new court commitments. For example, new court commitments have increased by 15 percent since 1998, whereas parole violator commitments increased, but by less than 2 percent (Harrison & Beck, 2005:6).

Another factor contributing to increases in the prison population is the popularity of life sentences. According to Davenport (2005), one in 11 offenders in federal and state prisons is serving a life sentence. All but six states have some sort of provision for the possibility of parole consideration for inmates sentenced to life imprisonment. Pennsylvania is one of the states that does not allow these offenders to become eligible for parole; it is estimated that there are more than 4,000 offenders serving life sentences in Pennsylvania (Davenport, 2005:1).

Correctional reforms in the next decade must include a review of existing correctional policy for drug offenders and nonviolent offenders. In addition, greater attention will have to be focused on sentencing statutes. If the statutes that mandate long sentences and the abolition of parole persist, prison overcrowding and the attendant costs will force states and the federal government to realign their priorities and allocate more money for the construction, expansion, and renovation of existing institutions. This will necessitate decreases in spending on education, health care, elderly services, homeland security, and transportation.

REENTRY: STRATEGIES FOR SUCCESSFUL REINTEGRATION

The sentencing policies discussed above and the get-tough politics of the 1980s and 1990s were characterized by a "lock them up and throw away the key" mentality. Some of the salient consequences of this legislation included increases in both the number of offenders sentenced to prison and the length of their sentences (Austin, 2001). The focus was on fighting crime by eliminating criminals via exclusionary, punitive, and harmful policies. Rehabilitation was deemphasized, and incapacitation (i.e., warehousing) was promoted. Clearly, the classical ideology of crime control underscored these developments. Apparently little thought was given to the inevitable release of these offenders.

By 2000, concerns about the increasing number of offenders being released—and the fact that they were ill-prepared for transition and at-risk for failure and subsequent return to prison—precipitated a "Reentry Roundtable" sponsored by the Urban Institute (Travis, Solomon & Waul, 2001:2). Several questions were addressed including:

- Who is coming home?
- How are they released?
- How are they prepared for release?
- What is post-release supervision?
- What happens to parole violators?

The forum identified several concerns: residential concentrations of ex-offenders and parolees, employment and housing needs, substance abuse problems, inadequate supervision and service delivery, collateral problems affecting families and communities, and public safety (Travis, Solomon & Waul, 2001). Similarly, Seiter reviewed the problems facing returning inmates: "finding housing, creating ties with family and friends, finding a job, addressing alcohol and drug abuse, continued involvement in crime, and the impact of parole supervision" (2002:51).

When Martha Stewart emerged in March 2005 from the Women's Federal Prison in Alderson, West Virginia, media attention focused on the prisoner reentry issue. Unfortunately, the problems faced by the typical inmate dealing with reentry are far more complicated. Marc La Cloche's case is probably more indicative of the barriers confronted by an offender trying to find employment in the community with the vocational training and skills acquired in the prison. In 2000, after he served an 11-year sentence in New York prisons for first-degree robbery, La Cloche attempted to secure gainful employment as a barber. Although he was initially denied his license to cut hair, that decision was reversed by a hearing officer. Then, the secretary of state for New York appealed the decision and won. The administrative judge determined that La Cloche's "criminal history indicates a lack of good moral character and trustworthiness required for licensure" (Haberman, 2005:A16).

In 2003, La Cloche went before a Supreme Court judge in Manhattan, and that judge ordered the authorities to review the case again. In short, the judge determined that the authorities had never really given La Cloche the chance to prove that he was of good moral character and trustworthy because it was the criminal record alone that resulted in the denial of a license. After an administrative judge reviewed the case, La Cloche was again denied the license. In this review, he was denied due to his "minimization" of the nature of the crime he committed. Although La Cloche was still hoping to secure his license and asked the state courts to help, he was on public assistance (Haberman, 2005:A16).

The barriers to employment that characterize La Cloche's case occur repeatedly for ex-offenders. According to Anne Page, the executive director of the Fortune Society, "the question is how long do you hold that albatross around a person's neck?" (Haberman, 2005:A16). It is that albatross that often precludes offenders from successfully making the transition from prison to home.

In her treatise on prisoner reentry, Petersilia (2003) clearly explained the problem, identified the challenges, and presented several comprehensive recommendations. "How we plan for inmates' transition to free living—including how they spend their time during confinement, the process by which they are released, and how they are supervised after release—is critical to public safety" (2003:3). Essentially, prisoner reentry is exacerbated by the number of returning offenders and the extent of their problems. More than 1,600 prisoners are released each day (approximately 600,000 year) and as a result of fewer prison programs, they are not prepared to reenter society and are therefore at greater risk for recidivism and revocation. An often-cited study of prisoner recidivism by the Bureau of Justice Statistics concluded that after 12 months, 44 percent of released prisoners were rearrested, and after 36 months, 68 percent were rearrested (Langan & Levin, 2002). Similarly, a study of prisoner recidivism in Pennsylvania concluded that after three years of release, the prison reincarceration rate was 46 percent (Flaherty, 2004).

Travis, Solomon, and Waul summarize the problem (2001:1):

> . . . the age-old issue of prisoner reintegration is taking on new importance. More prisoners are returning home, having spent longer terms behind bars, less prepared for life on the outside, with less assistance in their reintegration.

With attention to the challenges of prisoner reentry, Petersilia discusses four areas of opportunity to address the problems and improve both prisoner reintegration and public safety (2003:171):

- Alter the in-prison experience.
- Change prison release and revocation practices.
- Revive post-prison services and supervision.
- Foster collaborations with the community.

As mentioned earlier, the acknowledgement by Governor Schwarzenegger that corrections needs to correct and prisons need to rehabilitate reflects Petersilia's first recommendation that *prison experiences* have to be viewed as the beginning of the reentry process. In her discussion of reentry, Taxman (2004) emphasized that offenders need to become "active participants" as opposed to "active recipients" in their prison and release programs. Taxman describes two prison-based initiatives that support reentry by empowering prisoners and supporting their responsible planning: "to assist the offender to determine reintegration goals and to link the programming to transitional planning" (2004:33). These goals are similar to those that have also been endorsed by Schriro, who supports the strategy of "parallel universe" (2000:1): "the notion that life inside prison should resemble life outside prison and that inmates can acquire values, habits, and skills that will help them become productive, law-abiding citizens."

Regarding the *release process*, Petersilia advocates returning "risk-based discretion" to parole boards, and providing incentives and rewards to prisoners for their engagement in rehabilitation programming (2003:187). While predicting parole success or failure is not effective ("an imperfect science"), risk prediction instruments have been improved and can be a useful tool in determining release decisions. She identifies states that have had success with reforming release decisionmaking.

The third category of recommendation, changing the role of *parole supervision*, has been studied by Seiter (2002), who surveyed parole officers in St. Louis on what they considered important strategies for improving prisoner reentry. Parole officers reported that casework rather than surveillance supervision not only improved their jobs but contributed to "activities that emphasize assisting offenders in their success in the community" (2002:53). In commenting on the current state of parole supervision, Seiter concluded, "It is possible that we have pushed the emphasis on surveillance and risk reduction to a point where the casework activities become second priority, triggering more failures in reentry than in the past" (p. 53). By reaffirming the casework model of parole and emphasizing interventions such as drug treatment, job training, work release, and halfway house programs, Seiter believes that this not only holds offenders accountable but also increases parole success and enhances public safety. Similarly, Petersilia concluded "that programs must deliver high 'doses' of both treatment and surveillance to assure public safety and reduce recidivism" (2003:235).

Petersilia's final recommendation, *collaboration*, addresses the importance of partnerships, especially reentry partnerships, and includes the principles of restorative justice. Contrary to the punitive, exclusionary experience that Marc LaCloche had in New York, Van Ness and Strong (2002) propose that the inclusionary principles of supportive restorative justice are better suited to improving reentry successes. In discussing the process of reintegration, the authors identify three areas of assistance that are needed to facilitate offender reentry (2002:121):

1. Affirmations of personal value and common humanity.

2. Help dealing with immediate practical and material challenges.

3. Moral and spiritual direction.

The restorative perspective recognizes that community, victim, and offender share the need for support and service to overcome the consequences of crime and to provide healing and community safety. From this perspective and recognizing that "[c]orrections systems alone cannot address reentry" (Lynch & Sabol, 2001:20), the Transition from Prison to the Community Initiative (TPCI) offers assistance in redesigning reentry practices, including collaborative problem solving (Mitchell, Parent & Barnett, 2002).

In Rhode Island, for example, the TPCI involves "multiple agencies"—e.g., corrections, human services, faith-based, neighborhood organizations—working together to "strengthen the capacity of communities" to deal with returning offenders and to ensure continuity of efforts. "Rhode Island, under the TPCI model, will find innovative ways to share case-level information among the agency (i.e., Rhode Island Department of Corrections) and community partners, improving case management" (Rhode Island Department of Corrections, n.d.:3).

The project includes: assessment of offe? gramming during confinement, preparatio? nity supervision. While offenders generally? reentering the community, housing and er? that require coordinated interventions. In r ter in Providence offers a one-stop, multi-servi? offenders and their families by providing long-ter? management services starting prior to release from prison and e?? ing up to 18 months thereafter" (Family Life Center, n.d.).

The impetus for these initiatives include:

- Prisoners are returning to communities in large number with greater needs.

- Strategies need to include comprehensive, coordinated interventions to help break the cycles of prisoner recidivism and reimprisonment.

- Collaborative efforts present opportunities to enhance community supervision and to promote public safety.

The TCPI and Rhode Island's program are consistent with Petersilia's recommendations. They also demonstrate that partnerships are providing pathways for efficiency and effectiveness among community and criminal justice agencies.

COLLABORATION: COMMUNITY PARTNERSHIPS

If the retributive era was characterized by crime and punishment, the new emphasis on reentry recognizes the importance of cooperation and partnership. An early demonstration of a successful model of partnership is Boston's Gun Project. This initiative not only involved cooperation among law enforcement agencies but also the partnering of community, education, and faith-based organizations (Kennedy, Braga, Piehl & Waring, 2001). By identifying gangs, guns, drugs, and violence as community-wide issues, leaders from various public and private agencies joined efforts and shared resources to address the problems.

Similarly, Operation Ceasefire in Los Angeles "borrowed" from the Boston strategy and established a community working group to target gun violence (Tita, Riley, Ridgeway & Greenwood, 2005). The Los Angeles collaboration involved nine local, state, and federal criminal justice agencies; seven community-based organizations; three faith-based institutions; and two research organizations (p. 5). Tita and colleagues concluded that "perhaps the most important success of the am was the working group" (2005:19). This project demonstrated the various organizations were able to "exchange ideas . . . and work together effectively . . . to build community support for the interventions" (p. 19).

In a collaboration that targeted domestic violence in Richmond, Virginia, the Richmond Police Department and the Richmond Department of Social Services established a multidisciplinary approach that included second responders (i.e., social workers) who were sent "to homes following a police report of domestic violence" (Police Foundation Reports, 2005:1). Evaluation of the project determined that targeted families "received more social services . . ., more services from police . . ., and were more satisfied with how officers handled their situation" (p.2). While initial mistrust and underutilization of services characterized the partnership, the outcomes suggest "that police perform better when social workers are present and that women who receive an immediate social service response at the time of the incident may experience less repeat violence" (p.2).

In assessing this "New Paradigm of Coordinated Response," the researchers recognize the importance of "communication, collaboration, and coordination" among the various agencies (Police Foundation Reports, 2005:3). Clearly, these collaborative efforts have the potential of improving agency effectiveness, citizen/victim satisfaction, and public safety. Another type of collaboration with police that has gained attention and acceptance in communities is police-corrections partnerships (PCPs) (Parent & Snyder, 1999).

Because police and probation/parole officers often target the same populations in the same neighborhoods, an "enhanced supervision" model identifies a "common mission" that emphasizes public safety. Various strategies include "sharing information about criminal activities . . . working in partnership with the communities . . . moving to a proactive involvement . . . and reaching out to other agencies and community-based organizations" (Crawford & Talucci, 2000:44). In their study of the partnership between the Phoenix Police Department and the Maricopa County Adult Probation Department, Griffin, Hepburn, and Webb described how "such partnerships promise to lend coherence and impetus to what often are fragmented efforts to apply problem-solving to the tasks of reducing crime and increasing public safety" (2005:19).

These promising partnerships can be developed in at least five ways or models (Parent & Snyder, 1999):

1. Enhanced supervision.

2. Fugitive apprehension.

3. Information sharing.

4. Specialized enforcement.

5. Interagency problem solving.

In their evaluation of the Richland County, Ohio, community policing and community corrections partnership, Leitenberger, Semenyna, and Spelman found that "unified supervision," which included cooperative assignments and sharing of information, was successful in lowering crime rates (2003:22). In Wisconsin, the Wausau Police Department and the Wisconsin Department of Corrections initiated an enhanced supervision program to target high-risk offenders (e.g., gang members, violent criminals, sex offenders) (Hagenbucher, 2003). The Wisconsin Proactive Gang Resistance Enforcement, Suppression, and Supervision partnership (PROGRESS) conducted team visits to homes and neighborhoods as well as to collateral contacts. The partnership demonstrated that police and parole officers "benefited greatly from the exchange of information and the atmosphere of cooperation" (p. 23).

In Washington state, probation and parole officers have collaborated with the Spokane Police Department and community volunteers for approximately 10 years. They have established storefront shops known as COPS (Community-Oriented Policing Services) in more than 10 locations throughout the city. For the community, these storefronts serve as one-stop shops. Offenders who are under correctional supervision stop at the COPS locations to check in and to participate in treatment programs. In addition, citizens have a convenient location where they can file reports with the police as well as learn about social services. Such collaboration has improved relations among corrections, law enforcement, and the community, and it has improved accountability (Vander Sanden & Faulkner 2003:58, 65).

Another partner variation was initiated in a project sponsored by the U.S. Department of Justice in Arizona. The Phoenix Police Department and the Maricopa County Adult Probation Department joined efforts to develop "a shared database and integration of selected data" in order for probation and police officers to participate in a "formal, systematic problem-solving process aimed at reducing regional instances of burglary" (Griffin, Hepburn & Webb, 2005:4). While the collaboration did not demonstrate "measurable reductions in crime" (p.5), the shared database was constructed (albeit with technological difficulties and organizational turf issues) and the researchers concluded that "data sharing can be successfully accomplished" (p.60).

Similar strategies are also reflected in "Weed and Seed" programs throughout the country, which have been "a positive force in the community as evidenced by the decrease in crime rates and significant improvement in quality-of-life issues" (McLean, 2004:9). The Weed and Seed programs as well as the enhanced supervision approaches reveal that criminal justice agencies can partner with community organizations in sharing a commitment to enhancing pubic safety and implementing collaborative services and programs. While programs have had varied success, evaluations underscore the importance for criminal justice agencies to involve the community, especially key stakeholders, as well as to define goals clearly (McLean, 2004).

In the Humboldt, Tennessee, Weed and Seed program, the goals include "increasing police presence in the neighborhood . . . providing additional educational assistance and after-school programs . . . and demolishing or cleaning up existing properties though code enforcement" (Massey, 2004:17). The results indicated that "interagency coordination among law enforcement agencies improved," (p.17) and the collaboration committee was successful in planning and implementing various programs (p. 18).

ASSESSING EMERGENT TRENDS

The decline in violent crime coupled with the increasing costs of a correctional policy that is heavily dependent upon incarceration may be the ideal time to reconsider and refocus policy efforts. There is some evidence that the punitive stance that traditionally characterized drug sentencing is eroding. For example, in 2004 in New York, legislators amended the state's 30-year-old drug laws. The new legislation reduces the sentences for those offenders who are convicted for the first time and whose offense is a drug crime. Rather than the mandatory 15 years to life, the new law will require that these offenders receive sentences of less than eight years. Inmates now serving longer sentences are authorized to petition the courts to examine their sentences and reduce them to the new statute's levels (Eaton & Baker, 2004). Legislators in Kansas and Arizona have also revisited their drug statutes and are now using community-based alternatives for drug offenders (Collis, 2004:13).

In California, Proposition 36, the Substance Abuse and Crime Prevention Act of 2000, permits drug treatment rather than incarceration for offenders convicted of drug possession. This legislation could dramatically reduce California's prison population. In 2003, there were 672 third-strike offenders serving 25 years to life for drug possession, compared to 62 third-strike offenders serving a sentence for second-degree murder (Ehlers, Schiraldi & Ziedenberg, 2004:8). In addition, as noted above, Governor Schwarzenegger has called for reemphasis on rehabilitation and corrections in the prison system, ostensibly to reduce recidivism, which will reduce the state's prison population (Warren, 2005).

Similarly, in Pennsylvania, legislators voted to establish state-wide intermediate punishments (SIPs) for drug offenders that emphasize treatment and community-based residential programming (Senate Bill 217, 2004). The legislation shortens the period of incarceration and essentially recognizes a category of offenders "who never should have been subjected to mandatory sentences in the first place" (Smith, 2004:par 4). The bill was unanimously passed by both houses.

In addition, there is some evidence of a possible softening in public opinion about offenders and lengthy prison sentences. Schiraldi, Colburn, and Lotke (2004) contend that polls indicate a shift in public opinion favoring a more balanced approach to crime. When comparing data from 1994 with 2001, Hart and Associates found that the percentage of respondents who favored tougher sanctions—such as stricter sentencing, increased use of capital punishment, and a decrease in the use of parole—dropped from 48 percent in 1994 to 32 percent in 2001 (Hart & Associates, 2002:2).

In the context of this type of public opinion, the reported abuses of Iraqi prisoners under the care and custody of the U.S. military at Abu Ghraib have raised questions about the condition of prisons and the mistreatment of prisoners in the United States, and prompted the Commission on Safety and Abuse in America's Prisons to conduct a series of public hearings that will "examine the nature and extent of violence, sexual abuse, degradation, and other serious safety failures and abuses in American prisons and jails" (2005:par. 1). According to the Commission's mission statement, "At this moment, the effectiveness and morality of America's approach to corrections has the attention of policy makers at all levels of government and in both political parties" (2005:par. 2).

To some extent, this attention is directed toward the increasing number of offenders being released from prison. Israel reports (2005:5) that there is "bipartisan support" to pass legislation that will allocate additional funding and program support for reentry initiatives for offenders returning from prison.

At the same time, there is still plenty of get-tough rhetoric that will affect correctional policies. When the U.S. Supreme Court determined that the state and federal sentencing guidelines were unconstitutional, Congress vowed to draft new laws that would be even tougher on offenders. Clearly, there is an ambivalence regarding offenders. On the one hand, the data suggest that, at least with respect to drug offenders, there is a greater commitment to treatment. Conversely, there is still plenty of evidence in states, such as Texas, that high incarceration rates are acceptable and should be continued.

It is this conundrum that the system will confront in the next 10 years. Part of the equation will focus on the costs of incarceration and the continuation of harsh sanctions, and part will emphasize how best to prepare offenders to become law-abiding and productive members of society. The discussion and the development of policy will require communities to think locally about criminal justice issues such as reentry, and to utilize local resources in responding to the challenges (Friday & Brown, 1995:201). It is in this environment that collaborative efforts can evolve. Ultimately, successful prisoner reentry might alter public perceptions on crime and the criminal justice system, and signal acceptance of inclusionary initiatives and implementation of programs that reflect principles of restorative justice. Greater collaboration among criminal justice agencies, service providers, community leaders, and faith-based institutions is one small step toward reaching that goal.

DISCUSSION QUESTIONS

1. What are some of the reasons for the overcrowded conditions in prisons? Has the declining crime rate affected prison populations? Why?

2. What did the U.S. Supreme Court decide in *Blakely* and *Booker*? What effect do you anticipate the *Blakely* and *Booker* decisions will have on prison populations? Do you think that these decisions signify a shift in perspective? Why?

3. If you were asked to describe the future of prisons and prison populations, what would you say? Are the chances of incarceration equal for white and minority offenders? Which states have the largest prison populations? What about the federal system?

4. Discuss the three-strikes law in California. Has there been a shift in the voters' perceptions on the effectiveness of the legislation? What are some of the long-term consequences of the legislation?

5. What effects do overcrowded institutions have on the inmates? What would you recommend to address these conditions?

6. How have new court commitments, lifers, and prison returnees affected the prison population? What kinds of policies would you implement to address prison overcrowding? Why?

7. Why is Martha Stewart not a good example of the issues in prisoner reentry?

8. What are some of the reasons why offender reentry has become a concern for criminal justice policymakers? What are some characteristics of prisoners being released?

9. Based on Petersilia's model, identify and explain the four strategies for improving the success of prisoner reentry.

10. Discuss the concepts of "active participant" and "parallel universe." What are the goals of these approaches? What are the limits and constraints of adopting these goals for prisoners and prisons?

11. Discuss the advantages of collaboration in criminal justice. What are the basic principles of collaborative strategies?

12. Discuss why police–corrections partnerships (PCP) can be effective in crime prevention and reduction.

13. What are some indications that crime policy is softening? What are some indications that a get-tough policy is still prevalent?

14. What do you think are the significant developments in criminal justice and criminal justice policies? How will these developments impact the future of criminal justice?

REFERENCES

Austin, James (2001). "Prisoner Reentry: Current Trends, Practices, and Issues." *Crime & Delinquency* 47(3):312-334.

Bonczar, Thomas P. (2003). "Prevalence of Imprisonment in the U.S. Population, 1974-2001." *Bureau of Justice Statistics Special Report*. Washington, DC: U.S. Department of Justice, Office of Justice Programs.

Cohen, Laurie P. (2004). "Double Standard: In Wake of Ruling, Disarray Plagues Federal Sentencing." *Wall Street Journal* (December 28):1-A4.

Cohen, Laurie P., and Gary Fields (2005). "New Sentencing Battle Looms After Court Decision." *Wall Street Journal* (January 14):1, A4.

Collis, Ann (2004). "Sentencing Alternatives to Incarceration: Senate Bill 217 Passes." *Correctional Forum* (December):1,13.

Commission on Safety and Abuse in America's Prisons (2005). Mission. Washington, DC: Commission on Safety and Abuse in America's Prisons. *http://www.prison commission.org/mission.asp*

Crawford, Cheryl, and Vincent Talucci (2000). "Partnerships for Public Safety." *Corrections Today* (February):42-45.

Davenport, Kenny B. (2005). "Nothing to Lose: Re-Examining the Issue of Life in Pennsylvania." *Graterfriends* XXVIII(1):1-2.

Denniston, Lyle (2004). "Justices Agree to Consider Sentencing." *New York Times* (August 3):A12.

DiMascio, William M. (2005). "The Good and the Bad." *Graterfriends* XXVIII(2):16.

Durose, Matthew R., and Patrick A. Langan (2004). "Felony Sentences in State Courts, 2002." *Bureau of Justice Statistics Bulletin*. Washington, DC: U.S. Department of Justice, Office of Justice Programs.

Eaton, Leslie, and Al Baker (2004). "Changes Made to Drug Laws Don't Satisfy Advocates." *New York Times* (December 9). *http://www.nytimes.org*

Ehlers, Scott, Vincent Schiraldi, and Jason Ziedenberg (2004). "Still Striking Out: Ten Years of California's Three Strikes Law." Washington, DC: Justice Policy Institute.

Family Life Center (n.d.). *http://www.ri-familylifecenter.org*

Flaherty, Robert (2004). *Recidivism in Pennsylvania State Correctional Institutions 1996-2002*. (September). Camp Hill, PA: Pennsylvania Department of Corrections.

Friday, Paul C., and Michael Brown (1995). "The Politics of Community Corrections." In Michael Tonry and Kate Hamilton (eds.), *Intermediate Sanctions in Overcrowded Times*, pp. 198-202. Boston: Northeastern University Press.

GovTrack (2005). *Gang Deterrence and Community Protection Act of 2005*. *http://www.govtrack.us/congress/record.xpd?id=h109-1279*

Greenhouse, Linda (2005). "Supreme Court Transforms Use of Sentence Guidelines." *New York Times* (January 13):A1, A27.

Griffin, Marie, John Hepburn, and Vincent Webb (2005). *Combining Police and Probation Information Resources to Reduce Burglary: Testing a Crime Analysis Problem-Solving Approach*. Washington, DC: National Institute of Justice.

Haberman, Clyde (2005). "He Did Time, So He's Unfit to Do Hair." *New York Times* (March 4):A16.

Hagenbucher, Greg (2003). "PROGRESS: An Enhanced Supervision for High-Risk Criminal Offenders—Proactive Gang Resistance Enforcement, Suppression, and Supervision." *FBI Law Enforcement Bulletin* 72(9):20-24.

Harrison, Paige M., and Allen J. Beck (2004). "Prisoners in 2003." *Bureau of Justice Statistics Bulletin*. Washington, DC: U.S. Department of Justice.

Harrison, Paige M., and Allen J. Beck (2005). "Prison and Jail Inmates at Midyear 2004." *Bureau of Justice Statistics Bulletin*. Washington, DC: U.S. Department of Justice.

Harrison, Paige M., and J.C. Karberg (2004). "Prison and Jail Inmates at Midyear 2003." *Bureau of Justice Statistics Bulletin*. Washington, DC: U.S. Department of Justice.

Hart, Peter D. Research Associates, Inc. (2002). "Changing Public Attitudes Toward the Criminal Justice System."

Hulse, Carl, and Adam Liptak (2005). "New Fight Over Controlling Punishments Is Widely Seen." *New York Times* (January 13):A27.

Institute of Governmental Studies (2004). "Proposition 66: Limitation on 'Three Strikes' Laws." Berkeley, CA: Institute of Governmental Studies, University of California. *http://igs.Berkeley.edu/library/htThreeStrikesProp66.htm*

Israel, Michael (2005). *Criminal Justice Washington Letter* (March 4).

Kennedy, David M., Anthony A. Braga, Anne M. Piehl, and Elin J. Waring (2001). *Reducing Gun Violence: The Boston Gun Project's Operation Ceasefire*. Washington, DC: National Institute of Justice.

Langan, Patrick, and David Levin (2002). *Recidivism of Prisoners Released in 1994*. Washington, DC: Bureau of Justice Statistics.

Lawrence, C., and K. Andrews (2004). "The Influence of Perceived Prison Crowding on Male Inmates' Perception of Aggressive Events." *Aggressive Behavior* 30(4):273-284.

Leitenberger, David, Pete Semenyna, and Jeffrey B. Spelman (2003). "Community Corrections and Community Policing: A Perfect Match." *FBI Law Enforcement Bulletin* 72(11):20-23.

Lynch, James P., and William J. Sabol (2001). *Prisoner Reentry in Perspective*. Washington, DC: The Urban Institute.

Massey, Donna M. (2004). "The City of Humboldt, Tennessee." *Weed and Seed Best Practices: Evaluation-Based Series*, pp. 15-19. Washington, DC: U.S. Department of Justice, Executive Office for Weed and Seed.

McGough, Michael (2004). "Sentencing Guideline Ruling Delayed." *Pittsburgh Post-Gazette* (December 20):A-6.

McLean, Beverly (2004). "Buffalo Weed and Seed Program." *Weed and Seed Best Practices: Evaluation-Based Series*, pp. 9-13. Washington, DC: U.S. Department of Justice, Executive Office for Weed and Seed.

Mitchell, Cranston, Dale G. Parent, and Liz Barnett (2002). *Transition from Prison to Community Initiative*. Washington, DC: National Institute of Corrections. *http://www.nicic.org/pubs*

New York Times (2005) "Maryland: New Warden for Baltimore Jail." (July 7):A18.

Parent, Dale, and Brad Snyder (1999). *Police-Corrections Partnerships*. Washington, DC: National Institute of Justice.

Petersilia, Joan (2003). *When Prisoners Come Home: Parole and Prisoner Reentry*. New York: Oxford University Press.

Police Foundation Reports (2005). "Richmond's Second Responders: Partnering with Police Against Domestic Violence." Washington, DC: Police Foundation Reports. *http://www.policefoundation.org*

Pollock, Joycelyn M. (2004). *Prisons and Prison Life*. Los Angeles: Roxbury.

Rhode Island Department of Corrections (n.d.). *Reentry Initiatives. http://www.doc.state.ri.us/rehabilitative/reentry.htm*

Sacramento County Deputy Sheriffs' Association (2005). "Governor Schwarzenegger's Plan for CA Prisons." (January 27). *http://www.scdsa.org/content/public/articles _pring/governor_schwarzeneggers_plan_for_ca_pri*

Schiraldi, Vincent, Jason Colburn, and Eric Lotke (2004). "Three Strikes and You're Out: An Examination of the Impact of 3-Strikes Laws 10 Years after Their Enactment." Washington, DC: Justice Policy Institute.

Schriro, Dora (2000). "Correcting Corrections: Missouri's Parallel Universe." *Sentencing and Corrections* (No. 8). Washington, DC: National Institute of Justice.

Seiter, Richard P. (2002). "Prisoner Reentry and the Role of Parole Officers." *Federal Probation* 66(3):50-54.

Senate Bill 217 (2004). The General Assembly of Pennsylvania. No. 1758 (June 28).

The Sentencing Project (2005a). "Retrospective from the Sentencing Project." Washington, DC: The Sentencing Project. *http://www.sentencingproject.org/booker-retro spective.cfm*

The Sentencing Project (2005b). "The United States House of Representatives Passes the Gang Deterrence and Community Protection Act of 2005." Washington, DC: The Sentencing Project. *http://www.sentencingproject.org/hr1279.cfm*

The Sentencing Project (2004). "New Incarceration Figures: Rising Population Despite Falling Crime Rates." Washington, DC: The Sentencing Project.

Smith, Elmer (2004). "A 'Quiet' Turnaround on Mandatory Terms." *Philadelphia Daily News* (December 10). *http://www.philly.com/mld/dailynews/*

Stephan, James J. (2004). "State Prison Expenditures, 2001." *Bureau of Justice Statistics Special Report.* Washington, DC: U.S. Department of Justice, Office of Justice Programs.

Taxman, Faye S. (2004). "The Offender and Reentry: Supporting Active Participation in Reintegration." *Federal Probation* 68(2):31-35.

Tita, George, K. Jack Riley, Greg Ridgeway, and Peter W. Greenwood (2005). *Reducing Gun Violence: Operation Ceasefire in Los Angeles.* Washington, DC: National Institute of Justice.

Tonry, Michael (2004). *Thinking About Crime: Sense and Sensibility in American Penal Culture.* New York: Oxford University Press.

Travis, Jeremy, Amy L. Solomon, and Michelle Waul (2001). *From Prison to Home: The Dimensions and Consequences of Prisoner Reentry.* Washington, DC: The Urban Institute.

Turpin, James S. (2000). "What's Happened to the Crime Issue?" *Corrections Today* (December):161.

Vander Sanden, Bruce, and Rick Faulkner (2003). "Accountability Through Innovation and Collaboration." *Corrections Today* (August): 56-58, 65.

Van Ness, Daniel W., and Karen Heetderks Strong (2002). *Restoring Justice,* 2nd ed. Cincinnati: Anderson.

Warren, Jenifer (2005). "Governor Aims to Rehabilitate Prison System." *Los Angeles Times* (February 13). *http://www.latimes.com*

CASES

Blakely v. Washington, 124 S. Ct. 2531 (2004).

United States v. Booker, 125 S. Ct.738 (2005).

United States v. Fanfan, 125 S. Ct. 738 (2005).

7

Changing Course

In the 1960s, the idealism of liberal thinking about crime supported Johnson's "war on poverty," the rehabilitation of criminals, and the optimism that everything done with good intentions would work. By the mid-1970s, the "Martinson Report" (1974) dampened this enthusiasm and was used to condemn rehabilitation as a bankrupt model of crime control and to declare that "nothing works" in corrections and offender treatment (Cullen & Gilbert, 1982; Walker, 1998). This provided justification for more conservative and punitive responses to crime and criminals. At that time, the cycle alternating between severity and softening was moving into a period of severity (Clear & Cole, 1997). As discussed in Chapter 1, the "nothing works" mantra that prevailed as public policy in the 1980s was fashioned into "wars" on crime and on drugs that emphasized deterrence, incapacitation, and punishment. This thinking coincided with the expanding "justice juggernaut" (Gordon, 1990) that included longer and mandatory sentences, the rapid increase in incarceration rates and prison populations, the net-widening of community controls, and the focus on law enforcement and policing effectiveness. The shift from "everything works" to "nothing works" in ideology and public policy illustrates a dualistic fallacy in crime policy by which extremes distort understanding and the "either/or" choice frustrates rational thinking and polarizes discussion and debate on crime.

When complex issues are simplified into dichotomies, and citizens and policymakers are presented with limited choices, policy is distorted and criminal justice fails to achieve or maintain balance in crime control efforts. For example, when issues were presented as either for or against capital punishment, treatment versus punishment, probation versus prison, juvenile versus adult court, the zeitgeist of the 1980s and 1990s favored capital punishment, prison, and adult jurisdiction for youthful offenders. Efforts to develop more balanced and comprehensive alternatives, however, have broadened the policy options: for example, life without parole, coercive treatment (e.g., drug courts), intermediate punishments (e.g., electronic monitoring), and blended sentences for serious, violent juvenile offenders.

As Sherman's report (1997) suggests, crime policies in the twenty-first century can emphasize promising strategies rather than the continuing search for ideological victories and panaceas. One of the lessons of this review is to transcend political rhetoric and media news that filter, distort, and simplify crime issues into sound bites (Kappeler, Blumberg & Potter, 1996; Potter & Kappeler, 1998), and to identify and support crime policies with successful outcomes. Before reviewing generalizations about the capacity and limits of criminal justice to achieve balanced strategies, a final look at the problem of drugs and crime will help to illustrate the conundrum of a complex social problem in search of a simple solution—and the implications for the criminal justice system.

DRUGS: CRIMINAL JUSTICE OR MEDICAL MODEL?

In an assessment of the history of drugs and public policy, Inciardi, McBride, and Rivers (1996) identified two questions that characterize the drug problem in the United States:

1. What is the drug–crime connection?
2. Is it a criminal justice problem or a medical problem?

They concluded that while criminal involvement can precede drug use, drug use often intensifies and perpetuates criminal behavior, thus creating a bidirectional effect or relationship (p. 14). While recognizing the limits of the research and data, they described how moral crusades and manipulation of (and by) the media resulted in distorted images of drug users as "dope fiends" and evil, immoral, and dangerous offenders. The image of "evil" rather than "sick" (i.e., dualism) helped criminalize addiction and drug use. Social control was designated as a law enforcement issue, and the war on drugs was initiated.

A comprehensive and compelling critique of anti-drug campaigns presented by Jensen and Gerber demonstrates five consequences of criminalizing drug use (1998:22-23):

1. Increased pressure on law enforcement to make arrests and to extend intrusiveness of drug enforcement techniques.

2. Huge profits from drug sales, which attracted more profiteers and contributed to the expansion of drug markets.

3. Pervasive social controls that extended beyond criminal justice to schools, employers, and hospitals.

4. A United States–led worldwide crusade against illegal drugs that emphasized punitive and prohibitionist policies.

5. A United States war strategy that "has completely failed" and "voices advocating alternative solutions to problems associated with illegal drugs [that] become increasingly louder."

Generally, in considering anti-drug policies, four strategies are recognized: (1) supply reduction, (2) demand reduction, (3) legalization, and (4) harm reduction.

Supply reduction (eradication, interdiction, and law enforcement) and demand reduction (increased and longer prison sentences) have predominated the war on drugs. As noted by Jensen and Gerber (1998), frustration and failure with these efforts have contributed to initiatives more aligned with a medical-model strategy. For example, Proposition 215 in California legalized marijuana use for medical reasons. This resulted in about 30 medical marijuana supply operations throughout the state (*New York Times*, 1998a). Since California became the first state to permit the use of medical marijuana in 1996, 10 additional states began active medical marijuana programs: Alaska, Colorado, Hawaii, Maine, Maryland, Montana, Nevada, Oregon, Vermont, and Washington (National Organization for the Reform of Marijuana Laws, 2004). Contrary to some expectations, in a study conducted by O'Keefe and Earleywine (2005), the researchers concluded that in those states with medical marijuana laws, teens were no more likely to use marijuana than in states without such legislation.

While the legislative debate and ballot initiatives will continue to generate some support, the dualistic basis of the debate is evident: if legalization is not favored or viewed as acceptable policy, the alternative is to continue with and to support criminalization.

ALTERNATIVES TO DRUG WARS AND DUALISTIC POLICY DEBATES

TASC: Treatment Alternatives to Street Crime

One compromise between these opposing policies is to integrate medical models and criminal justice models. This accomplishes two objectives: first, it acknowledges that the drug problem is not only a crime problem but a broader social, public-health issue; second, it announces a cooperative approach that joins resources and strategies that include more than a unidimensional perspective. In this context, Inciardi, McBride, and Rivers (1996) summarized the history and success of the Treatment Alternatives to Street Crime (TASC) initiatives of the 1970s. Heroin was considered the problem drug at that time, and TASC's goals included interventions (1) to reduce drug use and crime, (2) to shift drug offenders from the criminal justice system, and (3) to avoid the labeling, stigma, and social learning that resulted from the incarceration experience (p. 41).

While the TASC projects experienced some challenges requiring program and policy modifications (e.g., due process, confidentiality, offender as client, and program termination), important outcomes of TASC included new and successful links between criminal justice and treatment systems (Inciardi, McBride & Rivers, 1996:46). The researchers' assessment recognized that beyond improved performance, program completion, employability, abstinence, and cost-benefits for offender-clients, TASC demonstrated that treatment providers could intervene with—and monitor—drug offenders while cooperating with corrections and court personnel. Even though TASC was not a panacea for the drug-crime problem, this approach achieved better post-treatment outcomes than previous programs and established a model for coercive treatment (p. 53).

Drug Courts

The lessons of TASC show the difficulty of stopping drug abuse and the limits of treatment. The problems of drugs and crime, however, have continued to be major challenges to criminal justice. In the 1990s and 2000s, the main criminal justice and treatment initiative is the drug court. As a court-enforced drug treatment alternative, which began in Miami in 1989, "drug courts bring the full weight of all interventions to bear, forcing the defendant to address his or her underlying substance abuse problem" (Huddleston, 1998:98). Targeting drug-dependent offenders, these courts are specialty courts that focus on expediting pre-trial jail cases by actively involving judges as "managers" who coerce, monitor, and enforce treatment (see Chapter 5). In addition, drug courts involve a collaboration of various programs and staff (e.g., substance abuse treatment specialists, probation officers, corrections officers, community leaders, prosecutors, defense attorneys) that help "create a unified system" (Huddleston, 1998:98).

In addition to a management-oriented judge, C. West Huddleston, a former deputy director of the National Drug Court Institute, identified five common characteristics of the drug court model (p. 98):

1. expedited adjudication;

2. intensive long-term treatment and aftercare;

3. comprehensive and well-coordinated supervision;

4. offender accountability through graduated sanctions and rewards; and

5. mandatory and frequent drug testing.

A review of 30 evaluations of drug courts conducted by the National Center on Addiction and Substance Abuse (CASA) found consistent and encouraging results that offenders received closer supervision and more frequent drug testing—and demonstrated reduced drug use and criminal behavior—while under court-treatment monitoring (Belenko, 1998). The findings reported by Belenko also indicate that costs are reduced, offenders can be safely supervised, and criminal justice and treatment systems can cooperate effectively. While assessments of longer-term outcomes are more cautious, this probably reflects the "embeddedness" of the offender's involvement in drugs and criminal activity. In other words, the longer and more intense the drug history, the more likely that relapse will occur (see Chapter 4).

As with TASC, the drug-court model is not a panacea but a collaborative, treatment-based strategy that attempts to interrupt the drug-crime cycle. Since the first drug court was established in 1989, there are now more than 1,600 such specialty courts in all 50 states; 400 of these drug courts were established in 2004 (Walters, 2005). The evidence suggests a safe, intense, less costly, and more effective approach to demand reduction than the increased prison sentences characterized by the Rockefeller drug laws that have been in effect in New York since 1973, the Reagan–Bush drug wars of the 1980s, and the continuing drug war of President George W. Bush, which has demonstrated a renewed focus on marijuana (Eggen, 2005; King & Mauer, 2005). A study of 17,000 drug court graduates found that after one year, only 17 percent had been rearrested and charged with a felony offense; this compares to a 44 percent recidivism rate for non-drug court graduates (Walters, 2005:par. 7).

Harm Reduction

The harm reduction model is another type of approach that offers an alternative to both demand and supply reductions and avoids the legalization debate. This framework emphasizes "the reduction of adverse consequences rather than the elimination of drug use" (Erickson & Butters, 1989:179) and includes programs such as needle exchange, methadone maintenance, and even the decriminalization of some drugs. Harm reduction reflects a public health perspective by which adverse health risks (e.g., needle sharing, unprotected sexual activity, crime, victimization) are targeted. Erickson and Butters describe harm reduction as more of a conceptualization that recognizes (p. 189):

> ... a shift from criminal to health definitions of drug-related problems (which is) accompanied by the view of users as mainstream or potentially functional members of society rather than marginal, deviant misfits.

The authors suggest that this represents a significant shift in thinking from a criminalized model to a medicalized model. For example, consider the use of methadone maintenance programs as a treatment for drug addiction. While former Mayor Rudolph Giuliani was proposing to phase out all such programs in New York City in 1998, Barry McCaffrey, former director of drug policy, was promoting this as an effective treatment for heroin addiction. Giuliani's view was that methadone was another form of drug addiction (replacement for heroin), and he wanted to close the clinics and let addicts practice abstinence. McCaffrey was proposing to increase methadone programs and to allow doctors to "treat methadone users as regular patients in their offices" (Marks, 1998:31).

As a harm reduction or public health/medical response, methadone has had fairly extensive success beginning in the 1960s. In addition to reducing criminal behavior, methadone use has reduced the risk of transmitting disease and HIV through injection. Moreover, with methadone regulation, addicts can maintain employment and avoid criminal involvement (Erickson & Butters, 1998). In their review of the harm reduction movement, Erickson and Butters recognize the dominance of the criminal justice model but view the "non-coercive and non-abstinence approach" as an opportunity to develop broader, less "single-minded" strategies to control drugs (1998:195). Yale University child psychiatrist David Musto critiques drug strategies by stressing that simple and quick expectations for reducing drug use are unrealistic, create a sense of frustration and failure, and often lead to "more severe penalties" (1998:24). In a more critical statement, Hahn observed that:

it seems unconscionable for our advanced society to continue to devote itself to a reactive, negative, punitive "war on
drugs" that there is little chance of winning, at a huge cost to
the community at large and to the viability of the criminal justice system (1998:21).

These lessons apply not only to drugs but also to expectations
regarding crime reduction and crime prevention.

ISSUES IN CRIMINAL JUSTICE

In a review of initiatives and programs in corrections, Roberg
and Webb (1981) identified characteristics of crime and criminal justice that make crime reduction and system reform difficult to achieve.
Using the conceptualization of an "issue" as a situation, problem, or
condition that (1) is interrelated to other issues/problems, (2) has systemic qualities, (3) has an ideological element, and (4) is persistent over
time, the authors concluded that crime and criminal justice epitomized these characteristics (pp. 4-5). The implications are not encouraging and point to the intractable nature of crime.

As Walker (2006) discussed in his treatise on crime policy, responses
to crime are often more like "social tinkering" than agents of comprehensive change. In addition, solutions to crime are more realistically
developed outside the criminal justice system because crime control policy is generally reactive and fails to address the antecedents of crime
(e.g., Hahn, 1998; Walker, 1998, 2006). For example, incarcerating
more offenders does little to curb the conditions conducive to crime and
may result in unintended effects that exacerbate criminal behaviors and
fail to control crime.

These ideas are reflected in part by Rose and Clear (1998) in their
discussion of the implications of incarceration. The authors hypothesize:

> that an overreliance on formal controls may hinder the abil-
> ity of some communities to foster other forms of control. As
> a result, these communities may experience more, not less,
> social disorganization (p. 443).

Their argument is consistent with Black's (1976) conceptualization
regarding an inverse relationship between informal and formal social
controls: as informal controls (e.g., family, church, school) fail to
regulate behavior and restrain deviance, society turns to more official-
formal regulators (e.g., police, courts, prisons). This reinforces the public view of a "breakdown of society" and the need to impose stronger
controls. Unfortunately, as Rose and Clear discuss, this overreliance

on formal controls (i.e., incarceration) further weakens the informal efforts and sustains dependency and the rationale for continued reliance on external, official regulation (p. 442):

> When local controls are impaired, communities must rely more heavily upon the controls of the state. Partly this is because there is more crime in these areas so the communities need the added strength of formal law enforcement in their response to crime. However, it may be that increased state efforts shift control resources from local to public, thus making state efforts more necessary.

This model helps explain why incarceration rates have increased disproportionately to crime rates: it is not primarily crime that drives up prison populations but rather the consequences of using more laws and more law enforcement to respond to crime (i.e., public policy). This view is consistent with Walker's observation (1998:277) and Sherman's conclusion (1997) that strategies and programs dealing with crime prevention are most effective in the neighborhoods and with the people who least need them. In other words, where informal controls are evident, formal controls are effective but also less necessary. It is in the areas in which "breakdowns" are more evident and concentrated (i.e., unemployment, poverty, births to single teens, female head of households) that formal efforts are less effective in preventing crime. The review by Sherman and colleagues (1997) suggests, however, that promising strategies include those with community involvement (i.e., informal) and collaborative projects with other agencies and organizations. For example, Canada (1995) described the success of the Beacon Schools in New York and the importance of encouraging and supporting the informal controls that parents, schools, and neighborhoods can exert in partnership with other public agencies.

LIMITS OF LAW

An important lesson about criminal justice is that there are limits to what laws can accomplish in response to complex social problems and diverse deviant behaviors. The general notion that legislating more laws (and adding the enforcement responsibilities and expenses to the criminal justice system) will "solve" a crime problem is what Walker (1998, 2006) would call "nonsense." Consistent with the themes of this text, Hahn has noted:

that public fear of crime and anger about it culminate in pressure on politicians, who in most cases have little knowledge about crime control and little will to advance anything other than simplistic solutions (1998:7).

Consider the bandwagon effect of states passing sex offender notification laws like "Megan's Law" of New Jersey. The intent of such legislation was to inform parents and neighbors that a known sex offender was residing near their homes and schools. In the summer of 1998, however, Connecticut citizens and lawmakers learned that "the notification law (had) failed them" when an 11-year-old papergirl in Willimantic, Angelica Padilla, was killed, allegedly by a convicted sex offender living in the neighborhood (Allen, 1998). The responses to the murder of Padilla indicate how legislators, police, and citizens have different perspectives on the sex notification laws.

Citizens expected that police would provide notification when a convicted sex offender moved into a neighborhood. In Connecticut, however, "citizens have to ask the local police for the information instead of being told" (Allen, 1998). Police officials reported that the law was too vague to force sex offenders to update their addresses and that it is difficult to keep addresses current. One State Senator, Kevin Sullivan, acknowledged that "a law on the books is a beginning, not an end . . . This is a terrible way to learn that you need to do something more" (Allen, 1998). In response, other legislators called for a stronger law that would require police to "notify all residents within a half a mile of a convicted sex offender." Some police chiefs wanted the legislature to "tighten the rules about updating the addresses of convicted offenders" (Allen, 1998). The general sense of these responses was: "we had a law; it didn't work; therefore we need a tougher law."

Another celebrated murder in 1998 also prompted endorsement for more laws. The brutal beating and murder of Matthew Shepard, a gay student at the University of Wyoming, occurred in a state with a hate crime statute that did not include sexual orientation. At the time, only 21 states had such laws. This prompted calls to broaden federal hate crime laws "to cover crimes motivated by the victim's sexual orientation, disability or gender" (Will, 1998:A6). In the context of the classical crime control ideology, more hate crime laws would be deterrents to crimes motivated by homophobic prejudices. In James Jacobs's view, however, "such calls are well-meaning but misguided" (1998:A25).

Jacobs and Potter, co-authors of *Hate Crimes: Criminal Law and Identity Politics* (1998), argue that there are already laws that adequately punish offenders for such serious crimes, regardless of the motivation. For example, in Wyoming, the two suspects in the Shepard murder faced capital murder charges and the death penalty (Jacobs, 1998a). Because of the seriousness of the crime and the media attention to it, politicians evoked well-used slogans about "getting tough" on crime. Jacobs observed that "it is hard to see the current outcry as anything more than another chance for politicians to go out on a limb and declare themselves against hate and prejudice" (1998a:A25). While the message may be relevant, appropriate, and even necessary, calls for more federal laws are mostly symbolic because, as noted by Jacobs, federal investigators and prosecutors "could not possibly respond to even a fraction of the offenses labeled as bias or hate crimes" (1998a:A25). George Will is even more critical of this case of the politics of crime:

> Congress continually uses the criminal law as a moral pork barrel, for indignation gestures. Compassion is today's supreme political value, so politics is a sentiment competition. It is less about changing society than striking poses: theatrical empathy trumps considerations of mere practicality (1998:A6).

These cases of sex offender notification and hate crime statutes demonstrate the themes that have been discussed throughout the text:

- The news media focus attention on celebrated crimes that then become transfixed as national events.

- Politicians offer quick, simple solutions such as proposing more law, without addressing the economic or system impacts.

- Ideological concepts are used to justify and rationalize the legislation as the "best" policy to confront crime.

In addition to notification, another legislative response for monitoring and getting tough with sex offenders is the National Sex Offender Public Registry (see http://www.nsopr.gov). This is an attempt to have child sex offenders register or face up to 20 years in prison for noncompliance (H.R. 3132, 2005). The Children's Safety Act of 2005 would require "felony offenders to register for life [see Box 7.1, Information Required in Registration] and authorizes the death penalty for sex crimes that result in the killing of a child" (Abrams, 2005:par. 5).

Box 7.1
Information Required in Registration

(a) Provided by the Offender—The sex offender must provide the following information to the appropriate official for inclusion in the sex offender registry:

  (1) The name of the sex offender (including any alias used by the individual).

  (2) The Social Security number of the sex offender.

  (3) The address and location of the residence at which the sex offender resides or will reside.

  (4) The place where the sex offender is employed or will be employed.

  (5) The place where the sex offender is a student or will be a student.

  (6) The license plate number of any vehicle owned or operated by the sex offender.

  (7) A photograph of the sex offender.

  (8) A set of fingerprints and palm prints of the sex offender, if the appropriate official determines that the jurisdiction does not already have available an accurate set.

  (9) A DNA sample of the sex offender, if the appropriate official determines that the jurisdiction does not already have available an appropriate DNA sample.

  (10) Any other information required by the Attorney General.

Source: H.R. 3132, Section 114, 2005. http://thomas.loc.gov/cgi-bin/query/F?c109:3:./temp/
~c109qhCXrX:e17854:

With this House Bill, legislators announced "a 'national crisis' in child sex offenses" (see Box 7.2, Declaration of Purpose) and the need to locate 100,000 of "550,000 convicted sex offenders whose whereabouts are unknown" (Abrams, 2005:par. 5).

Box 7.2
Declaration of Purpose

In response to the vicious attacks by violent sexual predators against the victims listed below, Congress in this Act establishes a comprehensive national system for the registration of sex offenders:

(1) Jacob Wetterling, who was 11 years old, was abducted in 1989 in Minnesota, and remains missing.

(2) Megan Nicole Kanka, who was 7 years old, was abducted, sexually assaulted and murdered in 1994, in New Jersey.

(3) Pam Lychner, who was 31 years old, was attacked by a career offender in Houston, Texas.

(4) Jetseta Gage, who was 10 years old, was kidnapped, sexually assaulted, and murdered in 2005 in Cedar Rapids, Iowa.

(5) Dru Sjodin, who was 22 years old, was sexually assaulted and murdered in 2003, in North Dakota.

(6) Jessica Lunsford, who was 9 years old, was abducted, sexually assaulted, buried alive, and murdered in 2005, in Homosassa, Florida.

(7) Sarah Lunde, who was 13 years old, was strangled and murdered in 2005, in Ruskin, Florida.

(8) Amie Zyla, who was 8 years old, was sexually assaulted in 1996 by a juvenile offender in Waukesha, Wisconsin, and has become an advocate for child victims and protection of children from juvenile sex offenders.

(9) Christy Ann Fornoff, who was 13 years old, was abducted, sexually assaulted and murdered in 1984, in Tempe, Arizona.

(10) Alexandra Nicole Zapp, who was 30 years old, was brutally attacked and murdered in a public restroom by a repeat sex offender in 2002, in Bridgewater, Massachusetts.

Source: H.R. 3132, Section 102, 2005. http://thomas.loc.gov/cgi-bin/query/F?c109:3:./temp/~c109qhCXrX:e9070:

The legislation would also establish a Sex Offender Management Assistance program and amend the DNA Identification Act of 1994 in order to authorize the development a Combined DNA Index System (H.R. 3132, 2005).

Whether through the addition of tougher legislation, more police officers on the street, longer sentences for drug offenders, or more crimes punishable by execution, the momentum of the formal, punitive social control juggernaut continues to increase.

GOOD NEWS: DECLINE IN CRIME

According to the United States Department of Justice, data from the National Crime Victimization Survey indicate that "violent and property crime rates in 2004 remained at the lowest levels since the Bureau of Justice Statistics first conducted its annual survey" in 1973 (U.S. Department of Justice, 2005:par. 1). From 1993 to 2004, "the violent crime rate fell 57 percent and the property crime rate dropped by 50 percent" (2005:par. 4). Based on data reported in the Uniform Crime Reports, the FBI also reported this continued drop in violent and property crimes in 2004 (Federal Bureau of Investigation, 2005). The continued decline in crime in the 1990s and 2000s presented encouraging news to politicians and the public and provided what Currie referred to as "a respite . . . from the epidemic levels of violence" (1998:9). The respite also provided an opportunity to go beyond assessments of why crime had been increasing and to consider more timely questions, including why crime was decreasing and what were the consequences of the get-tough politics of the 1980s and 1990s.

Explanations for Crime Reduction

After nine years of consistent decline in violent crime rates, several explanations have been proposed for this downturn in crime trends (Blumstein & Wallman, 2000; Levitt & Dubner, 2005; Siegel & Welsh, 2005; Travis & Waul, 2002; Walker, 2006). Two "crucial" views have focused on the decline of the crack cocaine market and police initiatives to seize handguns (Butterfield, 1998). These focus topics were suggested by the sharp drop in homicide and robbery, two crimes "most often committed with handguns and most associated with the crack cocaine epidemic in the later 1980s" (Butterfield, 1998:1).

In a report on crime in Washington, DC, Fernandez deferred to police officials who admitted "it is difficult to cite precisely why Washington streets were safer" (1999:J01). Writing for the National Center for Policy Analysis, though, Reynolds was decidedly more certain why crime had declined: "A major reason for this reduction in crime is that crime has become more costly to the perpetrators" (1998:1). Reynolds was referring to the deterrent nature of incarceration (i.e., the increased expectation of punishment) demonstrated by the growth in prison population and the mandatory, get-tough sentencing policies (see Chapters 3 and 4).

Currie (1998) also acknowledged the popular view that increased incarceration in the 1980s and 1990s resulted in crime reduction. His analysis, however, is that "incarceration 'works' much better for property crimes than for crimes like homicide or assault" (p. 188). This would predict that with increases in incarceration, property crimes would show the most decreases; in fact, data suggest the opposite—"the fastest declines have been in homicide, and property crime has fallen more slowly" (p. 188).

In addition to the questionable effects of incarceration, Currie's explanation for reductions in crime includes the implementation of police tactics and the growth in community-based prevention programs. He also credits the consequences of a stronger economy and the availability of legitimate work coupled with reduced opportunities for illegitimate work (i.e., waning of the crack market). Finally, he offers some anecdotal evidence suggesting attitude changes among youths (p. 188):

> [T]he decline reflects, in part, a subtle cultural shift among the young, especially minority youths—a growing turn away from violence against their peers, driven by revulsion against the destructiveness of the epidemic that had destroyed the lives, bodies, and futures of so many of their relatives and friends.

In a sense, the explanations for crime reduction are as complex as those for the prevalence of crime and for the increases that have captured so much attention. Anderson (1998) examined this "mystery of the falling crime rate" by focusing on the "back-end/front-end" debate. Essentially back-enders are conservatives, who believe crime has been reduced because of deterrent policies such as capital punishment, longer prison sentences, and limited discretion for judges and parole boards. Front-enders are liberals, who see the benefits (i.e., crime reduction) resulting from gun control, early intervention, drug treatment, and alternative programs (p. 34). Anderson asks: Which is the better way to fight crime? He offers the following observation, which serves as a review of some of the perspectives presented in Chapter 1:

> While the question ought to be pursued seriously—it is richly complex in practical, economic and moral issues—it became hopelessly politicized during the decade that began around 1985, when crack and guns produced a surge of urban crime and politicians sought ways to exploit the fear it generated. As it turned out, this politics of crime heavily favored back-enders as it produced fervent support for capital punishment and a nationwide movement toward three-strikes and other mandatory-sentencing laws (pp. 34-35).

Anderson's discussion not only critiqued the claims of back-enders versus front-enders regarding efforts of crime reduction, but also suggested that the prevailing (back-end) politics and policies have influenced the direction of criminal justice. The next section considers some of the continuing consequences of the get-tough ethos on the criminal justice system.

CONSEQUENCES FOR CRIMINAL JUSTICE

Capital Punishment

In 1999, after serving 16 years on death row in San Quentin for two murders he was convicted of committing in 1981, Jatarun Siripongs, a 43-year-old immigrant from Thailand, asked former California Governor Gray Davis "to commute his sentence to life without parole" (Terry, 1999:A14). Siripongs admitted to taking part in a robbery but maintained that it was his accomplice who committed the double murders. Once a Buddhist monk, Siripongs sustained a "spotless prison record" (i.e., no misconduct reports or difficulties while in prison) and had the support of the former prison warden, the Roman Catholic Bishop of Sacramento, a juror who voted to convict him, and the husband of one of the two people he was sentenced to death for murdering (Terry, 1999:A14).

The case received prominent attention because of concerns regarding the incompetence of the court-appointed trial attorney, an unprecedented plea for clemency from former warden Daniel Vasquez (who had overseen other executions), and the political spotlight that the request placed on California's newly elected Governor Gray Davis (the first Democratic governor in 16 years). In his election campaign, Davis took "a very strong position in favor of the death penalty," which, in effect, quieted his Republican opponent, State Attorney General Dan Lungren, who was a "staunch death penalty advocate" (Terry, 1999:A14).

As discussed earlier, the politicization of crime has moved the discourse away from who favors or opposes severe punishments such as the death penalty to the question of which candidate is tougher on crime and criminals. As a new governor in 1999, Davis presided over the largest state prison system in the nation, which included more than 500 offenders on death row. The Siripongs case was his first "life-or-death" decision.

Jatarun Siripongs was executed on February 9, 1999. In responding to the Siripongs case, a Santa Clara University law professor, Gerald Uelman, noted the political risk of granting clemency (cited in Terry, 1999:A14):

> I think the political cost to Gray Davis would be enormous if he grants clemency. We're in a state where death penalty politics has a heavy hand in gubernatorial politics, and we've seen Democratic candidates, again and again, become vulnerable to the issue. But Davis got past it by taking a very strong position in favor of the death penalty.

It is apparent that the visibility and emotionality of the death penalty issue make politicians vulnerable to public opinion—and therefore more inclined to support capital punishment. Consider the results of focus groups on the impressions of New York Governor George Pataki's accomplishments in his first term in office (Kolbert, 1999:37): "[P]articipants could hardly come up with anything. Only the death penalty and the welfare cuts were mentioned by more than one group." Pataki, who campaigned to bring the death penalty back to New York, signed legislation to fulfill his campaign promise.

This suggests that one of the most evident manifestations of the back-ender emphasis on crime is capital punishment. In the most recent year-end analysis, the Death Penalty Information Center reported that since 1999, when 98 executions were carried out, the number of executions has maintained a steady decline to 59 executions in 2004 (2005a). The number of offenders sentenced to death has also decreased from 320 in 1996 to 125 in 2004 (Death Penalty Information Center, 2005a). Contrary to the punitive policies of the 1990s, these downward trends in executions and death sentences not only reflect the decrease in violent crimes committed but also a reluctance to sentence innocent offenders to death (Death Penalty Information Center, 2005b). The Death Penalty Information Center reports that from 1973 to mid-2005, 121 offenders have been released from death row with evidence of their innocence. DNA evidence was used to establish innocence in 14 of the cases (2005b). Surveys also demonstrate that public support for the death penalty has declined in recent years (see Box 7.3). This is in part due to the release of innocent offenders from death row and to the availability of life-without-parole sentences (Death Penalty Information Center, 2005c).

As discussed in Chapter 1, politics has narrowed the debate on crime and punishment. For Democrats to overcome the "Dukakis legacy" (i.e., soft on crime, opposition to the death penalty), they have had to appropriate the Republicans' high ground on law-and-order issues. As Governor of Arkansas and as President, Bill Clinton took crime away from the Republicans as a wedge issue (Weisberg, 1999:34) and effectively left minimal room for serious discussion or debate on crime. In fact, some political analysts have observed that with such issues as crime, "the line between Democrats and Republicans can be hard to find" (Berke, 1999:1). The political alternatives are to be "tough" or "tougher." Davis, for one, learned the lesson and reinforced the message for politicians.

Box 7.3
Public Opinion and the Death Penalty

The latest Gallup Poll found support for the death penalty at 74%, a figure equal to the level in 2003 and less than the 80% support registered in 1994. The poll found that support for capital punishment dropped to 56% when respondents were given the alternative sentencing option of life without parole, less than the 61% support in 1997 with the same question. The percentage of respondents who believe an innocent person has been executed in recent years has dropped from 73% in 2003 to 59% this year. (The Gallup Organization Press Release, May 19, 2005).

A recent CBS News Poll (April 17, 2005) found the public more evenly split on the death penalty. In response to the question "What do you think should be the penalty for persons convicted of murder— the death penalty, life in prison with no chance of parole, or a long prison sentence with a chance of parole?", only 39% chose the death penalty, 39% chose life with no parole, 6% said a long sentence with parole, and 13% volunteered the answer "depends." (Roper Center at Univ. of Conn., May 17, 2005).

Source: Death Penalty Information Center (2005). News and Developments – Public Opinion. Reprinted with permission of The Death Penalty Information Center.

Police

In addition to political party convergence on issues of crime and punishment (Walker, 2006), the consequences of get-tough policies also renew concerns about the enforcement policies that are used by police (and supported by politicians) to bring down the crime rates. As noted earlier in the text, national attention was focused on police enforcement policies as a result of the criminal trial of four New York City police officers charged with sexually assaulting Abner Louima in 1997 and the incidence of the fatal shooting of Amadou Diallo, a 22-year-old West African immigrant from Guinea, by four other New York City police officers in early 1999. In the Louima case, Officer Justin Volpe entered a guilty plea and was convicted of aggravated sexual abuse and first-degree assault. One officer was convicted of restraining Louima while Volpe assaulted him, and the other three officers were acquitted (*New York Times*, 1999f). In the Diallo case, four officers fired 41 rounds at an unarmed citizen who had no police record (he was hit by 19 bullets) (McFadden & Roane, 1999). While former New York City Mayor Rudolph Giuliani counseled against a rush to judgment, a *New York Times* editorial reported that "while the city says that more than 90 percent of New York's police officers never fire their guns, three of the four officers in this case have been involved in shootings before, with two found to have acted properly and one incident still under review by the Brooklyn District Attorney" (1999b:A30). This incident "brought renewed scrutiny to the Street Crimes Unit, which had been criticized before for its aggressive tactics. The unit is assigned to seek out and stop crime before it happens. Its motto is 'We Own the Night'" (*New York Times*, 1999c:A23).

The media attention on Diallo's death focused on the "dark side" of aggressive policing and the climate of brutality that it creates (Bumiller & Thompson, 1999). In 1997, New York City received 4,769 complaints of police misconduct; in 1998, it received 4,976, a relatively small 4 percent increase. The number of substantiated cases declined from 448 in 1997 (8% of the allegations) to 300 in 1998 (6% of the allegations) (Cooper, 1999:A19). Another measure of police misconduct is the payments made by the city to settle misconduct claims. In 1997, more than $27.5 million was paid to settle lawsuits of police misconduct, compared to $20 million in 1993, a 38 percent increase (Berger, 1999:A31). In fiscal year 2005, New York City paid out $68.6 million dollars to settle 1,269 tort dispositions for the police department (New York City Law Department, n.d.).

The Street Crime Unit (SCU) was also plagued with allegations of racial profiling in addition to accusations of using aggressive tactics. In 1999, the SCU made one arrest for every 16 African Americans that were stopped (i.e., 6.3%) (Center for Constitutional Rights, 2005). Of 45,000 stops and frisks reported by the unit in 1997 and 1998, 22 percent resulted in an arrest. After the Diallo killing and a subsequent class action lawsuit, the SCU was disbanded and racial profiling was banned (Center for Constitutional Rights, 2005:par. 5).

However, the issue of racial profiling and police relations with black and Hispanic populations remains problematic. Recently, the Bureau of Justice Statistics released information about its study that involved interviews with 80,000 people in 2002. The research indicates that white, black, and Hispanic drivers in the United States were stopped by police at approximately the same rate, about 9 percent (Lichtblau, 2005A9). Although the researchers could not identify the reasons, it was clear that blacks and Hispanics were not treated as leniently as white drivers. The researchers "uncovered evidence of black drivers having worse experiences—more likely to be arrested, more likely to be searched, more likely to have force used against them—during traffic stops than white drivers" (Lichtblau, 2005:A9).

Prominent cases portray illegal arrests, excessive use of force, police shootings, and an ineffective review process. As a monitor of police misconduct cases from 1988 to 1996, Joel Berger expressed concern that the New York Police Department "fails to take any action in nearly two-thirds of the cases substantiated," a practice that he believes tends to promote police misconduct (1999:A31). The other side of this story is that the elite Street Crime Unit, which represented less than 2 percent of the entire New York City police force, "has been responsible for nearly 40 percent of all gun arrests annually" and has been "instrumental in reducing the number of reported shootings to fewer than 1,000 during the first half of 1998, compared with 2,500 in the first half of 1993" (Roane, 1999:1).

Berger's implication is that crime reduction comes with the expense of aggressive policing, which may generate more citizen complaints and cost the city more money to settle the cases. The Giuliani administration endorsed zero-tolerance, take-back-the-streets policing tactics and pointed to the sharp drop in crime, especially homicide [2,262 murders in 1990 to just over 600 in 1998 (Morrow, 1999); fewer than 600 homicides in 2004 (New York Police Department, 2005)], as evidence that these policies were effective. The goals of reducing crime and getting tough with criminals may have been demonstrated, but the consequences have generated concerns about police brutality, minority distrust of the police, tolerance for police misconduct, and the impact on the rest of the criminal justice system. "Police abuse has a long and tragic history in this country . . . The central question is how to achieve the proper balance between the two dimensions of accountability: serving the public while respecting the rights of citizens" (Walker, 2001:7).

Courts

Aggressive policing in New York City has resulted in more arrests and an emphasis on lower-level crimes such as street-level drug arrests that have overwhelmed the city's court system and slowed down the judicial process (Rohde, 1999). The number of "lesser offenses" increased by about 85 percent, but the number of judges remained about the same, resulting in an increase in the number of cases dismissed. In other words, the attention to making more arrests has not been accompanied by an increase in the number of judges.

As with New York City, in Baltimore, aggressive policing appeared to reduce serious crimes, including homicides, but created "such a backlog of cases" that a circuit judge dismissed first-degree murder charges against four men who had been awaiting trial for almost three years (Janofsky, 1999:A14). Postponements and delays burdened the courts and resulted in additional dismissed cases because no judges were available to hear them. The chaos prompted former Maryland Governor Parris Glendening to propose that the state take over the administration of the criminal courts because they were so backlogged (*New York Times*, 1999d).

One explanation for the judge shortage in New York City points to politics:

> New Criminal Court judgeships in the city, for example, would require Democrats in the Legislature to approve the jobs, which would be filled, at least temporarily, by Mayor Rudolph Giuliani, a Republican. In other parts of the state, Republicans oppose adding judgeships in areas controlled by Democrats (Rohde, 1999:1).

Budget concerns were also a factor. While New York City court administrators estimate the need for at least 23 more criminal court judges, politics impedes necessary action. Not only does this demonstrate the fragmented nature of criminal justice (i.e., an increase in the number of police officers and an increase in the number of arrests, but no proportionate increase in court personnel to accommodate additional criminal cases), but it also underscores how partisan politics confounds criminal justice. In general, "getting tough" on the front end of the system by cracking down on street-level crimes and making more arrests has the unintended (but not unanticipated) consequences of clogging the courts, slowing the judicial process, and resulting in more cases being dismissed (including those for serious felonies). These developments suggest a dysfunctional system focused on suppressing crime but not attending to the context of criminal justice. The impact on corrections has also been discouraging.

Corrections

The media attention and news headlines about the Diallo shooting coincided with reports of inmate deaths and guard brutality in jails, prisons, and detention centers. Increased complaints regarding corrections officers abusing and beating inmates in Nassau County Correctional Center (New York) prompted renewed investigations into previous allegations as well as a specific inquiry into the death of Thomas Pizzuto, who died in 1999 while serving a 90-day sentence for traffic violations (leaving the scene of an accident and driving under the influence of drugs) (Halbfinger, 1999:A23). According to the investigations, Pizzuto was "brutally attacked by guards after he loudly demanded his daily methadone treatment" (Halbfinger, 1999:A23). Afterward, at a hospital, he died of abdominal bleeding from a lacerated spleen; the death was ruled a homicide. Investigations further revealed that several inmates had filed complaints of brutality, but, over a period of 10 years, only one case had been prosecuted, and no correctional officer had been convicted of attacking an inmate. The reports of abuse were seen as more credible when one of the inmates filing a complaint about a beating was a former New York City police officer confined for violating an order of protection from abuse. The news media stories suggested that guards did not expect to be disciplined and in fact believed that violence was condoned by their supervisors (Halbfinger, 1999).

Similar concerns about excessive use of force by corrections officers occurred in Indiana, where two former sheriff's deputies were indicted for the death of an inmate who died from a blow to the head (*New York Times*, 1999e:A24). In this case, a 30-year-old man (Christopher Moreland) was found dead eight hours after being booked on charges of drunk driving. Reportedly, he became "combative" and two deputies used pepper spray and a restraining chair to subdue him. Apparently, they also used excessive force on Moreland's head, which was ruled as the cause of death.

Another case in this "wave" of inmate abuses and deaths was the healthcare-related death of a Dominican immigrant who was in federal detention in New York City awaiting deportation. The death of Miguel A. Valoy-Nunez prompted the Immigration and Naturalization Service (INS) to cite the deplorable overcrowding conditions in jails and detention centers. According to a news story, ever since a 1998 federal law mandating the detention of all noncitizens who commit deportable crimes went into effect, immigration centers have been "filled to capacity," provoking hunger strikes, attempted suicide, and confrontations with guards (Ojito, 1999:A25). Valoy-Nunez died from lack of medical care for a treatable viral infection; he was treated for a cold but did not see a doctor. Although the number of immigration detainees has increased, no additional medical personnel have been assigned to the detention centers.

The Pizzuto, Moreland, and Valoy-Nunez incidents are noteworthy because they leave impressions of nonviolent, less-serious offenders confined for relatively short periods of time whose deaths resulted from either officer brutality or neglect. The inmates had alcohol- or other drug-related charges (Pizzuto: driving under the influence of drugs; Moreland: drunk driving; and Valoy-Nunez: possession of heroin), and their offenses were targets of get-tough laws and enforcement strategies. Like the jails, the nation's prisons also continue to experience the consequences of the politicization of criminal justice and the punitive policies of the 1990s.

After the notorious photographs of detainees at Abu Ghraib prison became public and captured world attention, questions were raised about conditions in U.S. prisons (Clear, Cole & Reisig, 2006:284). The images of prisoners being "sexually humiliated and physically abused" caused concern that prisoner maltreatment and official denial could also reflect circumstances in U.S. correctional institutions. In 2005, when

U.S. Army Pfc. Lynndie R. England is escorted out of the courtroom after receiving a three-year sentence for her role in the Abu Ghraib scandal. She was in several of the best-known photos taken by U.S. guards at Abu Ghraib in late 2003. In one image she held a naked prisoner on a leash, while in others she posed with a pyramid of naked detainees and pointed at one man's genitals. England's defense attorney Capt. Jonathan Crisp is seen in the background. *(AP Photo/Tony Gutierrez)*

Army Pfc. Lynndie England was convicted of prisoner mistreatment and sentenced to three years in prison, photographs of her posing "with a pyramid of naked detainees" and "holding a naked prisoner on a leash" prompted renewed concern about abuse of authority and administrative failure to control guards (Badger, 2005:par. 10). Some of these same charges surfaced in the officer-on-inmate violence and killing that occurred at the California State Prison at Corcoran in the early 1990s (Clear, Cole & Reisig, 2006). At Corcoran, guards "instigated fights between rival gang members" and then tower guards would shoot the prisoner "gladiators" (Clear, Cole & Reisig, 2006:284). These "gladiator days" resulted in the killing of seven inmates and wounding of 43. "Each shooting was justified by state-approved reviewers" (p. 284).

As discussed earlier, while crime rates have been steadily decreasing, prison populations have continued to grow. According to Clear, Cole, and Reisig, "the skyrocketing prison population has created a correctional crisis of overcrowding" (2006:461). This has required hiring more corrections officers, spending larger portions of state budgets on prisons, and rethinking some of the reactionary sentencing policies that have increased the number of prisoners by about 7 percent per year since 1990. Butterfield reported that as prison populations have grown, the "number of prison and jail guards nationwide has increased by about 30 percent, to more than 600,000" (1997:1). States that have led the growth (such as California) are now experiencing difficulty supporting the prison system because voters refuse to approve more money for prison construction. Beginning in the late 1970s, California built 21 new prisons but "added only one university" to the public university system (Butterfield, 1997). Not surprisingly, the proportion of the state budget allocated to corrections has increased while the proportion for the university system has dropped: "From 1984 to 1994 prison spending in California rose 209 percent, compared with 15 percent for higher education" (Archibold, 1998:1). In California, from 1990 to 1998, "the higher education budget dropped 3 percent while spending for prisons and jails rose 60 percent" (Clear, Cole & Reisig, 2006:459). This trend reflects a public policy and budget dilemma: spending for prisons is a trade-off.

A similar pattern has been reported in New York, where state support for public universities dropped 29 percent while prison funding increased 76 percent. The state spent "$275 million more on prisons" than on higher education (Clear, Cole & Reisig, 2006:459). The growth in prison population that necessitated the construction of new prisons was due in part to mandatory sentences for minor drug offenses. "About one-third of the prisoners (70,000 total) are in for drug offenses" (Archibold, 1998:1). The implications of this war on drugs for minorities are devastating: even though more whites than blacks use crack, enforcement has focused on street-level, inner-city arrests, which has resulted in a higher rate of incarceration for blacks. According to the Drug Policy Alliance, 93 percent of the 16,000 offenders in the New York prison system who were sentenced under the Rockefeller Drug Laws are black and Latino (Drug Policy Alliance, 2005:par. 2). "In California, five black men are behind bars for each one in a state university" (Egan, 1999:A1). Barry McCaffrey, the former director of the National Drug Control Policy Office, called the drug war a failed social policy that has the potential to "bankrupt ourselves because we can't incarcerate our way out of this problem" (cited in Egan, 1999:A20).

In addition to tougher sanctions for drug offenders, truth-in-sentencing (TIS) laws, which were passed in several states to target violent offenders, have increased the average time served by inmates from 43 months in 1993 to 49 months in 1997, also contributing to the growth in state prison populations (Ditton & Wilson, 1999). For example, Pennsylvania has the record for keeping inmates incarcerated the longest. In 2001, the average length of incarceration for an offender in Pennsylvania was 69 months (DiMascio, 2004:3). This is another example of a shift in policy that exacerbated prison populations. Policies that abolished parole boards and discretionary release contributed to prison population growth and have precipitated their own unintended consequences: "Three states reinstituted parole boards after eliminating them because the resulting increase in inmates crowded prisons so much that the states were forced to release many of them early" (Butterfield, 1999b:A11).

As state executives and legislators continue to seek ways to respond to growing prison populations and escalating costs, two developments have occurred that further underscore the consequences of the punitive era of criminal justice. In New York State, Chief Judge Judith Kaye proposed a reduction in sentences "for some defendants found guilty of selling or possessing narcotics" (Finder, 1999:A23). In response to criticisms of New York's harsh drug laws, she recommended that 15-year minimum drug sentences be reduced to five-year minimum sentences and that low-level drug offenders be eligible for deferred prosecution and drug treatment (Finder, 1999). These proposals endorse case-by-case decisions that would be made by judges exercising renewed discretion and using treatment alternatives for appropriate defendants. While these changes are made in the context of (and reaction to) New York's overcrowded, costly prisons, they are significant because they articulate expanded judicial discretion and authority in the wake of legislative sentencing policies that characterized get-tough reactions to crime.

Truth-in-sentencing and mandatory sentences have removed some discretion from the criminal justice system and in some states "prison admissions for property and drug offenses outpaced admissions for violent offenses" (Rosich & Kane, 2005:21). Initiatives such as reinstating expanded authority to parole boards and increasing the judicial role in sentencing, however, may be indicative of an emerging view of criminal justice policy that recognizes and incorporates the expertise of professionals as opposed to politicians. For example, the option of drug treatment through drug courts rather than punishment through mandatory prison sentences coincides with reports that drug treatment is an effective crime prevention strategy (Butterfield, 1999c).

This also reflects statements made by Barry McCaffrey that question the assumptions behind punitive laws and endorse treatment for "low-level users" (Egan, 1999:A21). Moreover, even though New York's Governor Pataki has been skeptical of the changes proposed by Kaye (he proposed abolishing the state's parole board), he has at least called her proposal "thoughtful and intelligent" (Finder, 1999:A23). In August of 2004, Governor Pataki signed a bill that reformed the Rockefeller Drug Laws, albeit minimally. The legislation will enable 540 inmates convicted under the Rockefeller Drug Laws to apply for resentencing (Drug Policy Alliance, 2005). In one sense, this is an encouraging opening in contrast to reactive, emotional, and short-sighted proposals that continue to exacerbate the problems in the criminal justice system.

The discussion initiated by Kaye references treatment, case-by-case sentencing decisions, and judicial discretion as ways to deal with less-serious drug offenders, who constitute one of the major targets of the war on drugs and get-tough legislation of the 1990s. This suggests a departure from extreme conservative and punitive policies in which "all too often judges played no role in formulating sentencing polices" (American Judicature Society, 1998:1). The direction appears to support an effort to do more about drug-crime prevention than simply building more prisons. On the other hand, the building, managing, and staffing of prisons has become an industry that "has created its own growth dynamic" and will not easily be curtailed (Butterfield, 1997:2).

Prison–Industrial Complex

In a well-documented analysis of prevailing prison policy, Schlosser (1998) describes the development and momentum of a prison-industrial complex that is influencing the direction of criminal justice in the United States. He concludes that this complex:

> is not a conspiracy guiding the nation's criminal justice policy behind closed doors. It is a confluence of special interests that has given prison construction in the United States a seemingly unstoppable momentum. It is composed of politicians, both liberal and conservative, who have used the fear of crime to gain votes; impoverished rural areas where prisons have become a cornerstone of economic development; private companies that regard the roughly $35 billion spent each year on corrections not as a burden on American taxpayers but as a lucrative market; and government officials whose fiefdoms have expanded along with the inmate population (p. 54).

This perspective reinforces the themes presented in this book and raises questions about the future of criminal justice, especially corrections. If, as in the case of prisons, the "lure of big money is corrupting the nation's criminal justice system," then Schlosser may be correct in arguing that the drive for higher profits is replacing concepts of public service and will continue to affect the direction of criminal justice policy (p. 55). In addition, the confluence of a profit motive and the expanding number of prisoners also has the potential for abuse. In Florida, the state overpaid $13 million to two private prison companies (Corrections Corporation of America and the GEO Group) for positions that were unfilled and facility maintenance that was not completed (James, 2005).

Schlosser presents a critical review of the privatization of prisons and the growing "market share" being cornered by private prison companies. He is concerned that state and federal governments are looking to private enterprises as a less expensive alternative to building the additional prisons needed to incarcerate more prisoners. He concludes that most of the savings achieved by private companies are derived from using nonunion workers (p. 65). One company, formerly Corrections Corporation of America (CCA) (which merged with Prison Realty Corporation in 1999), was so confident of the expanding market that it planned to build "three prisons in California entirely on spec—that is, without any contract to fill them" (p. 76). In 2005, CCA was the "sixth largest corrections system in the United States" and the "nation's largest owner and operator" of private prisons, with 67,000 beds in 19 states and the District of Columbia (see http://www.correctionscorp.com). The company trades on the New

York Stock Exchange as CXW and has experienced a growth in prisoners in part due to contracts to house federal inmates and noncitizen immigrants (Crary, 2005).

The consequences of the punitive policies of the 1980s and 1990s are efforts to develop alternatives to incarceration (e.g., crime prevention programs, drug courts, reduced sentences, renewed judicial discretion, intermediate punishments) while at the same time funding "large-scale prison and jail construction projects" that have "not been able to keep pace with burgeoning correctional populations" (Bureau of Justice Assistance, 1998:1). Arguably, "the imprisonment of almost two million Americans has prevented some crimes from being committed," but as one of the legacies of politicized, exclusionary, and punitive public policy, prisons will be remembered at the end of the twentieth century as "the nation's largest public works"(Schlosser, 1998:77). Preoccupation with crime and emphasis on crime control are persistent social issues but, as Currie has cautioned, it is important for policymakers, criminal justice professionals, and citizens to be concerned with how the nation attempts to reduce crime (1998:193).

CHALLENGES AND CONTEXT FOR THE TWENTY-FIRST CENTURY

This sampling of news about capital punishment, police and correction officer brutality, court overloads, prison overcrowding, and privatization conveys that much of the information presented to the public reflects negative images of the criminal justice system. The predominant theme is that as the system continues to expand, its dysfunctions become more dynamic. Currie's optimism, however, maintains that the respite from crime, coupled with renewed concerns about these consequences and developments, provides an opportunity to reevaluate criminal justice philosophies, policies, and future directions. One critique of the current state of the system focuses on how politics and ideology have co-opted criminal justice.

Federalization

In early 1999, the Criminal Justice Section of the American Bar Association (ABA) released a report that was critical of the growth in the number of federal crimes and the expansion of federal jurisdiction into state powers of law enforcement (American Bar Association, 1999a). The report faulted lawmakers for being politically motivated to appear tough on crime by expanding federal criminal statutes. An ABA press release cited the Task Force's chair, former Attorney General Edwin Meese III, who raised concerns about the detrimental consequences of federalizing crimes, including "an unhealthy concentration of policing power at the federal level" (American Bar Association, 1999b:2). Meese stated that "this current phenomenon is capable of altering the careful decentralization of criminal law authority that has worked well in America" (1999b:1).

The study noted the dramatic growth in expenditures for the federal criminal justice system and criticized Congress for not considering the dire economic consequences of the federalization of crime. In addition to unnecessary expense and adverse consequences on the federal judicial system, the panel concluded that:

> increased federalization is rarely, if ever, likely to have any appreciable effect on the categories of violent crime that most concern Americans, because in practice federal law enforcement can only reach a small percent of such activity (1999b:1).

The report strongly characterized the political nature of federal criminal laws that were enacted in response to sensationalized crimes and the pressure on Congress to "do something." This politicization of crime was also viewed as diverting federal criminal justice away from "activity which only federal prosecutors can address" (1999b:2). The report underscored how the politics of get-tough legislation have actually been detrimental to federal law enforcement and have created inappropriate federalization. Although the juggernaut of crime control has been expanded, the impact on crime reduction is questioned by the task force.

In 2005, in the aftermath of the destruction and tragedy of Hurricanes Katrina and Rita, President Bush expressed his support for amending federal law to expand the powers of the military to take responsibility in domestic disasters (Sanger, 2005). In response to the "crisis" and in addition to providing disaster relief, the president proposed a larger role in local social control for the federal government. Even though exceptions have been made in using federal troops for domestic matters, an 1878 law, *Posse Comitatus*, "prohibits the military from engaging in domestic law enforcement" (Sanger, 2005:par. 4). Military leaders "expressed concern about broadening the military's responsibilities to include what would, in effect, be police work" (par. 5).

Partially in response to terrorism, the federal government is also expanding its role at airports by utilizing new technology. Five airports have allowed travelers to forego random searches at airport security areas in exchange for providing extensive personal information, having the irises of their eyes scanned, and submitting to being fingerprinted (Associated Press, 2004). In 2005, for about $80 a year, a private company in Orlando, Florida—Verified Identity Pass—began offering a service called "Clear" to frequent travelers. The service includes a private, voluntary, biometric "fast pass" system whereby one card grants members expedited security screening at multiple venues. Initially, more than 1,700 travelers signed up for the program. While previous tests were conducted by the Transportation Security Administration, this one is being conducted by a corporation. Whether these kinds of security services are performed by government employees or contracted out to private corporations, one of the goals is to make the technology available at all airports (Long, 2005).

Nationally, services for the approximate 600,000 offenders who are released each year have been lacking. Recently, Congress designated $100 million to the Department of Labor, Department of Health and Human Services, and Department of Justice to initiate reentry programs such as housing, employment, and mentoring (The Urban Institute, 2005; U.S. Department of Labor, 2005). In his State of the Union message, President Bush advocated for faith-based community organizations to become involved in and to receive funding for programs aimed at prisoner reentry (U.S. Department of Labor, 2005). Faith-based organizations could develop or expand job training programs and housing for offenders, and help ease their transition from prison to community.

There is some evidence that the government is also taking a more active stance in determining which federally funded research findings will be released to the public. In August of 2005, information was released about a national study that had been conducted on racial profiling. The Bureau of Justice Statistics chief was asked to resign after he refused to delete the references from the press release summarizing the study's findings that blacks and Hispanics were more likely to be searched and to have force used against them (Lichtblau, 2005:A9).

Public Perception

Coincidental to the Task Force Report, the American Bar Association announced a symposium to report research findings "on the public's current understanding and attitudes about the American justice system" (American Bar Association, 1999c:1). Topics included "the role of the media in promoting public understanding" of criminal justice and "the limitations on fulfilling that role" (p. 1).

Similarly, the American Judicature Society held a symposium in 1997 to consider sentencing and judicial responses to crime (Sampson, 1998). The symposium was convened in response to extensive changes in sentencing policies and their impact on the judiciary, especially a loss of judicial independence. One concern was that "all too often judges played no role in formulating new sentencing policies" (1998:1). The implication was that the judiciary has been excluded from this important dimension of criminal justice because of legislation and the politics dominating sentencing policy. The American Judicature Society recommended education for "the problem of the public's lack of knowledge about and trust in the criminal justice system generally, and the courts in particular" (p. 2). The recommendations also called for more proactive leadership from the judiciary, including attention to sentencing disparities, lack of resources, coalition building, and informed policymaking.

These two organizations, the American Bar Association and the American Judicature Society, responded to the politicization of crime (federal crime statutes and sentencing policies), which they viewed as detrimental to criminal justice and a disservice to the public. Some of this, no doubt, was in reaction to the co-optation of their professional authority and judicial independence that resulted from the politics of crime. Their efforts, however, suggest initiatives: (1) to promote more informed, less political policies; (2) to provide less media-sensationalized messages to the public about crime and criminal justice; and (3) to assert a more professional presence in the development of criminal justice policy.

Reports of federal judges who deviated from the sentencing guidelines by sentencing offenders more leniently than prescribed were wildly exaggerated. In 2003, the Attorney General notified all federal prosecutors that any judges who did not adhere to the guidelines were to be reported to the Department of Justice within 14 days (Kappeler & Potter, 2005:326). In this context, and in the "excessively politicized" nature of the attacks on judicial independence, Stanford University Law professor Kathleen Sullivan observed that "Congress has stripped federal courts of jurisdiction over prison litigation and immigration appeals." She expressed strong concern that "some conservative critics have talked of impeaching federal judges for their rulings or subjecting court decisions to congressional veto by majority vote" (1999:23). Similarly, the Chief Justice of the Massachusetts Supreme Judicial Court, Justice Margaret Marshall, spoke to the graduating class at Brandeis University in 2005 and noted that rather than attacks on individual judges or the decisions that they make, she is concerned about "attacks leveled at the very foundation of our legal system—the principle that judges should decide each case on its merits . . . independent of outside influence" (Russell, 2005, par. 2). Finally, Judge Joan Humphrey Lefkow, whose husband and mother were murdered by a defendant who had appeared in front of her, testified before the Senate Judiciary Committee in 2005 and asked the Senators to ". . . publicly and persistently repudiate the gratuitous attacks on the judiciary" (*The Chicago Tribune*, 2005, par. 5).

Early Intervention

These critiques of punitive ideology, get-tough legislation, and co-optation of the courts coincide with increasing evidence that the public is supportive of alternatives to incarceration, such as treatment programs (e.g., drug courts) and early intervention initiatives (e.g., Head Start, parental training, and drug education). For example, a survey of citizens in Tennessee conducted by Cullen and colleagues revealed that "a clear majority still favored governmental efforts designed to intervene with families and children" (1998:197). In spite of the fashionable view that incarcerating more offenders is the best way to reduce crime, the researchers found support for early intervention with youths that suggested that "policies that seem harsh toward at-risk children are inconsistent with the public mood" (p. 198). With evidence to support the effectiveness of some intervention strategies (see Chapter 5), the costs and consequences of the punitive era of politics and criminal justice may be the necessary initiative to give larger voice to a new proactive, progressive era of criminal justice.

Cullen and his colleagues are optimistic that as the punitive emphasis continues to wane, criminologists have an opportunity to articulate effective strategies, such as early intervention, that are publicly supported and now politically feasible (p. 200). In addition, his research over the last two decades on public opinion about rehabilitation has also consistently demonstrated that Americans still support rehabilitation for offenders (Cullen, 2005:12-13). The pendulum appears to be swinging; the context for criminal justice in the twenty-first century includes empirical knowledge of what works, public support for efforts to break the cycles of crime, and dissatisfaction with extreme conservative reactionary politics and the costly policies that have evolved. While the legacies of the 1980s and 1990s will persist, the emerging agenda challenges the myths and misconceptions that have propelled the criminal justice juggernaut. It presents an opportunity for more balanced efforts to control crime and maintain social order. It is with guarded optimism that we welcome the new era.

DISCUSSION QUESTIONS

1. What can be done to involve more communities in collaborative crime prevention strategies? What informal controls can be developed and utilized to prevent crime?

2. What is wrong with sex offender notification laws? Can they prevent the sexual molestation of children? What are some alternative attempts that could be utilized?

3. Explain the reduction in officially reported violent crime in the United States. Who is to be partly credited for this decrease: back-enders or front-enders? Why?

4. Using death penalty statutes and the likelihood of governors granting clemency as an example, explain the politicization of criminal justice policy in the United States.

5. Defend the criminal courts against allegations of inefficiency. How do you explain the problems with the criminal courts? Elaborate on the interdependence of the system in its response to new initiatives.

6. Provide an argument of guarded "optimism" regarding the criminal justice system and its crime policy in the next century. Now, prepare an argument of "pessimism" regarding the criminal justice system and its crime policy in the next century. Which view do you expect to predominate? Why?

7. Develop a strategy to reduce the federal government's role in crime control initiatives. What alternative role can the federal government have?

8. Briefly elaborate on drug policy in the United States. What are the "lessons" we have learned that we might want to share with other countries? What strategies and/or programs merit greater utilization? What role can the media and politicians have in this process?

9. What's "right" with criminal justice? Respond to the criticisms of the system.

10. Identify a current serious criminal justice problem or issue. Evaluate the influence of ideology, the media, and politics on it. What is the current approach being utilized? What do you recommend for the future?

REFERENCES

Abrams, Jim (2005). "House Passes Stricter Sex Offender Bill." *Boston Globe* (September 15). *http://www.bostonglobe.com*

Allen, Mike (1998). "Connecticut Killing Shows Limits of 'Megan's Law.'" *New York Times* (August 28). *http://www.nytimes.com*

American Bar Association (1999a). *The Federalization of Criminal Law*. Chicago: American Bar Association.

American Bar Association (1999b). "Creating Too Many Federal Crimes is Dangerous and Counterproductive, ABA Task Force Warns." *http://www.abanet. org*

American Bar Association (1999c). "ABA Symposium to Focus on Public Perceptions of the Justice System." See *http://www.abanet.org/publiced/lawmatters/symposium. html* for more information.

Anderson, David C. (1998). "The Mystery of the Falling Crime Rate." In Lawrence M. Salinger (ed.), *Deviant Behavior 98/99*, pp. 34-40. Guilford, CT: Dushkin/McGraw-Hill.

Archibold, Randal C. (1998). "Colleges Fall, but Prisons Rise in State Support." *New York Times* (December 2).

Associated Press (2004). "Quick Airport Screening Gets First Test." *St. Petersburg Times*. Online (July 8). *http://www.sptimes.com/2004/07/08/Worldandnation/ Quick_airport_screeni.shtml*

Badger, T.A. (2005). "Pfc. England Says She Was Used by Granger." *New York Times* (September 27). *http://www.nytimes.org*

Belenko, Steve (1998). "Research on Drug Courts: A Critical Review." *National Drug Court Institute Review* 11(1):1-42.

Berger, Joel (1999). "The Police Misconduct We Never See." *New York Times* (February 9):A19.

Berke, Richard L. (1999). "Republicans Face Identity Crisis." *New York Times* (January 31). *http://www.nytimes.com*

Black, Donald (1976). *The Behavior of Law*. Orlando, FL: Academic Press.

Blumstein, Alfred, and Joel Wallman (eds.) (2000). *The Crime Drop in America*. New York: Cambridge University Press.

Booth, William (1998). "Longing for the Good Old Golden Days: As Problems Mount in California's Schools, Reform Becomes a Political Priority." *The Washington Post National Weekly Edition* (November 30):32.

Bumiller, Elisabeth, and Ginger Thompson (1999). "Thousands Gather Again to Protest Police Shootings." *New York Times* (February 10):A24.

Bureau of Justice Assistance (1998). *Critical Elements in the Planning, Development, and Implementation of Successful Correctional Options*. Washington, DC: Department of Justice.

Butterfield, Fox (1997). "Crime Keeps on Falling, but Prisons Keep on Filling." *New York Times* (September 28).

Butterfield, Fox (1998). "Sharp Drop in Violent Crime Traced to Decline in Crack Market." *New York Times* (December 28).

Butterfield, Fox (1999a). "Prison Population Increases as Release of Inmates Slows." *New York Times* (January 11):A10.

Butterfield, Fox (1999b). "Eliminating Parole Boards Isn't a Cure-All, Experts Say." *New York Times* (January 10):A11.

Butterfield, Fox (1999c). "Offenders' Drug Use Increases but Treatment Declines, Study Finds." *New York Times* (January 6):A12.

Canada, Geoffrey (1995). *Fist, Stick, Knife, Gun: A Personal History of Violence in America*. Boston: Beacon Press.

Center for Constitutional Rights (2005). *CCR Achieves Historic Settlement in Street Crime Unit Class Action. http://www.ccr-ny.org*

The Chicago Tribune (2005). "Testimony of Joan Humphrey Lefkow United States District Judge of Northern District of Illinois before the Judiciary Committee of the United States Senate." (May 18). *http://www.chicagotribune.com*

Clear, Todd R., and George Cole (1997). *American Corrections*, 4th ed. Belmont, CA: Wadsworth.

Clear, Todd R., George Cole, and Michael D. Reisig (2006). *American Corrections*, 7th ed. Belmont, CA: Thomson Wadsworth.

Common Sense for Drug Policy (2004). *Factbook: Medical Marijuana* (October 10). *http://www.drugwarfacts.org/medicalm.htm*

Cooper, Michael (1999). "Complaints Against Police Rise by 4.3%." *New York Times* (January 14):A19.

Crary, David (2005). "Private Prisons Experience Business Surge." *Washington Post* (July 31). *http://www.washingtonpost.com*

Cullen, Francis T. (2005). "The Twelve People Who Saved Rehabilitation: How the Science of Criminology Made a Difference: The American Society of Criminology 2004 Presidential Address." *Criminology* 43(1):1-42.

Cullen, Francis T., and Karen E. Gilbert (1982). *Reaffirming Rehabilitation*. Cincinnati: Anderson.

Cullen, Francis T., John Paul Wright, Shayna Brown, Melissa M. Moon, Michael B. Blankenship, and Brandon K. Applegate (1998). "Public Support for Early Intervention Programs: Implications for a Progressive Policy Agenda." *Crime & Delinquency* 44(2):187-204.

Currie, Elliot (1998). *Crime and Punishment in America: Why the Solutions to America's Most Stubborn Social Crisis Have Not Worked—And What Will*. New York: Henry Holt and Company.

Death Penalty Information Center (2005a). *Facts About the Death Penalty*. Washington, DC: Death Penalty Information Center. *http://www.deathpenaltyinfo.org*

Death Penalty Information Center (2005b). *Innocence and the Death Penalty*. Washington, DC: Death Penalty Information Center. *http://www.deathpenaltyinfo.org*

Death Penalty Information Center (2005c). *Life Without Parole*. Washington, DC: Death Penalty Information Center. *http://www.deathpenaltyinfo.org*

DiMascio, William (2004). "A Question of (Public) Interest." *Correctional Forum* (September):2-3.

Ditton, Paula M., and Doris James Wilson (1999). "Truth in Sentencing in State Prisons." *Bureau of Justice Statistics Special Report*. Washington, DC: Department of Justice, Office of Justice Programs.

Drug Policy Alliance (2005). "Reform of Rockefeller Drug Laws Takes Another Small Step in Right Direction." (September 28) *http://www.drugpolicy.org/news/83105rockyreform.cfm*

Durose, Matthew R., and Patrick A. Langan (2003). "Felony Sentences in State Courts, 2000." *Bureau of Justice Statistics Bulletin*. Washington, DC: Department of Justice, Office of Justice Programs.

Egan, Timothy (1999). "The War on Drugs Retreats, Still Taking Prisoners." *New York Times* (February 28):A1, 20-21.

Eggen, Dan (2005). "Marijuana Becomes Focus of Drug War." *Washington Post* (May 4). *http://www.washingtonpost.com*

Erickson, Patricia G., and Jennifer Butters (1998). "The Emerging Harm Reduction Movement: The De-Escalation of the War on Drugs?" In Eric L. Jensen and Jurg Gerber (eds.), *The New War on Drugs: Symbolic Politics and Criminal Justice Policy*, pp. 177-196. Cincinnati: Anderson.

Federal Bureau of Investigation (2005). "Preliminary Crime Statistics for 2004." *http://www.fbi.gov/pressrel/pressrel05/preliminary060605.htm*

Fernandez, Maria Elena (1999). "No Rhyme or Reason to City's Crime Decline." *Washington Post* (February 4):J01.

Finder, Alan (1999). "Top New York Judge Calls for Easing Some Drug Laws." *New York Times* (February 9):A23.

Gordon, Diana (1990). *The Justice Juggernaut: Fighting Street Crime, Controlling Citizens*. New Brunswick, NJ: Rutgers University Press.

Hagenbucher, Greg (2003). "PROGRESS: An Enhanced Supervision for High-Risk Criminal Offenders—Proactive Gang Resistance Enforcement, Suppression, and Supervision." *FBI Law Enforcement Bulletin* 72(9):20-24.

Hahn, Paul H. (1998). *Emerging Criminal Justice: Three Pillars for a Proactive Justice System*. Thousand Oaks, CA: Sage.

Halbfinger, David M. (1999). "Inmates Say Brutality is the Rule in Nassau Jail." *New York Times* (February 1):A23.

H.R. 3132 (2005). Children's Safety Act of 2005. *http://thomas.loc.gov*

Huddleston, C. West (1998). "Drug Courts and Jail-Based Treatment." *Corrections Today* 60(6):98-101.

Inciardi, James A., Duane C. McBride, and James E. Rivers (1996). *Drug Control and the Courts*. Thousand Oaks, CA: Sage.

Jacobs, James B. (1998). "New Laws Won't Stop Hate." *New York Times* (October 14):A25.

Jacobs, James B., and Kimberly Potter (1998). *Hate Crime: Criminal Law and Identity Politics*. New York: Oxford University Press.

James, Joni (2005). "Audit: State Overpaid $13 Million for Prisons." *St. Petersburg Times* (July 26). *http://www.sptimes.com*

Janofsky, Michael (1999). "Baltimore's Push on Crime Creates Backlog of Cases." *New York Times* (January 7):A14.

Jensen, Eric L., and Jurg Gerber (eds.) (1998). *The New War on Drugs: Symbolic Politics and Criminal Justice Policy*. Cincinnati: Anderson.

Kappeler, Victor E., Mark Blumberg, and Gary W. Potter (1996). *The Mythology of Crime and Criminal Justice*, 2nd ed. Prospect Heights, IL: Waveland.

Kappeler, Victor E., and Gary W. Potter (2005). *The Mythology of Crime and Criminal Justice,* 4th ed. Long Grove, IL: Waveland.

King, Ryan S., and Marc Mauer (2005). *The War on Marijuana: The Transformation of the War on Drugs in the 1990s.* Washington, DC: The Sentencing Project. *http://www.sentencingproject.org*

Kolbert, Elizabeth (1999). "The Charisma of No Charisma." *The New Yorker* (January 18):34-37.

Levitt, Steven D., and Stephen J. Dubner (2005). *Freakonomics: A Rogue Economist Explores the Hidden Side of Everything.* New York: William Morrow.

Lichtblau, Eric (2005). "Profiling Report Leads to a Clash and a Demotion." *New York Times* (August 24):A1, A9.

Long, Phil (2005). "Airport to Test Pilot Program for Screening of Passengers." *The Miami Herald* (June 26). *http://www.miami.com/mld/miamiherald/news/11987365.htm*

Marks, John (1998). "Mayor vs. Drug Czar: New York's Giuliani Claims That Methadone is Merely Another Form of Addiction." *Newsweek* (October 12):31.

Martinson, Robert (1974). "What Works? Questions and Answers About Prison Reform." *The Public Interest* (Spring) 35:22-54.

McFadden, Robert D., and Kit R. Roane (1999). "U.S. Examining Killing of Man in Police Volley." *New York Times* (February 6). *http://www.nytimes.com*

Morrow, James (1999). "The Incredible Shrinking Crime Rate." *U.S. News & World Report* (January 11):25.

Musto, David R. (1998). "This 10-Year War Can Be Won." *The Washington Post National Weekly Edition* (June 22):24.

National Organization for the Reform of Marijuana Laws (2004). Medical Use: Active State Medical Marijuana Programs. *http://www.normal.org*

New York City Law Department (n.d.). Tort Reform. *http://www.nyc.gov*

New York Police Department (2005). Press Release 217-05. "Mayor Bloomberg and Police Commissioner Kelly Announce FBI Report Shows Safest Big City Got Even Safer in 2004." (June 6). *http://www.nyc.gov*

New York Times (1998a). "California Pot Club Closed by Feds." (October 20). *http://www.nytimes.com*

New York Times (1998b). "Chiefs Oppose Drug Legislation." (October 20). *http://www.nytimes.com*

New York Times (1999a). "2 Executed in Oklahoma, Arizona." (February 4). *http://www.nytimes.com*

New York Times (1999b). "Holding Fire." (February 9):A30.

New York Times (1999c). "NYC Protests Police Shooting." (February 9):A23.

New York Times (1999d). "Governor Seeks Takeover of Criminal Court System." (January 13):A16.

New York Times (1999e). "2 Ex-Deputies Indicted in '97 Death of an Inmate." (February 14):A24.

New York Times (1999f). "History of a Brutality Case." (June 9). *http://www.nytimes.com*

New York Times (1999g). "Violent Crime Falls 7 Percent to Lowest Level in Decades." (July 19):A10.

Ojito, Mirta (1999). "Immigrant's Death in Detention Prompts New Criticism." *New York Times* (February 9):A25.

O'Keefe, Karen, and Mitch Earleywine (2005). "Marijuana Use by Young People: The Impact of State Medical Marijuana Laws." Washington, DC: Marijuana Policy Project. *http://www.mpp.org*

Potter, Gary W., and Victor E. Kappeler (1998). *Constructing Crime: Perspectives on Making News and Social Problems*. Prospect Heights, IL: Waveland.

Reynolds, Morgan O. (1998). *Crime and Punishment in America: 1998*. Washington, DC: National Center for Policy Analysis. *http://www.ncpa.org/studies/s219.html*

Roane, Kit R. (1999). "Elite Force Quells Crime, But at a Cost, Critics Say." *New York Times* (February 6). *http://www.nytimes.com*

Roberg, Roy R., and Vincent J. Webb (eds.) (1981). *Critical Issues in Corrections: Problems, Trends and Prospects*. St. Paul, MN: West.

Rohde, David (1999). "Arrests Soar in Giuliani Crackdown." *New York Times* (February 2). *http://www.nytimes.com*

Rose, Dina R., and Todd R. Clear (1998). "Incarceration, Social Capital, and Crime: Implications for Social Disorganization Theory." *Criminology* 36(3):441-479.

Rosich, Katherine J., and Kamala Mallik Kane (2005). "Truth in Sentencing and State Sentencing Practices." *NIJ Journal*. Washington, DC: U.S. Department of Justice, National Institute of Justice.

Russell, Jenna (2005). "SJC Chief Decries 'Attacks' on Judges." Bostoncom.news (May 23). *http://www.boston.com*

Sampson, Kathleen M. (1998). *A National Symposium on Sentencing: The Judicial Response to Crime—Report and Policy Guide*. Des Moines, IA: American Judicature Society.

Sanger, David E. (2005). "Bush Wants to Consider Broadening of Military's Powers During National Disasters." *New York Times* (September 27). *http://www.nytimes.com*

Schlosser, Eric (1998). "The Prison-Industrial Complex." *The Atlantic Monthly* (December):51-77.

Sherman, Lawrence W. (1997). "Policing for Crime Prevention." In Lawrence W. Sherman, Denise Gottfredson, Doris MacKenzie, John Eck, Peter Reuter, and Shawn Bushway (eds.), *Preventing Crime: What Works, What Doesn't, What's Promising*, pp. 8-1–8-58. Washington, DC: Office of Justice Programs.

Sherman, Lawrence W., Denise Gottfredson, Doris MacKenzie, John Eck, Peter Reuter, and Shawn Bushway (1997). *Preventing Crime: What Works, What Doesn't, What's Promising*. Washington, DC: Office of Justice Programs.

Siegel, Larry J., and Brandon C. Welsh (2005). *Juvenile Delinquency: The Core*, 2nd ed. Belmont, CA: Thomson Wadsworth.

Snell, Tracy L. (1998). "Capital Punishment 1997." *Bureau of Statistics Bulletin*. Washington, DC: Department of Justice, Bureau of Justice Statistics, Office of Justice Programs.

Sullivan, Kathleen M. (1999). "The Law: Put Politics Back Where It Belongs." *The Washington Post National Weekly Edition* (January 11):23.

Terry, Don (1999). "Term Just Begun, Governor Faces Life-or-Death Choice." *New York Times* (February 4):A14.

Travis, Jeremy, and Michelle Waul (2002). *Reflections on the Crime Decline: Lessons for the Future?* Washington, DC: The Urban Institute. *http://www.urbaninstitute.org*

Urban Institute (2005). "Prisoner Reentry: Overview." (September 27). *http://www.urbaninstitute.org*

U.S. Department of Justice (2005). "Violent Crimes and Property Crimes Remain at 30-Year Lows." Washington, DC: Bureau of Justice Statistics. *http://www.ojp.usdoj.gov/bjs/pub/press/cv04pr.htm*

U.S. Department of Labor (2005). "President Bush's Prisoner Reentry Initiative: Protecting Communities by Helping Returning Inmates Find Work." (September 26) *http://www.dol.gov/cfbci/reentryfactsheet.htm*

Walker, Samuel (1998). *Sense and Nonsense About Crime and Drugs: A Policy Guide*, 4th ed. Belmont, CA: West/Wadsworth.

Walker, Samuel (2001). *Police Accountability: The Role of Citizen Oversight*. Belmont, CA: Wadsworth/Thompson Learning.

Walker, Samuel (2006). *Sense and Nonsense About Crime and Drugs: A Policy Guide*, 6th ed. Belmont, CA: Wadsworth.

Walters, John P. (2005). "Drug-Court Programs Save Money and Get Better Results." (May 11). *http://www.whitehousedrugpolicy.gov/news/oped05/051105.html*

Weisberg, Jacob (1999). "The Governor-President." *New York Times Magazine* (January 10):30-35, 41, 52, 65.

Will, George (1998). "Just Execute Them; No Need for 'Hate Crime' Laws." *Erie Morning News* (October 15):A6.

Name Index

Subject Index

Brutality, police. *See* Police
Budget constraints. *See* Costs of incarceration; Courts
Bullying, 176, 181
Bureaucratic efficiency model, 40-41
Bureau of Justice Statistics, 134, 210-211, 235, 240, 250

California Court of Appeals, 82-83
California Department of Corrections and Rehabilitation, 203
California State Prison at Corcoran, 244
California Supreme Court, 83
California Youth and Adult Correctional Agency, 114
Call-outs, reaction-oriented, 56
"Capable guardians" in third-party policing, 52
Capital punishment, 14
 Bill Clinton and, 17
 decline of, 89-91, 217, 237-239
 for hate crimes, 232
 in juvenile justice, 170
 public support of, 65-67
 sexual offenders and, 232, 234
Carjacking, 88
Casework supervision, in parole, 212
Catholic Church, sexual abuse and, 63
Center for Constitutional Rights, 240
Centers for Disease Control and Prevention, 118
Center for the Study and Prevention of Violence, 181
Central Intelligence Agency (CIA), 53
Chemical, biological, and radiological (CBR) attacks, 53
Chicago's Alternative Policing Strategy (CAPS), 51
Children, 70-71, 140. *See also* Sexual offenders
Children and Youth Services Agency, 171
Children's Defense Fund, 161
Children's Safety Act of 2005, 137, 232-234
Citizen involvement. *See* Community policing
Citizenship, inmate loss of, 134
Civil commitment statutes, 116
Civil liberties, 42, 55-56
Civil rights, 19

Classical model of criminal justice, 10-12, 15
Clemency, 237
"Clenched fist and outstretched hand," in Boston Gun Project, 184
Cocaine, 20-22, 78-79, 85, 120, 122, 204, 235
Coercive treatment, 224
Collaborative Intensive Community Treatment Program (CICTP), Erie County, PA, 186
"Collective use of force" concept, 24
Columbia University, 138, 227
Columbine High School, Littleton, CO, 28, 154, 163
Combined DNA Index System, 234
Commission on Safety and Abuse in America's Prisons, 217
Communities
 correctional services based in, 122
 courts based in, 99
 get-tough legislation *versus* partnerships in, 213-216
 incarceration and, 229
 juvenile justice mobilization of, 184-185
 reentry to, 209-213
 sex offenders notification to, 94
Communities in Schools (CIS), 175, 178
Community Oriented Policing Services (COPS), 45, 57, 182, 215
Community policing, 28, 45-56
 critique of, 45-48
 goals of, 49
 homeland security and, 53-56
 successful, 50-52
 by third-parties, 52-53
Community service, in sentencing, 69, 96, 127
Commutation, 17, 237
Comprehensive Crime Control Act of 1984, 76
Comprehensive Youth-Oriented Prevention Strategy, Office of National Drug Control Policy (ONDCP), 174
Computer-related crimes, 71
"Condensation symbol," 167
Conflict resolution, 102, 181
Consent decrees, 128
Contagious disease, in prisons, 207
Content analysis of crime news, 6

About the Authors

Peter J. Benekos is Professor of Criminal Justice and Sociology at Mercyhurst College, Erie, Pennsylvania. He earned his B.S. at Clarion University of Pennsylvania, his M.A. at the University of Cincinnati, and his Ph.D. in Sociology/Criminology from the University of Akron. He was a corrections counselor with the Pennsylvania Department of Corrections and a child care worker, and has conducted research and published in the areas of juvenile justice, corrections, and public policy. He is the co-editor (with Alida V. Merlo) of *Controversies in Juvenile Justice and Delinquency* (LexisNexis/Anderson, 2004) and *Corrections: Dilemmas and Directions* (Anderson, 1992) and co-author (with Alida V. Merlo) of *What's Wrong with the Criminal Justice System? Ideology, Politics, and the Media* (Anderson, 2000). He is past President of the Northeastern Association of Criminal Justice Sciences and recipient of the Association's Fellow and Founder's Award.

Alida V. Merlo is Professor of Criminology at Indiana University of Pennsylvania. She earned her A.B. at Youngstown State University, her M.S. in Criminal Justice at Northeastern University, and her Ph.D. in Sociology at Fordham University. Previously, she was a faculty member in the Criminal Justice Department at Westfield State College in Westfield, Massachusetts, and a juvenile probation officer and intake supervisor in Mahoning County Juvenile Court in Youngstown, Ohio. She has conducted research and published in the area of corrections, juvenile justice, and women and the law. She is co-editor (with Joycelyn M. Pollock) of *Women, Law & Social Control*, Second Edition (Allyn & Bacon, 2006); co-editor (with Peter J.

Benekos) of *Controversies in Juvenile Justice and Delinquency* (Lexis-Nexis/Anderson, 2004) and *Corrections: Dilemmas and Directions* (Anderson, 1992); and co-author (with Peter J. Benekos) of *What's Wrong with the Criminal Justice System? Ideology, Politics, and the Media* (Anderson, 2000). She is the past President of the Academy of Criminal Justice Sciences (1999-2000) and recipient of the Academy's Founder's Award and the Fellow Award.